Enacting a Pedagogy of Teacher Education

John Loughran's *Developing a Pedagogy of Teacher Education* poses a broad range of challenges for teacher educators around the globe. As a companion volume, *Enacting a Pedagogy of Teacher Education* offers insights into the work of individual teacher educators who have accepted Loughran's challenges and begun to modify their personal practices. The 16 contributors include experienced teacher educators, individuals in their early years as teacher educators, individuals preparing to enter the role, a school administrator supporting in-service teacher development and a student teacher whose personal experiences of pre-service teacher education emphasize the importance of this work.

The evolution of personal teacher education practices is a central theme in many of the chapters. Teaching students of teaching requires deep and well-conceptualized understandings of pedagogy that are developed, articulated, critiqued and refined in the crucible of practice itself. Necessarily, these accounts focus on the complexity of enacting one's values and the excitement of coming to understand one's values more fully by studying one's own personal practices. Listening to the voices of those learning to teach is often a central element in a teacher educator's self-study, and articulating personal principles of practice is another key element.

Reflective practice is illustrated throughout the collection, as is the development of personal values in relation to both theory and practice. Those who are willing to take up the question, "As a teacher educator, how do you develop and enact your pedagogy of teacher education?", will find in this collection a range of engaging narratives to start them on their journey of personal professional development.

Tom Russell is a Professor of Teacher Education at Queen's University, Canada.
John Loughran is Professor of Education at Monash University, Australia.

Enacting a Pedagogy of Teacher Education

Values, relationships and practices

Edited by

Tom Russell and John Loughran

Routledge
Taylor & Francis Group

LONDON AND NEW YORK

To LaVerne and Airlie, who understand our passion for improving teacher education.

First published 2007
by Routledge
2 Park Square, Milton Park, Abingdon, Oxon OX14 4RN

Simultaneously published in the USA and Canada
by Routledge
270 Madison Ave, New York, NY 10016

Routledge is an imprint of the Taylor & Francis Group, an informa business

Typeset in Galliard by RefineCatch Limited, Bungay, Suffolk
Printed and bound in Great Britain by
The Cromwell Press, Trowbridge, Wiltshire

British Library Cataloguing in Publication Data
A catalogue record for this book is available from the British Library

Library of Congress Cataloging in Publication Data
A catalog record for this book has been requested

ISBN10: 0–415–41899–2 (hbk)
ISBN10: 0–415–41900–X (pbk)
ISBN10: 0–203–96244–3 (ebk)

ISBN13: 978–0–415–41899–7 (hbk)
ISBN13: 978–0–415–41900–0 (pbk)
ISBN13: 978–0–203–96244–2 (ebk)

Contents

Contributors

Amanda Berry is a Senior Lecturer in the Faculty of Education, Monash University, Australia, where she works mainly in the areas of pre-service and in-service science teacher education. Amanda's research focus is the self-study of teaching practice, an interest that began during her career as a high school teacher before joining Monash University. She has a keen interest in the collaborative learning about teaching that can take place between teacher education colleagues and in the power of modeling in teaching about teaching.

Shawn Michael Bullock taught physics at the secondary and post-secondary level prior to beginning his PhD studies at Queen's University, Ontario, Canada. His long-standing interest in teachers' professional development has been informed by two years as professional development leader for the staff of a large secondary school. As a teacher-educator-in-training, he is particularly interested in self-study and in prospective teachers' responses to pedagogy.

Alicia R. Crowe is Assistant Professor of Middle and Secondary Social Studies Education in the Department of Teaching, Leadership, and Curriculum Studies at Kent State University, Ohio, USA. She teaches undergraduate and graduate students who are preparing to be teachers. Her areas of interest and research include self-study of teacher education practices, social studies education and teacher learning.

Ruth Kane is Director of Teacher Education at the Faculty of Education at the University of Ottawa. Beginning her career as a secondary school teacher in New Zealand and Australia, she has worked for 20 years as teacher educator at universities in Australia and New Zealand. Her recent research projects include a national study of teacher education in New Zealand, a study of perceptions of teachers and teachers' work in New Zealand, and two ongoing studies that examine the preparation and induction of beginning secondary teachers in New Zealand and Québec.

Cristy L. Kessler is an Assistant Professor in the Institute for Teacher Education at the University of Hawaii at Manoa. She received National Board Certification in Adolescence and Young Adulthood/Social Studies-History in 2005. She currently works with the Masters of Education in Teaching (MEdT) Program and is involved in purposeful ways of developing learning communities and building the relationships between the university and its partnership schools.

Fred Korthagen is a Professor of Education working at the Vrije Universiteit in Amsterdam, Utrecht University, and the Hogeschool Utrecht (as Chair of the Pedagogy of Teacher Education). He and Tom Russell edited the book, *Teachers who Teach Teachers*, and he is the lead author of *Linking Practice and Theory in Teacher Education*, which describes the pedagogy of teacher education developed at Utrecht University. In 2000 and again in 2006, he received the Exemplary Research Award of the Division of Teaching and Teacher Education of the American Educational Research Association.

Clare Kosnik is Executive Director of the Teachers for a New Era project at Stanford University, CA, USA. She is on leave from her position as Associate Professor and Director of the Elementary Pre-service Program at the Ontario Institute for Studies in Education, University of Toronto. Her recent publications include *Making a Difference in Teacher Education through Self-Study: Studies of Personal, Professional, and Program Renewal* and *Innovations in Teacher Education: A Social Constructivist Approach*. She is currently Chair of the Self-Study of Teacher Education Practices Special Interest Group of the American Educational Research Association.

Linda R. Kroll is Professor of Education in the School of Education at Mills College in Oakland, California. She teaches courses in development and learning and elementary literacy teaching methods, and her research interests focus on teacher development, self-study of teacher education practices, application of constructivist theory to educational practice, and development of children's literacy. She is co-author of *Teaching as Principled Practice: Managing Complexity for Social Justice*.

John Loughran is the Foundation Chair in Curriculum and Professional Practice in the Faculty of Education, Monash University, Australia, where he is also Associate Dean. His research fields include science education, self-study of teaching and teacher education practices, reflective practice and teacher research. His most recent books include *Developing a Pedagogy of Teacher Education: Understanding Teaching and Learning about Teaching*, *Understanding and Developing Science Teacher's Pedagogical Content Knowledge*, and *The International Handbook of Self-Study of Teaching and Teacher Education Practices*. With Tom Russell, he edits the journal *Studying Teacher Education*.

Mieke Lunenberg is Associate Professor at the Centre for Educational Training, Assessment and Research (CETAR) of the Vrije Universiteit in Amsterdam.

Her main professional interest concerns the professional development of teacher educators; her publications focus on value-based teacher education, teacher educators as role models, the identity of teacher educators and research by and with teacher educators. As assessor for the Registration of Experienced Teacher Educators in The Netherlands, she is also involved in a practical way in the professional development of teacher educators.

Andrea K. Martin is Adjunct Associate Professor in the Faculty of Education at Queen's University, Ontario, Canada. Her areas of interest and scholarship include the development of teachers' knowledge, pre-service teacher education, special education, and literacy development and interventions.

Matthew Olmstead completed a Master's Degree in Mechanical Engineering in 2002 and took time to train in improvised theatre and musical theatre in Toronto. This shift in career tracks led him to the stage as both performer and technical team member of "*Evil Dead 1&2 the Musical*" at the Just for Laughs festival in 2004. He completed a Bachelor of Education degree at Queen's University, Canada, in 2006 and anticipates a career combining science, education and entertainment.

Tom Russell is a Professor in the Faculty of Education, Queen's University, Ontario, Canada, where he has taught pre-service science methods courses and supervised practicum placements for the past 30 years. His early interest in science education quickly evolved into a broader interest in teachers' professional knowledge and how individuals learn to teach, and these interests soon evolved to include self-study of teacher education practices. With John Loughran, he edits the journal *Studying Teacher Education*.

Joseph C. Senese has taught high school English in public and private schools for over 33 years, most recently as an Assistant Principal at Highland Park (Illinois) High School, USA. His interest in and support of teacher development extend to teaching pre-service teachers in the graduate program at Northwestern University. Recipient of the award for Best Research in Staff Development for 1999 from the National Council of Staff Development, Joe has written about his experiences working with fellow teachers and conducting his own action research and self-studies.

Hildelien S. Verkuyl began her career as a primary teacher, studied the history and philosophy of education at Utrecht University, worked for more than 30 years as a pedagogue and a teacher educator, and has a growing private practice as a pedagogue. She has published articles and books about pedagogical issues, including a pedagogical workbook for prospective teachers. She now works full-time with pupils, parents and teachers, supporting pupils' identity development with a focus on balancing environmental influences and expectations with personal motives and goals.

Martijn Willemse has worked as a researcher, teacher educator, curriculum developer and consultant at the Centre for Educational Training, Assessment and Research (CETAR) of the Vrije Universiteit in Amsterdam and at the MHR Educational centre. As a researcher his main interest is value-based teacher education, which was the focus of his PhD research. Currently, he advises members of the Dutch parliament in the areas of education, culture and science.

1 Enacting a pedagogy of teacher education

John Loughran

> If the well entrenched, taken-for-granted aspects of teaching resulting from years of an *apprenticeship of observation* (Lortie, 1975) are to be seriously examined with students of teaching, then the "highly visible" teaching in teacher education must make clear all of that which has hitherto been unseen and unappreciated. To do so is obviously a demanding task and helps to account for the growing momentum for the articulation and development of a pedagogy of teacher education.
>
> (Loughran, 2006, p. 173)

Enacting a pedagogy of teacher education is enmeshed in the ways in which teacher educators knowingly and purposefully create opportunities for students of teaching to see into teaching. It is about how teacher educators are able to make teaching a site for inquiry. In so doing, students of teaching might see into practice (both their own and that of their teacher educators) in such a way as to gain a genuine appreciation of the skills, knowledge and abilities that shape practice. Such inquiry opens teaching to questioning, probing, reflection and critique that goes way beyond the technical. Enacting a pedagogy of teacher education matters so that practice is not simplistically viewed as just "doing teaching." As noted above, it is not easy work for either students of teaching or for teacher educators, yet it is fundamental to better understanding and valuing teacher education practices.

As the chapters in this book clearly illustrate, a pedagogy of teacher education requires a deep understanding of practice through researching practice. In order to develop such deep understanding, it is important not to be constrained by a teacher educator's perspective but to actively seek to better understand the perspectives of students of teaching. By drawing appropriately on both of these perspectives, the sometimes contradictory and competing agendas and insights into the ways in which teaching is conceptualized and practiced might then influence the way in which teaching *and* learning about teaching might be articulated and portrayed. Endeavouring to act in ways that are responsive to both of these perspectives is essential in enacting a pedagogy of teacher education.

Teaching about teaching

Teaching about teaching is complex work and demands a great deal of teacher educators (see, for example, Berry, 2004; Bullough, 1997; Bullough and Gitlin, 2001; Clarke and Erickson, 2004; Dinkelman *et al.*, 2006; Hoban, 2005; Korthagen, 2001a; Nicol, 1997, 2006; Northfield and Gunstone, 1997; Tidwell, 2002; Trumbull, 2004; Tudball, 2004). The complexity is embedded in the very nature of teaching itself, and thus when the focus is on teaching teaching, even more sophisticated understandings of practice are essential.

Deeper understandings of practice revolve around (at least) such things as: the problematic nature of teaching; making the tacit explicit; teaching as relationship; and challenging the tyranny of talk. Enacting a pedagogy of teacher education means that these elements must then be explicitly addressed through a teacher educator's practice.

Focusing on the problematic in teaching teaching

One approach to enacting a pedagogy of teacher education emerges through the ways in which a teacher educator questions—and encourages students of teaching to question—the taken-for-granted aspects of one's own practice. Seeing teaching as problematic, looking into and beyond the idiosyncrasies of practice, being able to abstract from the specific to the general—and vice versa—by developing an approach to pedagogical reasoning that genuinely informs teaching is important. Making that clear to oneself as a teacher educator matters, making it explicit for students of teaching is crucial. However, it does not follow that it is easy to do because:

> One difficulty with conceptualizing teaching as being problematic is that, for novices, the messiness, the apparent lack of a clear path . . . may create a yearning for a much simpler solution in order to fashion a sense of control over the impending uncertainty of teaching.
>
> (Loughran, 2006, p. 31)

Experienced teachers seem to effortlessly and confidently manage the uncertainty of practice. In so doing, to an observer (especially a novice), it can appear as though teaching progresses along a preordained path with little divergence from a well-established objective or goal. If this impression is gleaned, then in many ways it can be argued that the very act of good teaching actually masks the skilful ways in which teachers respond to the problematic nature of practice. Therefore, in teaching teaching, there is a pressing need for teacher educators to be able to bring to the surface the reactions, responses, decisions and moves that influence and shape their teaching during teaching. On the one hand, this is important in order for teacher educators to be cognizant of their own skills, knowledge and expertise in teaching. On the other, it matters if students of teaching are to see beyond the superficial and to engage with practice in more nuanced and sophisticated ways.

In the first instance, articulating a pedagogy of teacher education requires teacher educators to be aware of how they recognize and respond to the problematic nature of teaching. Yet as Korthagen makes clear, the problematic nature of teaching in teacher education is linked to the "technical-rationality model [that] still represents a very dominant line of thought" (2001b, p. 8). Thus it is important for teacher educators to be reminded about the fundamental nature of practice in order that they continue to question the taken-for-granted in their own teaching and not succumb to (or regress toward) a technical-rational approach to teaching teaching.

Enacting a pedagogy of teacher education means developing ways of delving into, and working with, the problematic nature of practice in order to highlight that teaching is much more than well-rehearsed scripts and routines. If pedagogical expertise is embedded in the ways in which a teacher skilfully manages the dilemmas, tensions, issues and concerns of practice during practice, then genuine examples of such situations must be made available to students of teaching, preferably through the very experiences of their own learning in their teacher education classes, as demonstrated by Clare Kosnik. The difficulty for teacher educators is in having the wisdom to know when they are confronted by a teachable moment (Van Manen, 1991) and how to productively open it up for inquiry in ways that do not become tedious or lead to an over-analysis of the simple or superficial.

Berry's experience offers insights into the dilemmas and difficulties of enacting this element of a pedagogy of teacher education:

> Usually, there is a multitude of thoughts running through my head as I teach. How do I know which of these is useful at any particular time to select to highlight for my students? . . . I had to choose carefully what I held up for public examination that would be useful and accessible for these student teachers . . . I wanted to convince them that it is OK to be unsure in your own practice, that teaching is problematic.
>
> (2001, p. 3)

Teacher educators need to be aware of the difficulties associated with attempting to make the problematic examinable for student teachers and the ways in which that might be done draws attention to the difference between teaching and telling; a major dilemma for many teacher educators. The way these two issues are intertwined is interesting in terms of a pedagogy of teacher education for it is not good enough to simply tell students of teaching that which appears problematic and that which does not. In a similar vein, nor is it helpful in learning about teaching to simply hear how to deal with such situations. Learning about the problematic nature of teaching is embedded in how teacher educators and students of teaching together recognize, respond to and are encouraged to explore the problematic. Such explorations offer insights into how some teacher educators enact a pedagogy of teacher education. Clare Kosnik in Chapter 2 captures the essence of one way of enacting this aspect of her pedagogy of teacher education by making the problematic a site for inquiry. In her chapter, she explains how she shares with her students her teaching intentions, thereby creating opportunities to examine the reasons for the sequence of her courses, her rationale for selecting particular readings and assignments, and her inevitable struggles with particular content and topics as well as with grading assignments. In so doing, she offers her students of teaching ways of "hearing her internal dialogue" and creates real possibilities for questioning that which happens in their shared teaching and learning experiences in their teacher education program.

In approaching her practice in this way, Kosnik highlights the importance of making the tacit aspects of practice explicit; initially for herself, but ultimately for her students of teaching so that they are offered useful ways of seeing into the complexity of practice. Her invitation to students of teaching to unpack their experiences of her teaching offers a concrete example of teaching teaching in accord with the needs and expectations of enacting a pedagogy of teacher education.

Making the tacit explicit

> Expert teachers possess richly elaborated knowledge about curriculum, classroom routines, and students that allows them to apply with dispatch what they know to particular cases. Where novices may focus on surface features or particular objects, experts draw on a store of knowledge that is organized around interpretative concepts or propositions that are tied to the teaching environment. Because the knowledge is tacit, it does not translate easily into direct instruction or formalization. This may help to account for the difficulty that teachers have in articulating the pieces that comprise their performance and knowledge base.
>
> (Munby *et al.*, 2001, p. 889)

Teachers' professional knowledge has long been recognized as largely being tacit. But for students of teaching to see into the complex nature of teaching, there is a need for teacher educators to be able to make the tacit explicit; something that as (or if they once were) classroom teachers they were perhaps less well versed in doing. There is a constant need for teacher educators to be able to answer questions from students of teaching such as: "Why does that teaching procedure work?"; "How does concept mapping enhance student learning?"; or "Why would I use a jig-saw method for groupwork?" Being able to articulate one's own knowledge of practice is vital to enacting a pedagogy of teacher education in order to be able to answer questions of this type. Scholarship in teaching and teacher education is evident when teaching procedures are used for particular reasons, in particular contexts, with particular content; not just because "they work." The expectation that teacher educators are scholars of teaching must then be a catalyst for making the tacit explicit.

Alicia Crowe and Amanda Berry in Chapter 3 offer insights into this aspect of enacting a pedagogy of teacher education. In developing and articulating their principles of practice they draw attention to ways of making the tacit explicit. Their second principle of practice, *Prospective teachers need opportunities to see into the thinking like a teacher of experienced others*, goes to the heart of what they describe as creating access to their pedagogical reasoning. Importantly, they do not see this as something to "build up to," rather, they launch into it at the outset. They describe how during the first day of classes their students of teaching are exposed to the thinking of a teacher as they are asked to consider the reasoning underpinning the actions of their teacher educator which creates a platform from which they can (together) examine fundamental principles of her practice. Through this approach, students of teaching begin to see below the surface of the teaching and learning episodes they have just experienced.

This approach to enacting a pedagogy of teacher education also illustrates the risks associated with attempting to make the tacit explicit. There is an inevitable vulnerability that accompanies making teaching about teaching a site for inquiry; placing one's own teaching on the table for dissection and analysis. Enacting a pedagogy of teacher education requires a confidence that might only be developed through learning to openly deal with the dilemmas, tensions and concerns of publicly examining the problematic nature of teaching in teaching teaching. Therefore, it is understandable that for some teacher educators there may well be a reluctance to overtly challenge their own teaching expertise; however, I would argue that such challenges are needed in order to begin to ask the hard questions about one's own pedagogical reasoning. Otherwise, it may well be that in modelling teaching, the impression gained by students of teaching is that being able to "do teaching" is all that matters. Thus, without intending it to be the case, a technical rational approach to learning about teaching may well prevail and create an unwitting counterpoint to any argument that teaching is a complex, messy yet sophisticated business.

As noted above, and further reinforced by Joe Senese in Chapter 4, making the tacit explicit is difficult for classroom teachers, and not necessarily something that is expected or encouraged. As a high school administrator, Senese has recognized the value in helping teachers begin to articulate what they think they are doing in the classroom in order to compare it to what they actually do; and to learn from the difference. He notes that teachers have little practice in articulating their pedagogical reasoning and that they are largely unaware of the "larger purposes, the overarching goals, and the deeper questions involved in teaching and learning." He draws attention to the personal and professional risks involved in examining the underpinnings of practice and how important it is for them to work with trusted colleagues in safe conditions. Yet, in so doing, teachers gain confidence and develop deeper understandings of what they do and why, which helps them to uncover assumptions about teaching and learning that then inform their practice.

The fact that it is difficult for experienced teachers to make the tacit explicit further reinforces why it is so important that teacher educators be skilled at so doing. Senese eloquently captures some of the difficulties and dilemmas of enacting this aspect of a pedagogy of teacher education. But, despite these difficulties he does not resile from the need for this to be a core attribute of teaching teaching for it is a conduit to teachers' professional knowledge.

Teaching as a relationship

Bullough and Gitlin offer a compelling argument about teaching as a relationship. They describe teaching as a way of being with, and relating to, others. When they extend this into teaching about teaching, they state that it requires more than "just dispensing information in a timely fashion but of building trust, of talking and problem-solving together" (2001, p. 3). Understanding teaching as a relationship hinges on a responsiveness to the dynamic nature of the teaching and learning environment and a sensitivity to its participants.

Coming to understand teaching in this way requires a commitment to looking more deeply into practice. For teachers this approach is sometimes captured through the notion of reflection (e.g., Dewey, 1933; Schön, 1983), for some teacher educators, it is most commonly displayed through self-study (Aubusson and Schuck, 2006; Hamilton *et al.*, 1998; Kosnick *et al.*, 2006; Samaras, 2006).

In Chapter 5, Ruth Kane highlights the ways in which honesty, trust and risk-taking must not only be reflected upon, but acted upon, in learning to articulate and better value professional knowledge of practice. Underpinning relationships is also important beyond the individual, and Kane shows clearly how her knowledge of teacher education practices also influenced the manner in which she conceptualized, and then constructed, a teacher education program.

In Chapter 6, Shawn Bullock offers an intriguing account of the development of his understanding of teaching as a relationship. Through analysis of his daily journal of his teaching, he came to see how important it was to the way in which he developed his practice to pay careful attention to relationships, particularly those between teacher and students. As he reflected on his practice he came to see that "recognizing the primacy of relationships in teaching represented a major shift in [his] thinking" about teaching. The primacy of relationships carried over in important ways into his learning in teaching about teaching and helped him to concentrate on appropriate ways of addressing the tensions and dilemmas associated with trying to teach (as opposed to telling) students of teaching about the complexity of practice. Bullock's efforts highlight how enacting a pedagogy of teacher education requires close attention to relationships and how sensitivity to situations is so important in shaping actions in action.

Relationships influence a great deal in learning and teaching about teaching. Whether intended or not, all that teacher educators do models something about practice. Maintaining a respect for the need to positively develop and respond to relationships is the key to enacting a pedagogy of teacher education and is hopefully something that is genuinely and purposefully modelled in teaching teaching.

Challenging the "tyranny of talk"

Bullock's chapter draws attention to the enduring effects of transmissive teaching. He describes the challenge he faced to his "default understanding of teaching as telling," as he confronted the need to challenge the tyranny of talk. Challenging the tyranny of talk requires looking into the relationship between teaching and learning and endeavouring to develop ways of engaging learners in learning. One way in which this might begin for teacher educators is through sustained efforts to encourage, support and learn through metacognition (theirs and their students).

In Chapter 7, Linda Kroll illustrates how her pedagogy of teacher education has been influenced by her thinking about her own learning and how that relates to students as learners of teaching and learning. By questioning her own history of learning and how that has been constructed, she is able to "unpack" some of the crucial relationships between teaching and learning that matter in the ways in which she thinks about how her students might learn.

Such thinking is indicative of learning through metacognition and, importantly, of doing so in a purposeful and serious manner. By linking teaching and learning in real ways, by contrasting the roles of teacher and learner, Kroll is able to construct pedagogy that is embedded in relationships. Doing this in her own practice brings to the surface (for herself) what this aspect of a pedagogy of teacher education entails, pursuing it with her students of teaching is how it is enacted in practice. Further to this, in being purposefully responsive to her students' perspectives on learning, a serious focus on learning about teaching emerges which then illustrates the complementarity necessary to balance the demands of teaching *and* learning about teaching in teacher education programs.

Learning about teaching

Understanding learning about teaching from the perspective of students of teaching is important in shaping a pedagogy of teacher education:

> [Yet] it is not sufficient for students of teaching to uncritically accept (or reject) the teaching approaches used in their teacher preparation programs. They need to be sensitive to the manner in which the teaching that they experience is conducted and to constantly be cognizant of the link between the teaching that they experience and the ways in which it influences their learning.
>
> (Loughran, 2006, p. 102)

Students of teaching are continually confronted by struggles, difficulties and dilemmas that affect their understanding of the nature of teaching as a consequence of their experiences in learning about teaching. Although they may not recognize it at the time, students of teaching are influenced by the *dual nature* of learning about teaching, for their experience involves being learners and teachers at the same time. By encouraging students of teaching to learn from the questions and critiques of the teaching used to teach them, teacher educators are able to enact another aspect of a pedagogy of teacher education so crucial to embedding such learning in their own experiences.

Being a student of teaching: knowing yourself

There is little doubt that the "apprenticeship of observation" (Lortie, 1975) that students of teaching have experienced as students influences profoundly their views and expectations of teacher education. It is important that teacher educators develop, and are able to enact, serious ways of challenging the many hidden assumptions about teaching that students of teaching have inevitably developed over time (but may not consciously recognize).

Enacting this aspect of a pedagogy of teacher education requires an ability to find a balance between responding appropriately to the apparent needs and concerns of students of teaching while at the same time creating an expectation for pedagogical development and challenge. As noted earlier in the chapter, because everything that teacher educators do models something to students of teaching, the ways in which this balance is managed is also dependent on teacher educators experiencing events in ways similar to that of their students of teaching. For example, in expecting students of teaching to meaningfully confront their own hidden assumptions, so too should teacher educators. It is in the common inability (or avoidance) of such actions to be publicly enacted in teacher education that students of teaching rightly become critical of teacher educators "saying one thing and doing another" or, expecting students of teaching to do things that "they do not do themselves," that highlights how everything that we do as teacher educators models something. Therefore, it is difficult to help students of teaching learn about teaching if we do not also learn ourselves. Hence, knowing yourself is an important precursor to being able to help others do likewise; and is an important element of learning, especially in regard of teaching.

The teaching behaviours and actions that come to the fore through the ways in which we work pedagogically must be able to be moderated, mediated and managed in ways that demonstrate a thoughtfulness about our own practice if we are to be seen as credible models for our students of teaching. Yet, modelling in teacher education can be a problem. In some instances, the use of the term modelling is as a synonym for demonstrating the "correct way" of doing something, and so, is set down as a form of blueprint or recipe for careful replication by learners. In contrast, I mean the term modelling to suggest that teacher educators' practice should be seen as offering ways of seeing into teaching; not to be mimicked or copied "letter perfect," but to be a case from which exploration, development, innovation and adaptation might be generated in different ways for different learners of teaching.

Fred Korthagen and Hildelien Verkuyl, in Chapter 8, illustrate this point vividly through the way their chapter illustrates the value of coming to better know and confront the self. What they expect of their workshop participants, they similarly expect of themselves. They draw attention to the interesting observation that many teacher educators "restrict themselves to promoting reflection with regard to behavior, competencies and perhaps beliefs about teaching and learning," thus avoiding the sense of doubt or confusion that can surround the gap between the personal motivation for being a teacher and the realities of teaching itself. In essence, the importance of coming to understand one's own professional identity and taking more active responsibility for the ways in which that is shaped and developed is a central purpose in Korthagen and Verkuyl's work: "We kept track of our own journey . . . repeatedly questioned each other, especially on issues such as our own ideals in education and the deeper sources of our ways of functioning as teacher educators."

By knowing what it is like to be a student of teaching, in coming to know oneself better, by feeling it as a learner, by creating opportunities and experiences that encourage deeper understandings of one's own practice, there is more likelihood that taken-for-granted aspects of practice and hidden assumptions that shape one's practice might be challenged by both teacher educators and students of teaching. In enacting this aspect of a pedagogy of teacher education, active and purposeful development of the personal and professional self is more likely to be encouraged. Such encouragement can be operationalized and formalized through self-study and, as Korthagen and Verkuyl demonstrate, the outcomes of self-study have the potential to influence practice dramatically. In a similar way, Cristy Kessler placed herself in the position of learner, in Chapter 9. Through her self-study she developed much deeper understandings about what a teacher must "know and be able to do" to successfully complete National Board certification.

Seeing through students' eyes

Munby and Russell (1994) coined the phrase "authority of experience" to capture the importance of knowing about practice by learning from one's own experiences of practice. Clearly, reflective practices are paramount in influencing the extent to which such "authority" might genuinely guide and inform the development of one's authority of experience, but without doubt, authority of experience would be impoverished if experience itself was lacking. Paradoxically, in some situations, teacher educators choose to organize alternatives to experience in order to convey what might be learnt through such experience. It stands to reason that in attempting to help students of teaching develop the authority of their own experience, teacher educators must also embark on experiences that can help them see situations through learners' eyes. Kessler did just that in choosing to submit for National Board certification.

In experiencing what was personally required to complete National Board certification, Kessler brought new meaning to the notion of "recent and relevant" experience for teacher educators. She felt what it was like to be a teacher traversing the complex path necessary for National Board Accreditation. In so doing, she developed her authority of experience as a teacher. As a beginning teacher educator, the experience was also powerful in shaping her understanding of, and developing identity as, a teacher educator in ways that dramatically reshaped her practice.

She could not help but see "the parallels between teaching and teaching about teaching [which also] made it almost inevitable that the process [became] a catalyst for [her] to study [her] own practice." Her self-study created new ways of understanding her growing knowledge of a pedagogy of teacher education and ways in which it might be enacted. Because she was "forced" to reconsider her own practice, she came to see modelling in new and different ways and so she purposefully developed ways for her students of teaching to experience flexibility and compassion and how important they were to creating and sustaining a positive classroom environment.

By submitting to the complex and difficult task of seeking National Board accreditation, Kessler learnt, first, about how to develop, and then, second, how to enact, a pedagogy of teacher education. Through her experience, she (re)learnt about planning and flexibility and how important they were to successful teaching. Through this process, she was able to see, feel and learn through the experience in ways that enabled her to be a much more informed and thoughtful teacher of teachers. She developed much deeper understandings of her own learning and it helped to better direct her teacher education practices, and ultimately, the learning about teaching of her students of teaching.

Seeing learning about teaching through the eyes of students of teaching is important. However, when such perspectives can be viewed through the eyes of students of teaching themselves, then the experiences take on a whole new level of meaning. In Chapter 10, Matt Olmstead does just that through his chapter's insights into learning about teaching from this personal perspective as a student of teaching. It is a perspective that teacher educators need constantly to be reminded of and to seek to encourage as a way of enacting their pedagogy of teacher education. Olmstead highlights again the importance of relationships in teaching. In this case, it is the relationship of associate teacher and teacher candidate and the dramatic impact that relationship can have on one's teaching identity and subsequent practices: "Almost right away I found myself wondering about my associate's classroom environment from her students' point of view. By the end of the first day I realized that my vision of teaching and my associate teacher's were very different."

What Olmstead's chapter highlights is the need for students of teaching to feel comfortable in an environment in which professional critique of practice is experienced as being helpful, informing and challenging in the pursuit of a growth of knowledge and practice in teaching. Such an experience is of course in stark contrast to experiences of personal criticism and an implicit learning about teaching message such as: "You need to learn to teach like me"; or even worse, "Do as I say, not as I do."

Enacting a pedagogy of teacher education that encourages and supports students of teaching to examine their developing practice in the way Olmsted demonstrates is surely a hallmark of quality in teacher education practices. To develop a trust in, and an explicit valuing of, a student-teacher as researcher stance

(Cochran-Smith, 1991; Loughran, 2004) brings to the fore the importance of a focus on the authority of experience in meaningful and applicable ways. Just as Olmstead demonstrates in his most compelling chapter, there is a great need for teacher educators to creating possibilities for realistic approaches to professional learning so that students of teaching can come to better understand and value the professional knowledge of practice. Teacher education is the starting point for creating that vision and so the way teacher education programs are conceptualized, structured and organized does matter; and does influence the ways in which a pedagogy of teacher education might be enacted.

Teacher education programs

Teacher preparation is a beginning, not an end unto itself. Therefore, when considering what can be done in a teacher education program, there is always a need to realistically respond to what is possible and reasonable; or, put another way, *teacher education is by definition incomplete* (Northfield and Gunstone, 1997). This is not meant as an excuse for what some might describe as "the things that ail teacher education," rather, it is a simple reminder that in many cases, the expectations and demands placed on teacher education go well beyond that which is fair and reasonable.

Teacher education is the beginning of the development of prospective teachers' conceptualization and practice of professional learning; a career-long undertaking. Hoban captures well an important way of thinking about structuring a teacher education program:

> [There is no] "one best way of educating teachers" for that would be nonsensical. Teacher preparation programs vary according to the goals, course content, beliefs of the teacher educators, students and teachers, as well as the social-cultural contexts of schools involved. However, I do argue that a quality teacher education program needs to be guided by a coherent conceptual framework with interlinked elements. Such a program would help pre-service students to learn about teaching and understand its complex nature.

> (2005, p. 1)

The notion of a conceptual framework is important because almost regardless of the words that comprise a teacher education program's mission, or vision or philosophy, the words themselves carry little meaning if they are not enacted in the practices of the program's teacher educators. Hoban identifies four links that together comprise a coherent conceptual framework for teacher education program design: (1) conceptual links across the university curriculum; (2) theory–practice links between school and university settings; (3) social-cultural links among participants in the program; and (4) links that shape the identity of participants in the program. Although I concur with Hoban about the importance of a conceptual framework that embodies program structure, in terms of enacting a pedagogy of teacher education, I also see a pressing need for such conceptualizations to be explicitly realized in practice.

Andrea Martin's Chapter 11 offers insights into what it means to enact a pedagogy of teacher education through a reconsideration of the structure and organization of a teacher education program and how it so dramatically shapes teacher educators' teaching and pre-service teachers' learning. Martin describes how teaching in a restructured program with an extended fall practicum from the first day of the school year forced her to confront her assumptions about teaching about teaching. She found that "it quickly became apparent that traditional, transmission models of teaching were both inadequate and inappropriate. Teaching experience-rich pre-service teachers would require us to develop a new pedagogy of teacher education." The overall result was as an epiphany that continues to shape her thinking and practices.

Importantly, the challenges of a change in the traditional teacher education program structure led her to genuinely pursue, in practice, the development of a community of learners with a shared sense of purpose. Her sensitivity to what structural changes meant for the learning of students of teaching led her to enact new approaches to teaching about teaching as she questioned her fundamental beliefs and values in ways that helped her better walk her talk. She demonstrates that program structures necessarily influence teacher educators' practices as well as the learning by students of teaching. Hoban's point about a well-conceptualized teacher education program being important in shaping a pedagogy of teacher education is certainly reinforced by Martin's chapter.

In Chapter 12, Mieke Lunenberg, Fred Korthagen and Martijn Willemse consider the importance of a conceptual framework in shaping the nature of teacher education through the manner in which they explore "value-based teacher education." They are concerned to better understand the way in which a teacher's norms and values, as they are played out in practice, influence the way in which students might develop their own. They illustrate how relationships, identity formation, professional learning and personal growth are then key concepts in shaping a conceptual framework on which teacher education program structuring might not only be designed but also enacted.

In their chapter, Lunenberg *et al.* raise an interesting issue that is not prominent in the literature—the professional development of teacher educators. In considering the way in which teacher educators themselves shape the curriculum, they remind us of the need to seriously question what is taught, how and why. Further to this, the role of language and the importance of meta-awareness for recognizing possibilities for unpacking practice is crucial for delving into what they describe as "golden moments." In drawing attention to the possibilities inherent in the professional development of teacher educators, they represent teaching teaching as a rich and complex pursuit in which both teacher and student interact to shape the learning outcomes. Therefore, no matter how well a teacher education program might be structured, organized or conceptualized (or not), the need for teacher educators to have rich understandings and practices of teaching *and* learning about teaching is vital. Hence, it seems reasonable to suggest, that developing and enacting a pedagogy of teacher education are paramount to quality teacher education.

In Tom Russell's closing chapter, his reconsideration of his teaching about teaching is catalysed through aspects of teacher education that should be important in shaping the nature of program organization and structure. He describes in detail how his pedagogy of teacher education has developed and changed in response to two important elements: students' reactions and research findings. As a consequence, the conceptual framework that directs his responsibilities in the Queen's University's teacher preparation program is focused on "teacher candidates learning to study their own development as teachers." By conceptualizing teacher education in this way, Russell intends that reflective practice and constructivist teaching approaches become more meaningfully embedded in teaching *and* learning about teaching.

Again, the centrality of relationships comes to the fore as Russell explains his own development as a teacher educator and the manner in which that has informed the ways in which he conceptualizes teacher education as a "teaching–learning relationship [that is a] fundamental block from which all else follows." Thus it can well be argued that the teacher education practices at the heart of enacting such a conceptualization must be based on shared experiences.

The value of shared experiences seems self-evident, yet it is not a theme or issue commonly noted in the teacher education literature. Russell illustrates clearly how "the important messages conveyed to students by how a teacher teaches" demand that teacher education be built on shared experiences from which more personally meaningful unpacking and learning from those episodes and events might occur and positively shape the development of knowledge of practice for students of teaching.

Through his conceptualization of teacher education, Russell aims to ensure that constructivism, metacognition, and reflective practice are not simply idle terms and phrases but that teacher education is indeed a beginning point in bringing them to life. In so doing, it becomes more likely that students of teaching (and their teacher educators) are able to build on the meaning of terms such as these and that they will have real implications in teaching learning not only in teacher education classrooms, but in school classrooms as well.

Conclusion

Self-study of teacher education practices has gained a strong foothold in the teacher education literature over the past 15 years. Scholarship in this field has been important in bringing to the surface aspects of teaching and learning about teaching that previously were less well understood and considerably less well researched. The research findings have been much more applicable to teacher education generally because those involved in the enterprise of teacher education are increasingly those doing the research and those who are framing the questions being asked, the methodological approaches to data collection and analysis and the manner in which participants' perspectives shape the research. Just as the transition from student to teacher offers new and important insights into learning about teaching when developed from the perspective of a student of teaching, so too the shift from classroom teacher to teacher educator is equally important when framed from a teacher educator's perspective.

Enacting a pedagogy of teacher education requires much more than simply delivering whatever it might be that is variously described as the curriculum of teacher education. Doing teaching with students of teaching requires deep and well-conceptualized understandings of pedagogy that are developed, articulated, critiqued and refined in the crucible of practice itself. Shulman (2000) has focussed much attention on the scholarship of teaching, and the scholarship of teacher education practices is equally important. Such scholarship is evident in the way in which teacher educators actively pursue the development of their pedagogy of teacher education. It seems reasonable, then, that we should all be challenged to respond to the question, "As a teacher educator, how do you develop and enact your pedagogy of teacher education?"

References

Aubusson, P. and Schuck, S. (eds.) (2006) *Teacher education: The mirror maze.* Dordrecht: Springer.

Berry, A. (2001) Making the private public: Using the WWW as a window into one teacher educator's thinking about her practice. Paper presented at the meeting of the International Study Association of Teachers and Teaching, Faro, Portugal, September.

Berry, A. (2004) Self-study in teaching about teaching. In J. Loughran, M. L. Hamilton, V. K. LaBoskey and T. Russell (eds.), *International handbook of self-study of teaching and teacher education practices.* Dordrecht: Kluwer, pp. 1295–1332.

Bullough, R. V. J. (1997) Practicing theory and theorizing practice in teacher education. In J. Loughran and T. Russell (eds.), *Teaching about teaching: Purpose, passion and pedagogy in teacher education.* London: Falmer Press, pp. 13–31.

Bullough, R. V. J. and Gitlin, A. (2001) *Becoming a student of teaching: Linking knowledge production and practice.* 2nd edn. London: RoutledgeFalmer.

Clarke, A. and Erickson, G. (2004) The nature of teaching and learning in self-study. In J. J. Loughran, M. L. Hamilton, V. K. LaBoskey, and T. Russell (eds.), *International handbook of teaching and teacher education practices.* Dordrecht: Kluwer Academic Press, pp. 41–67.

Cochran-Smith, M. (1991) Reinventing student teaching. *Journal of Teacher Education,* *42*(2), 104–118.

Dewey, J. (1933) *How we think.* Lexington, MA: D.C. Heath and Company.

Dinkelman, T., Margolis, J., and Sikkenga, K. (2006) From teacher to teacher educator: Experiences, expectations, and expatriation. *Studying Teacher Education, 2,* 5–23.

Hamilton, M. L., with Pinnegar, S., Russell, T., Loughran, J., and LaBoskey, V. (eds.). (1998) *Reconceptualizing teaching practice: Self-study in teacher education.* London: Falmer Press.

Hoban, G. F. (ed.) (2005) *The missing links in teacher education design: Developing a multi-linked conceptual framework.* Dordrecht: Springer.

Korthagen, F. A. J. (2001a) Building a realistic teacher education program. In F. A. J. Korthagen, J. Kessels, B. Koster, B. Lagerwerf, and T. Wubbels, *Linking practice and theory: The pedagogy of realistic teacher education.* Mahwah, NJ: Lawrence Erlbaum Associates, pp. 69–87.

Korthagen, F. A. J. (2001b) Teacher education: A problematic enterprise. In F. A. J. Korthagen, J. Kessels, B. Koster, B. Lagerwerf, and T. Wubbels (eds.), *Linking practice and theory: The pedagogy of realistic teacher education.* Mahwah, NJ: Lawrence Erlbaum Associates, pp. 1–19.

Kosnick, C., Beck, C., Freese, A., and Samaras, A. (eds.) (2006) *Making a difference in teacher education through self-study: Studies of personal, professional, and program renewal.* Dordrecht: Springer.

Lortie, D. C. (1975) *Schoolteacher.* Chicago: University of Chicago Press.

Loughran, J. J. (2004) Student teacher as researcher: Accepting greater responsibility for learning about teaching. *Australian Journal of Education, 48*, 212–220.

Loughran, J. J. (2006) *Developing a pedagogy of teacher education: Understanding teaching and learning about teaching.* London: Routledge.

Munby, H. and Russell, T. (1994) The authority of experience in learning to teach: Messages from a physics method class. *Journal of Teacher Education, 4*, 86–95.

Munby, H., Russell, T., and Martin, A. K. (2001) Teachers' knowledge and how it develops. In V. Richardson (ed.), *Handbook of research on teaching.* 4th edn. Washington, DC: American Educational Research Association, pp. 877–904.

Nicol, C. (1997) Learning to teach prospective teachers to teach mathematics: Struggles of a beginning teacher educator. In J. Loughran and T. Russell (eds.), *Teaching about teaching: Purpose, passion and pedagogy in teacher education.* London: Falmer Press, pp. 95–116.

Nicol, C. (2006) Designing a pedagogy of inquiry in teacher education: Moving from resistance to listening. *Studying Teacher Education, 2*, 25–41.

Northfield, J. R. and Gunstone, R. F. (1997) Teacher education as a process of developing teacher knowledge. In J. Loughran and T. Russell (eds.), *Teaching about teaching: Purpose, passion and pedagogy in teacher education.* London: Falmer Press, pp. 48–56.

Samaras, A. (2006) *Self-study of teaching practices.* New York: Peter Lang.

Schön, D. A. (1983) *The reflective practitioner: How professionals think in action.* New York: Basic Books.

Shulman, L. S. (2000) From Minsk to Pinsk: Why a scholarship of teaching and learning? *The Journal of Scholarship of Teaching and Learning, 1*(1), 48–52.

Tidwell, D. (2002) A balancing act: Self-study in valuing the individual student. In J. Loughran and T. Russell (eds.), *Improving teacher education practices through self-study.* London: RoutledgeFalmer, pp. 30–42.

Trumbull, D. (2004) Factors important for the scholarship of self-study of teaching and teacher education practices. In J. J. Loughran, M. L. Hamilton, V. K. LaBoskey, and T. Russell (eds.), *International handbook of self-study of teaching and teacher education practices.* Dordrecht: Kluwer Academic Publishers, pp. 1211–1230.

Tudball, L. (2004) Listening and responding to the views of my students: Are they ready to teach in a diverse world? Risking self-study of the internationalization of teacher education. In D. Tidwell, L. Fitzgerald, and M. Heston (eds.), *Journeys of hope: Risking self-study in a diverse world*, Proceedings of the fifth international conference of self-study of teacher education practices, vol. 2. Cedar Falls, IA: University of Northern Iowa, pp. 250–254.

Van Manen, M. (1991) *The tact of teaching: The meaning of pedagogical thoughtfulness.* Albany, NY: State University of New York Press.

2 Still the same yet different

Enduring values and commitments in my work as a teacher and teacher educator

Clare Kosnik

Becoming a teacher educator involves much more than a job title. Even if one becomes a teacher educator at the moment one becomes a teacher educator, one's professional identity as a teacher educator is constructed over time. Developing an identity and a set of successful practices in teacher education is best understood as a process of becoming. Although the work of teaching has much in common with the work of teacher education, the two positions are significantly different in important ways.

(Dinkelman *et al.*, 2006, p. 6)

In many ways my efforts as a teacher educator are a continuation of my work as a classroom teacher. In other ways my teaching is different, particularly my intentionality about making the thinking behind my teaching visible and about conducting research on the impact of my teaching. I recognize that my pedagogy of teacher education continues to evolve as I continue to study my practice:

It is not just the experience that matters, it is the learning through experience that needs to be reflected upon and shared, as the nature of the deliberations within the teacher education learning community are critical to the development of a pedagogy of teacher education.

(Loughran, 2006, p. 23)

Loughran writes compellingly that we need a pedagogy of teacher education. In this chapter, I describe elements of my philosophy of education that shaped my work as a classroom teacher and that continue to frame my work as a teacher educator. I discuss these values and principles because they are the foundation of my work in teacher education. I provide examples from both my current practice and from my work as a classroom teacher. Although I have organized the chapter into three sections, my development as a teacher educator did not follow a linear path. In fact, I see my career as a continuous looping back as I reconsider avenues taken and not taken, overlapping interests, a recanting of some sacred beliefs, and development of new values, at times being clear-sighted while at other times being confused about the next steps. My career continues to involve ongoing readjusting and reframing of beliefs and practices.

Recognizing that teacher education can be done differently

Teacher education is often criticized for being irrelevant, separate from theory, repetitive, and demeaning (Darling-Hammond and Bransford, 2005; Ducharme and Ducharme, 1999; Labaree, 2004). I can relate to many of the stinging judgments because I completed an 8-month, post-baccalaureate program that was a cobbled together string of courses and experiences that lacked coherence and vision. I began my teaching career with few of the basic skills of teaching but I learned on the job, supported by outstanding colleagues. Because my teacher education program was so dismal, I quickly sought professional development opportunities and enrolled in in-service and graduate courses. Thus my poor experience of pre-service teacher education cultivated my enduring commitment to ongoing learning about teaching.

Different is not necessarily better

Like many other teacher educators, I began my career as a teacher. Becoming a teacher educator is something I fell into by default, having to assume the work for a school district superintendent who was too busy to become involved in a school–university project. Although I enjoyed the work, I was often wracked with self-doubts, believing that I was not qualified to teach at a university because I was *just* a teacher. My approach to my first few teacher education courses was quite simple: give the student teachers an endless stream of practical resources, tips, strategies, and materials. Knowing how unprepared I had been as a first-year teacher, and knowing the enormous effort required to locate and develop essential resources, I wanted to save my often naïve and innocent students from that horrendous first year of teaching. I concluded that they should focus on their students rather than spend endless hours searching for materials and then being too exhausted to teach. They appreciated the binders and boxes of materials I carted into class each week, believing these resources would help them be effective teachers. I was acting as a curriculum resource clearing house, drawing on many examples that gave me credibility in the eyes of my students. Like my students, I was shortsighted and did not deserve the title of teacher educator:

> One difficulty associated with framing professional identity through the lens of the ex-school teacher is that the teacher educator may be viewed as simply being a teacher teaching in teacher preparation rather than as a teacher educator with an expertise in teaching and learning about teaching.
>
> (Loughran, 2006, p. 13)

Early in my career as a teacher educator, both my identity and my practices were closely tied to being a classroom teacher of children and I had not made the transition, with the accompanying skills and knowledge, to being a teacher educator teaching about teaching.

I soon sensed there was something wrong with my approach to teacher education but I could not define the problem. When a colleague introduced me to action research, I immediately realized that my lack of theory and my inattention to helping student teachers develop as thinking, inquiring, and decision-making professionals could actually do them harm. I seemed to be fooling them into believing that a few good resources, a caring approach, and good classroom management were all they required. When I read reports of classroom teachers doing research on their work (Patterson *et al.*, 1993), I immediately recognized the potential of teacher inquiry.

Although I had no examples of teacher educators adopting such a radically different approach, I set out to integrate action research into my course. Action research has become more common in teacher education programs, but in the early 1990s this was a radical step. A willingness to "think outside the box" and be experimental are now enduring traits of my practice. At times, my innovations have caused problems but I am not one to simply do something in a particular way because it is the way it has always been done.

Developing an inquiry-based program

Introducing action research into my course was not a simple curriculum modification. I struggled with students who craved and demanded to be told how to teach; I struggled with some of my colleagues who resented my advocacy for teachers examining their practice. They complained that it was causing too much upheaval in the program. Loughran argues for the inclusion of teacher research in a pre-service program:

> There is also a realization that there is no educational change without teacher change and by focusing on personal practice and experience, teachers may undertake genuine enquiry that can lead to a better understanding of the complexities of teaching and learning.
>
> (2006, p. 138)

Although I encountered resistance, I persevered, modified my practice, drew on some successes, found some examples in the literature (Ross, 1987), and began to collaborate with like-minded colleagues. Eventually, action research became more accepted and the faculty team grew to include individuals with similar interests. Coinciding with this shift, I became Coordinator of the Mid-Town cohort of pre-service teachers. Not satisfied with my earlier efforts, I wanted to move inquiry from being an activity in one course to setting the framework for our entire program. This was coupled with my strong interest in helping our cohort become a community. A colleague and I wrote a vision statement for our program that led to the faculty team jointly planning the program and devising a series of community-building activities.

Having an inquiry-based program is not an easy task, and each year I tried to explain to my student teachers why I wanted them to do action research. I explained my belief that it empowers teachers and provides insights into one's teaching, through the continuous cycle of observation, reading, curriculum modification, data-gathering and assessment, and reflection. Despite my extensive explanations, I realized that student teachers could not "hear my rationale":

> Seeing ourselves through students' eyes often leads to our realizing that we have to pay much more attention than we thought was necessary to explaining and justifying our actions. We have to create windows into our minds so that students can see the workings of our own teaching rationales. Laying bare our pedagogic reasoning helps students understand that our actions are not arbitrary or haphazard. They see that our choices and injunctions spring from our past experiences as teachers, from our convictions about what we're trying to accomplish, and from our knowledge of students' backgrounds, expectations, cultures, and concerns.
>
> (Brookfield, 1995, p. 108)

I had to find ways to make my rationale explicit in a language my students could understand. I shared pieces of reflective writing about action research done by previous student teachers in the Mid-Town cohort and I involved them in my personal action research (e.g., improving small-group discussion). Eventually, I realized that it was not sufficient for me to talk about the value of action research; the student teachers needed to experience it firsthand. Over the course of the academic year they begin to see the value of action research. An especially powerful teaching strategy involved inviting graduates from Mid-Town to talk to the current student teachers about action research. One described the impact of action research as follows:

> It really shaped the way I perceived the role of the teacher. In any other program you'd probably hear the phrase reflective practitioner but I think until you live it you can't really understand it. And with the action research we really learned that we had to read. We had to read, we had to reflect, we had to consult, we had to talk, we had to observe our kids, we had to implement changes. You can't understand it unless you're really immersed in it.
>
> (Kosnik, 1999, p. 7)

Another Mid-Town graduate made these comments:

> Action research gives credence to teachers' observations and reflections. Where the thoughtful practitioner's final analysis may have been based upon intuition, experience, and hearsay, action research empowers the teacher by answering why the implementation worked or did not work and why he/she

observed what he/she did. Action research simply allows for more focus and empowers teachers to empower their students to learn.

(ibid., p. 11)

Experiencing action research and meeting with new teachers who had done action research were two very good pedagogies, but I did not find these strategies in books on either teacher education or action research. Rather, I discovered them by listening to students try to figure out why they seemed resistant to action research and then by thinking outside the box for solutions.

Examining teaching practices critically was akin to my work as a classroom teacher because I had a long history of constantly assessing and modifying my teaching. As a classroom teacher, I was not familiar with the theory of action research; I did not call my efforts "inquiry" but my approach was definitely a simple form of teacher research. Once I had the language, I could more fully describe my approach and involve others in dialogue. Using an inquiry approach has become an central element of personal practice and my current work as a researcher builds on my work as classroom teacher.

Being deliberate in my choices

As I became a more able teacher educator, I began to view myself and my work through a different lens. I saw the need to model effective teaching, reflect openly about my work, and be more deliberate in my work. I also came to appreciate the power of my actions:

> A teacher's norms and values, and the extent to which they are enacted in practice, influence the manner [in] which students develop their own. Thus personal relationship between teachers and students is crucial as identity for-mation and personal growth combine to shape the nature of pedagogy itself.
> (Loughran, 2006, p. 2)

Loughran's conclusion has been borne out repeatedly in our follow-up studies of graduates from the Mid-Town cohort. For example, our emphasis on care and community profoundly shaped our program. As one graduate noted:

> All of our professors were caring for us, and they taught us it's not just curriculum, curriculum, curriculum, or this is what you need to learn to be a good teacher. It's more to help us become [caring] like that, and I think that's what a lot of us are going to remember.
> (Beck and Kosnik, 2002, p. 428)

Making explicit my values and decisions

Lortie's research clearly illustrated that the decisions teachers make are often invisible to pupils and the long apprenticeship of observation has its limitations:

Students do not receive invitations to watch the teacher's performance through the wings; they are not privy to the teacher's private intentions and personal reflections on classroom events. Students rarely participate in selecting goals, making preparations or analyzing the class later. Thus they are not pressed to place the teacher's actions in a pedagogically oriented framework.

(Lortie, 1975, p. 62)

Similarly, the choices and struggles of teacher educators are frequently not apparent to student teachers. I continue to be astounded that student teachers are often unaware of the challenges I face as a teacher educator as they are becoming increasingly aware of the complexity and demands of teaching; they tend not to appreciate that teacher educators face many of the same issues they themselves face as teachers.

As a teacher educator, I have become more aware of the need to walk my student teachers through my decision-making process. As Loughran (2006, p. 5) notes:

If students of teaching are to genuinely "see into teaching," then they require access to the thoughts and actions that shape such practice; they need to be able to see and hear the pedagogical reasoning that underpins the teaching that they are experiencing.

Given that modeling is not sufficient, I have tried to make my teaching more transparent to my students; however, Loughran cautions that there "was a danger that talking aloud about what I was or was not doing, and why, could be interpreted as lacking appropriate direction" (1995, p. 434). I concur with Loughran's warning because some of my students have been surprised and unsettled that their teacher educator, a university professor, had feelings of uncertainty. Nevertheless, I believe that thinking aloud helps my student teachers understand that the process of teaching is not simply communicating a given body of information to students and that teachers do not have all the answers.

I continue to share with my students my intentions—the reasons for the sequence of courses, my rationale for selecting particular readings or assignments, the struggle I have when I need to delete or shorten particular topics, the stress of grading assignments, and so on. Sharing my thinking with my students has had many benefits: it helps them hear my internal dialogue, it gives them comfort when they have similar struggles, and it has led to interesting discussions about the teaching–learning process. For example, in a course on classroom culture, I struggled to set assignments that were relevant. I shared my dilemma with my students and, at first, I was met with stony silence; as the term progressed, we worked out assignments that were highly useful and met the goals of the course. This proved highly informative to them as beginning teachers because they experienced first-hand the value of seeking student input. As a classroom teacher I used a similar approach, although in that context, it was much less explicit. I often gave the students choice in their work assignments. In a unit on poetry, children could choose four assignments from the list and, in some instances, I let them suggest or create their own assignment. After relating to my student teachers the need for pupil involvement and their own experience at helping me shape our course, I noticed that some experimented with a less prescriptive style of teaching themselves.

As part of my efforts to make the teaching–learning process more transparent, I share with my student teachers the story of my career. This allows them to have a greater understanding of who I am as a person and teacher; it also leads many to begin to think about their own story and choices. The three fundamental principles of teaching and learning identified by the National Academy of Sciences are designed to guide teaching practices for children, but I believe they apply equally well to teaching about teaching and are relevant in this discussion of making values and beliefs explicit. The three principles are summarized as:

1   Students come to the classroom with prior knowledge that must be addressed if teaching is to be effective.
2   Students need to organize and use knowledge conceptually if they are to apply it beyond the classroom.
3   Students learn more effectively if they understand how they learn and how to manage their own learning.

(Darling-Hammond, 2006, p. 9)

The first principle is critically important because our student teachers are not blank slates waiting to be filled by us. Sharing my story and encouraging students to recount their own stories leads many to appreciate that their experiences as pupils strongly influence who they are as teachers. By helping student teachers make their implicit values explicit and by recognizing that their prior knowledge about teaching and learning influences how they respond to my teaching and messages about teaching, I believe that I increase the likelihood of the teacher education experience building on their strengths and talents. As Loughran (2006, p. 124) wrote, "the transition from student to teacher involves a realization that some changes are quite personal (e.g., coming to know oneself) while others are more generalizable (e.g., initially identifying more strongly with students than teachers) concerns about subject matter knowledge." Student teachers cannot interrogate their personal beliefs if we pretend that those beliefs do not exist. I also tell my student teachers how I told my own pupils about some of the rationale for the work that I was asking them to complete. Even though I taught mainly in the lower primary grades, I tried to explain to the children why we were doing what we were doing. I tried to avoid statements such as, "when you are working, you will need to know how to write a proper paragraph." Rather, I tried to explain the rationale for work in terms the children could relate to. Involving students in the learning process, regardless of age, is an enduring value.

Modeling effective teaching

Finding ways to help student teachers acquire the knowledge, skills, and attitudes of effective teachers is an ongoing challenge. I have begun to model a variety of teaching strategies, yet modeling alone is not sufficient because student teachers can be dazzled by our teaching or they can just take our teaching for granted:

> Teaching about teaching goes beyond the traditional notion of modeling, for it involves not just teaching in ways congruent with the expectations one has of the manner in which pre-service teachers might teach, it involves unpacking teaching in ways that give students access to the pedagogical reasoning, uncertainties and dilemmas of practice that are inherent in understanding teaching as being problematic.
>
> (Loughran, 2006, p. 6)

Modeling must be accompanied by an appropriate narrative that explains one's teaching. Student teachers must begin to understand the complexity and challenge of teaching, even at the university level because "what may well be difficult or perplexing pedagogical situations are made to look simple to the students of teaching" (ibid., p. 41). Through think-alouds and discussions, I work to reveal the complexity of teaching and thereby provide a more realistic view of the teaching process. On-going discussions in class and analysis of their own learning helps them study teaching in more informed ways, perhaps leading to more powerful teacher education experience.

Beyond modeling teaching strategies, I believe we need to model all aspects of effective teaching, such as reflective practice and self-study. Each year, I tell my students about my research, including my self-study activities. I have even shared some of my reflective writing and my students are often surprised that I do walk my talk about reflecting on practice being a critical aspect of teaching. When I was doing a self-study on collaboration recently, I told my students about it, described the methodology, and read them excerpts from the paper.

Emphasizing community

The bulk of my elementary school teaching was in urban areas where many of my students found school to be one of the few safe environments in their lives. This led me to focus on helping the class become a strong, supportive, friendly community. Two texts helped me build upon my intuitive sense that community was a necessity. *Life in a crowded place: Making a learning community* (Peterson, 1992) provided many practical strategies, while *The schoolhome: Rethinking schools for changing families* (Martin, 1992) grounded community-building in theory. As a teacher educator, I remain strongly committed to community. Helping a group of student teachers become a community is somewhat different from my work with Grade 1 children, but many of the principles are the same. "Teaching is a relationship, a way of being with and relating to others, and not merely an expression of having mastered a set of content-related delivery skills" (Bullough and Gitlin, 2001, p. 3). Regardless of age, learners need a sense of security and acceptance; student teachers need a place to openly share their questions about becoming a teacher. I spend time getting to know my student teachers both inside and outside my classes. A recent pre-service class included a group of knitters and we would regularly get together for knitting nights. Being with my student teachers outside the regular classroom allowed me to see them more as individuals and to appreciate their individual struggles as they become teachers.

To help my student teachers experience community, I am intentional in my efforts, as I was as a classroom teacher. One of my first forays into building community at the university level involved organizing a retreat for my student teachers. Our two days at a beautiful retreat center outside the city included team-building activities, identifying one's learning style, working in small groups on the goals for education, and plenty of time to socialize. One of the main activities was the sharing of the *All about me* books that each person made prior to the retreat. The students used a variety of formats to tell their stories: newspaper, poems, comics, dioramas, picture books, even mystery stories. Sharing our books was a poignant time as the students learned about each other and experienced the power of story. In our follow-up research we have found that many beginning teachers had their pupils do *All about me* books as part of their community-building work.

By taking the time for community-building and talking explicitly about our community and its values, each year's cohort did become a community. However, like elementary school classes, each cohort had a unique personality and ways of interacting. Each year I emphasize that community is not an add-on or frill but a central part of the teaching–learning process. In follow-up research on our program, graduates have repeatedly discussed the positive experience of being part of the Mid-Town community. For example, Kathryn said she had been influenced by our creating a community, showing that it can be done: "I mean, if you can do it with adults coming from who knows where, you can certainly do it with children. So I think that a lot of what I want to see happen in my classroom has actually happened in the program" (Beck and Kosnik, 2001, p. 487). Heather commented:

> Inside of me there are two little battles going on. There's the one that says just grow up and be tough and do the work and don't have needs. And then there's the other part of me that knows I have needs and is drawn towards this kind of warm, welcoming atmosphere . . . I think it's good to have standards and to really command excellence but to know that within that we can be nurtured as humans.
>
> (Beck and Kosnik, 2001, p. 493)

Framing and reframing my identity

I have come a long way from the nervous teacher educator who carted boxes of curriculum resources into class for her student teachers. I now see my work as much more complete, thoughtful, and effective. It is not only that I have gained confidence and acquired a greater repertoire of teaching skills; it is also that my concept of who I am as a teacher educator has become richer and more complex. Murray and Male describe a study of 26 new teacher educators that is relevant to the discussion about developing an identity as a teacher educator:

> The transition from the first-order setting of school teaching into the second-order setting of HE [higher education]-based teacher education was constructed by the majority of the interviewees as a distinct and stressful career change, characterized by high levels of uncertainty and anxiety. Recurring feelings about the early years of HE work were of being "de-skilled", of "struggle", and of "masquerading". These feelings were particularly acute during the first year. Learning to become a teacher educator was seen as a slow, uncertain process, requiring the acquisition of new professional knowledge and understanding.
>
> (2005, pp. 129–130)

Being a researcher

In addition to teaching my courses, being a teacher educator means that I am also a researcher. I both conduct research and draw on it. I vividly recall the first time that I described myself as a researcher and then quietly admitted that my field of research was teacher education. I was nervous about describing myself as a researcher and wondered if someone would call me a fraud. I could relate to the participants in Murray and Male's study who "questioned their credentials as 'academics' or doubted their own abilities to research and publish at the levels required by their institutions" (ibid., p. 132). It has taken time for me to be comfortable with this description but I feel it is incredibly important to my work as a teacher educator to be both teacher and researcher. Being a researcher has strengthened my work as a teacher educator because I have systematically studied many aspects of teacher education. I have spent hundreds of hours interviewing student teachers and beginning teachers about their views on teacher education and the challenges they face.

When I secured a tenure-track position at the Ontario Institute for Studies in Education, University of Toronto (OISE/UT), there was a sense of urgency to publish a significant number of articles in order to gain tenure. In many ways, this period involved a constant stream of self-study projects seeking to understand teacher education through the eyes of both our student teachers and those who teach in the program, with particular attention to appreciating the challenges faced by beginning teachers. By studying aspects of the program and its redesign, I developed an in-depth understanding of the Mid-Town program. Without a thorough understanding of my own work, I could not appreciate the discipline of teacher education. This led me to think seriously about the pedagogy of teacher education. As I researched, I saw more clearly the distinctions between teaching children and student teachers (for whom I need to make the teaching process explicit). I also saw the common features (regardless of age, all students need a safe community).

I believe it is important to make my work as a researcher visible to my student teachers. I share with them the research that I am conducting and regularly take to class research articles that I am reading, especially if they relate to the work of beginning teachers. Because my area of research is teacher education, I regularly invite my students to be involved in the research (e.g., through completing a survey, being interviewed, sharing their papers with me) and I have taken increasingly to following them into the first few years of teaching to determine the impact of the teacher education program on their practices. I also emphasize the need to draw on the research regarding effective teaching practices that support pupil learning. For example, in my course on classroom culture, I shared statistics about inclusive teaching practices so students could see that my position is well grounded in the research literature. I want my students to be deliberate in their choices about teaching and assessment practices and to resist the temptation to use materials simply because they are readily available. This means drawing on research about effective teaching practices and about being teacher researchers, even when that research at first seems unrealistic because of their pressing needs to know how and what they will teach the next day. As Loughran (2006, p. 145) notes, the student teacher as a researcher is a principle that applies throughout a pre-service program:

> A student-teacher as researcher stance requires trusting that students of teaching are able to learn from their own experiences and that teacher educators' expertise is not necessarily bound up in just "passing on" their experience to their neophytes but in helping their learners to see, and respond to, the teaching and learning opportunities they experience; all the more so when teacher educators purposefully create such pedagogic episodes for their learners.

Even as beginning teachers, I want my student teachers to have research as part of their philosophy and repertoire of skills. Their approach to teaching must have pupil achievement and well-being at the core, and this requires them to be teacher-researchers. I want them to develop habits of professionals, using methods and practices that are proven to be effective.

As noted above, as a teacher, I regularly enrolled in courses to improve my knowledge and practice and, as a researcher, I continue to grow and develop. Improving my work through study is an enduring value. As a classroom teacher, I told my pupils about the courses that I was taking and now, as a teacher educator, I tell my students about the research I am doing and the conferences that I attend.

Searching for community

As a teacher, I was part of many communities and networks within my school, in the district, and in provincial-level organizations. Having begun my teaching career in an open area arrangement, working in a community or team is part of my teacher identity. As a teacher educator, I describe to my student teachers these communities so that they begin to think about which communities they will be a part of after graduation.

When I became a professor at OISE/UT, I was not immediately welcomed into a particular community and there was no obvious home for me. A major reason for my isolation was that particularly tumultuous period in OISE/UT's history. Pre-service and graduate-degree programs had been separate entities and were being merged, leaving many feeling displaced. The upheaval was especially pronounced for those involved in pre-service teaching. There was an exodus of faculty from the pre-service program and those of us who remained were viewed suspiciously. At times, I yearned for the communities that I had belonged to when I was teacher. I felt as thought I did not belong at OISE/UT, yet I was no longer part of the teacher communities. It took time to find and help build a new set of communities. Becoming part of the Self-Study of Teacher Education Practices (S-STEP) Special Interest Group (SIG) within the American Educational Research Association (AERA) was a professional turning point.

Through the SIG, I found colleagues who gave me not only companionship but also a tremendous boost professionally. Anne Freese, Anastasia Samaras, and I became instant friends and colleagues. Although we work at three different universities, we have engaged in numerous collaborative projects. Two notable joint endeavors were our teamwork as program chairs and editors of the proceedings of the Fourth International Conference on Self-study of Teacher Education Practices and as co-editors of a book on the contributions of self-study to teacher education (Kosnik *et al.*, 2006). Our emails and meetings at conferences such as the biennial international self-study conference and annual meetings of AERA allow us to engage in continuous and productive dialogue.

Coming full circle back to focusing on pupils

As Director of the Teachers for a New Era (TNE) project at Stanford University, I am working in a new university, in a new country, with a new set of colleagues. What would have been so unsettling a few years ago has been a highly rewarding experience, both personally and professionally. Teachers for a New Era is an initiative designed to strengthen K-12 teaching by developing state-of-the-art programs of teacher education. This reform endeavor aims to strengthen teacher education by creating strong links among departments of humanities and sciences, schools of education, and the local schools where teachers are trained. The Stanford Teacher Education Program (STEP) was selected for this award because of its many initiatives that include enhancing the curriculum, strengthening clinical training, and adding an undergraduate component to the traditional graduate program.

Teachers for a New Era has many facets and the emphasis on research is particularly interesting. I am part of a team conducting the project, How does teacher education make a difference? An exploration of the relationships among teacher education, teaching practices, and student learning. The overall goal of the research is to study the influence of teacher education and ongoing professional development experiences on teachers' practices and their pupils' achievement. More than 300 teachers in our six Professional Development Schools will be surveyed, and data on the pupil achievement of about 2000 pupils will be collected. The scope and complexity of the study could be daunting, but I am a member of an impressive team that has supported my learning. In many ways, this study of pupil achievement takes me full circle back to my roots as a classroom teacher. One of my enduring commitments has been to make a difference in the lives of children and this study is examining how teaching practices and practices taught in teacher education support pupil learning and growth.

Next steps in developing my pedagogy of teacher education

The stories above reveal a set of enduring values and practices: thinking outside the box, being a lifelong learner, building community, adjusting my theories as I learn more, and using research to guide my teaching. My work as a teacher educator is different from my work as a classroom teacher, yet both are based on many of the same values and principles. I concur with Loughran that the two teaching roles have significant differences, yet I also believe the principles of both are the same. In the end, I am developing a pedagogy of teacher education, and I hope that this chapter illustrates how I am working to enact that pedagogy in real and meaningful ways in my teacher education classes. For me, this pedagogy of teacher education is based on the literature and research of teacher education and also informs the field as I study how I enact that pedagogy in my teacher education practices. What I have come to see through this process of development and enactment supports Loughran's sense that we need a more widely agreed upon pedagogy if we are to move the field of teacher education forward.

The path I have followed has had many obstacles and my work in teacher education will continue to present challenges. Being an innovative teacher educator requires patience, fortitude, and skill. Having my work and decisions guided by a set of values and beliefs is important. Although my work as a teacher educator has been fulfilling, it has not been without its moments of self-doubts and obstacles. As Loughran notes, "teaching about teaching demands a great deal from teacher educators. There is a continual need for teacher educators to be conscious of not only what they are teaching, but also the manner in which that teaching is conducted" (2006, p. 11). Part of the challenge has been trying to create an innovative, research-based teacher education program. We must also think beyond our own students and classrooms to consider issues at the institutional level and at the level of the international community of teacher educators:

> First is the institutional level whereby the practices inherent in a pedagogy of teacher education need to be explicitly played out not only through individual teacher educators' practice, but also in the manner in which program organization and structure reflect the way in which a pedagogy of teacher

education is inherently intended to shape teacher education as a whole. Finally, there is the collective responsibility of the community of teacher educators, for it is through [that] community that ideas, issues, concerns and conceptualizations might be developed, debated, articulated and portrayed in ways that will progress the field of teacher education.

(ibid., p. 176)

I do not believe that we should have a one-size-fits-all teacher education program, but I do believe that we can be using best practices and draw on research to develop common goals and practices. We need to make explicit pedagogies of teacher education that help to guide both new teachers and experienced teacher educators. Developing such pedagogies is fraught with challenges, but that is what teacher education is all about.

References

Beck, C. and Kosnik, C. (2001) From cohort to community in a pre-service teacher education program. *Teaching and Teacher Education, 17*, 925–948.

Beck, C. and Kosnik, C. (2002) The importance of the university campus program in pre-service teacher education: A Canadian case study. *Journal of Teacher Education, 53*, 420–434.

Brookfield, S. D. (1995) *Becoming a critically reflective teacher.* San Francisco: Jossey-Bass Publishers.

Bullough, R. V., Jr. and Gitlin, A. (2001) *Becoming a student of teaching: Linking knowledge, production and practice*, 2nd edn. London: RoutledgeFalmer.

Darling-Hammond, L. (2006) *Powerful teacher education: Lessons from exemplary programs.* San Francisco: Jossey-Bass.

Darling-Hammond, L. and Bransford, J. (eds.) (2005) *Preparing teachers for a changing world: What teachers should learn and be able to do.* San Francisco: Jossey-Bass.

Dinkelman, T., Margolis, J., and Sikkenga, K. (2006) From teacher to teacher educator: Experiences, expectations, and expatriation. *Studying Teacher Education, 2*, 5–23.

Donovan, M. S. and Bransford, J. (eds.) (2005) *How students learn: History, mathematics, and science in the classroom.* Washington, DC: National Academy Press.

Ducharme, E. and Ducharme, M. (1999) Teacher educators and teachers: The need for excellence and spunk. In R. Roth (ed.), *The role of the university in the preparation of teachers.* London: Falmer Press, pp. 41–58.

Kosnik, C. (1999) The transformative power of the action research process: Effects of an inquiry approach to pre-service teacher education. *Networks: An On-Line Journal for Teacher Research, 2*(1). Retrieved September 6, 2006, from http://education.ucsc.edu/faculty/gwells/networks/journal/Vol%202(1).1999march/article3.html

Kosnik, C., Freese, A., and Samaras, A. (eds.) (2002) Making a difference in teacher education through self-study. *Proceedings of the Fourth International Conference on Self-study of Teacher Education Practices.* Retrieved August 16, 2006, from http://educ.queensu.ca/~ar/sstep/

Kosnik, C., Freese, A., Samaras, A., and Beck, C. (eds.) (2006) *Making a difference in teacher Education through self-study: Studies of personal, professional, and program renewal.* Dordrecht: Springer.

Labaree, D. (2004) *The trouble with ed schools.* New Haven, CT: Yale University Press.

Lortie, D. (1975) *Schoolteacher: A sociological study.* Chicago: University of Chicago Press.

Loughran, J. (1995) Practicing what I preach: Modelling reflective practice to student teachers. *Research in Science Education, 25,* 431–451.

Loughran, J. (2006) *Developing a pedagogy of teacher education: Understanding teaching and learning about teaching.* London: Routledge.

Martin, J. R. (1992) *The schoolhome: Rethinking schools for changing families.* Cambridge, MA: Harvard University Press.

Murray, J. and Male, T. (2005) Becoming a teacher educator: Evidence from the field. *Teaching and Teacher Education, 21,* 125–142.

Patterson, L., Santa, C. M., Short, K., and Smith, K. (eds.) (1993) *Teachers are researchers: Reflection and action.* Newark, DE: International Reading Association.

Peterson, R. (1992) *Life in a crowded place: Making a learning community.* Richmond Hill, Ontario: Scholastic Press.

Ross, D. (1987) Action research for pre-service teachers: A description of why and how. *Peabody Journal of Education, 64*(3), 131–150.

3 Teaching prospective teachers about learning to think like a teacher

Articulating our principles of practice

Alicia R. Crowe and Amanda Berry

Teaching is a complex endeavor in which there are few absolutes and even fewer algorithms for practice (Hoban, 2005). Beginning teachers need more than a set of activities, ideas, and techniques to help them become deliberate, thoughtful teachers who understand the relationship between their teaching and the quality of their students' learning. Teachers need to be able to think creatively about complex situations, consider multiple options, make decisions about best courses of action, and understand why they do what they do. Show-and-tell teaching by teacher educators cannot help prospective teachers to think in more complex ways about their practice (Myers, 2002).

One way that teacher educators can begin to address the challenge of supporting the development of thoughtful new teachers involves having a clear sense of the principles of practice that guide their work. By making these principles explicit not only to themselves but also more broadly to the community of teacher educators, the principles can be discussed, challenged and developed as a powerful form of knowledge of practice. This chapter focuses on the principles of practice developed by two teacher educators for teaching prospective teachers to think like teachers. We consider the manner in which these principles are understood and enacted and the challenges associated with enacting one's principles.

We conceptualize the process of becoming a new teacher as teacher *education* rather than as teacher *training*. Programs based on a transmission model of teacher training deliver knowledge about teaching in the form of skills and theories to be acquired mindlessly and applied unproblematically in the practice context (Wideen *et al.*, 1998; Korthagen and Russell, 1995). Research about learning to teach suggests that such a transmission model, although widespread, is not helpful in influencing the practice of new teachers (Korthagen *et al.*, 2001; Wideen *et al.*, 1998). An alternative view of teacher education, as we envision it, involves a process of cognitive and affective development and change as prospective teachers learn to negotiate their developing identities as teachers. As teacher educators who embrace such a view of teacher education, we must do more than provide recipes for prospective teachers' classroom success; we must actively facilitate their becoming a teacher (Pinnegar, 2005).

Learning to think like a teacher

One important aspect of our view of becoming a teacher involves learning to think like a teacher. We want to encourage prospective teachers' learning to think like teachers through "being awake to, and aware of, their practice, not just immersed in it" (Mason, 2002, p. 15) so that the knowledge developed through their experiences of teaching and learning can inform and improve future practice. For us, thinking like a teacher involves developing a sensitive awareness of one's actions and a consistent focus on recognizing alternative perspectives and approaches to learning situations. Here we draw on Schön's (1983) perspective on reframing of practice situations. This view of teaching as pedagogical reasoning and decision-making contrasts with the entering assumptions of many prospective teachers for whom teaching appears to be the enactment of a series of uncomplicated routines and learning as something that is done to learners. Furthermore, prospective teachers' prior experiences as students often mean that they do not expect to take into account anything beyond their own perspective in a learning situation. The "different worlds" (Perry, 1988) that exist in a classroom and the range of ways in which teaching actions can be interpreted are not relevant to those whose primary interest is predominantly focused on themselves. As teachers of teachers, then, we see our role as crucial in supporting prospective teachers' transition from thinking as a student (in the ways described above) to thinking as a teacher, one who is richly aware of, and responsive to, the complexities that comprise the pedagogical environment.

As teacher educators with several years' experience working with prospective teachers, we have initiated a collaborative self-study investigating the ways in which each of us acts to facilitate prospective teachers' learning to think like a teacher, the reasons we act in the ways that we do, and the challenges associated with our efforts (Berry and Crowe, 2006). Although we work in different institutions (Kent State University and Monash University), in different countries (the USA and Australia) and in different subject disciplines (social studies and biology), our informal, shared conversations have led us to recognize that we face similar problems as teacher educators in facilitating the process of learning to think like a teacher and that we are developing similar responses to deal with these problems.

As an approach to researching practice, self-study is driven largely by the concerns of teaching, the development of knowledge about practice, and the development of learning (Berry, 2005). Hence self-study in this research is a means of formalizing our research approach as the vehicle through which our individual and shared understandings of learning to think like a teacher can be explored and developed.

Our initial research efforts led to the development of a set of shared "principles of practice" (Loughran, 2006) that we have identified as shaping our approach to supporting prospective teachers' learning to think like a teacher. Our principles were developed through conversations in which we worked to articulate to each other the knowledge of practice that we have developed in our experiences of teaching teachers. As Loughran pointed out, many have argued the need to clearly identify and explain the principles that guide one's practice as a teacher educator. Aligning our principles and our practice as well as making explicit to ourselves and to our students the framework that guides our practice is very important "if we expect our practice to influence our students' developing views of, and actions in, their own teaching" (ibid., p. 84).

Our principles represent a conceptualization of the knowledge of practice of teacher education developed through our personal experiences of teaching prospective teachers and through ongoing efforts to derive meaning from these experiences. While the particular ways in which we enact these principles may be context- and individual-specific, they represent a big-picture view of what matters in our teaching about teaching. They also provide a basis for shared reflection on practice and a "catalyst for researching teaching" (Loughran, 2006, p. 98) collaboratively through self-study. As we have considered our practice, we have developed five principles that capture the essence of our pedagogical practices in supporting prospective teachers learning to think like teachers:

Principle One: Thinking like a teacher involves learning to see teaching from the viewpoint of the learner. Experiencing the role of learner is an important means of developing an understanding of the learner's viewpoint.

Principle Two: Prospective teachers need opportunities to see into the thinking like a teacher of experienced others.

Principle Three: Prospective teachers need opportunities to try out thinking like a teacher in order to develop their thinking as a teacher.

Principle Four: Prospective teachers need scaffolding (guidelines, questions, structures) to support them in the process as they begin thinking like a teacher.

Principle Five: Developing responsive relationships is at the heart of learning to think like a teacher and at the heart of supporting our students (relational support).

In presenting these principles in a list, we do not intend that they be interpreted in a hierarchy or progression, nor do we wish to suggest that they can be distinguished individually within our work. Rather, we see the principles as an explanatory pathway into a complex set of interconnected ideas that comprise learning to think like a teacher. The principles are enacted differently with different students and at different times of the year, according to the concerns, contexts and challenges that we and our students encounter.

In order to illustrate how these principles are infused in our approach, we offer an extended vignette, constructed from our experiences over several years of learning to help prospective teachers begin to understand our expectations for their learning to think like a teacher. The vignette is written to capture some of the ways in which we have come to know what we know about teacher education and to illustrate features of how we work and what matters to each of us in our work. Our use of a vignette highlights our view of teacher education as one that is embedded in personal experience, where experience provides a personally meaningful context for the development of understanding. Thus the vignette itself represents a way to experience our teaching vicariously. Consistent with our view of teacher education, the vignette takes place within a first meeting with a new group of prospective teachers, illustrating our belief that from the moment we begin to teach, we aim to develop our students' sensitivities to thinking like teachers. Although the vignette is set within the context of Alicia's social studies methods class, the pedagogical features we describe are intended to be representative of how we both work and could be situated in classes taught by either of us. (Numbers in brackets refer to the principles being illustrated.)

As I prepare for another year of teaching prospective teachers, I wonder again: "How will I help these individuals move from being students in a university class and thinking like students in a university class to becoming teachers and thinking as teachers do?", "What do I know that will help me engage these students so that they might begin to think like a teacher?" With these questions going through my mind, I begin to craft our first session.

Walking into the seminar room on the first day of the semester, I see that one or two students are already seated, some are milling around in small groups and chatting, while others slowly drift into the room. In these moments before the class officially begins, it may seem to the students as though nothing much is happening (and when I first began in the role of teacher educator, I would have thought the same), but over the last few years I have come to recognize this time as important for my learning (as a teacher educator) about each new group of prospective teachers. So I listen a little to their conversations, I watch their actions as they enter the room, I look at their clothing, and I try to pick up on some clues that will help me know something about how these future teachers will develop this year. [5] I try to figure out where these students are, right now, in their thinking about teaching. I ask myself, "Which of them will struggle the most? Will it be the person sitting quietly flicking through the pages of the books, or the one loudly joking at the back of the room? Which of them will 'soar' within a few weeks? How will I know? And, will I get all of them, by the end of the year, to think like teachers, when right now they look and sound so much like students?" For me, and hopefully for them, the feelings of anticipation are great. What will this year bring for us?

In a confident and friendly tone, I begin. "Welcome to your first social studies teaching and learning course . . . My name is Alicia . . ." I know that, right from the start, relationships matter. As we move through introductions, I work to make eye contact with people and listen carefully to how they speak and what they say. I want to send a clear message that I am interested in each of them as individuals. I am learning about each person from the words they choose, their tone and their gestures. [5]

We work through a series of planned activities, both so that I can get a sense of where they are in their thinking about teaching, learning, and social studies and so that they can begin to learn about the course, each other and me. Things progress pretty smoothly; so far, so good. With 15 minutes left, the class session nears its end and I know the time is approaching for me to begin explicitly modeling my teacher thinking about the session for them, to give them a chance to share insights and connections of their own, and to start supporting them in the development of their thinking as teachers. [2, 3, 4]

"O.K., we'll draw the session to a close today by spending some time thinking about what we have been doing together and why." [1] I pause, look around and check that I have their attention. "One of the most important aspects of teaching that I want you to learn this year is how to develop your 'teacher eyes.' That means moving away from being a student who 'receives' teaching to being a teacher who thinks about and actively engages in all that is going on around you, including the curriculum, the students, the instructional approaches, the classroom climate, everything." Another pause. I wonder if they are with me. "To help you start to do this, we are going to recount what we did during this session and then begin to analyze it. Let's start by talking about what we did in class. How did the class begin? What activities did we do?" [4]

I know that I have told them a lot in these few statements. I know that some will be struggling to understand what I mean while others will be beginning to make sense of it. At this point, my aim is to help them think about how they participated in the class and to introduce some useful language that we can keep using, such as "teacher eyes." [4]

Dana begins with specific answers. "First, we did a KWL chart, then we had a small-group activity, then we learned each other's names." "Thanks, Dana," I respond. Then I begin to probe a little. "Why would I do a KWL? [2] What did it help you do as a learner? [1] What does it help me do as your teacher?" Now, I want to dig underneath the surface of the session to help them explore the thinking behind it. [2] We discuss each aspect of the class and, as we do, I am aware of who is participating, when, and the ways in which different individuals respond.

Robert, the student who was flicking through the pages of his book at the start of the session, suddenly speaks up: "So, why did we do that KWL thing?" At this stage I am not sure whether his question is intended as provocative or a genuine inquiry. Was he not listening or did he not fully understand? Either way, it gives me a chance to add some explicit detail to illustrate my thinking that must not have been clear. "Thanks for that, Robert. [5] I chose the KWL not only to provide some support for you to think about what you know but also to initially assess what you know about social studies teaching and learning, to model a tool you can use with your students, and to convey a message that I value you as an integral part of this classroom and the teaching and learning process. Multiple reasons for one action." [2] He looks satisfied, for the moment.

"There's something that I noticed!" declares Doug. "You use our names every time you address us. That seems to help us feel more comfortable and it seems like you already have a certain level of respect for us." [1, 3, 5] "Great! Doug has articulated another level of thinking about the session that is important for students to recognize. It is not only the content of what we do but the environment that is being constructed that matters." Doug's and Robert's confidence to speak their thoughts encourages a couple of others to contribute. I stand back and listen as more ideas are put forward about how different individuals experienced my teaching and their learning.

The next 15 minutes fly by. It's time to go and I remind them to read the syllabus and section of the text for next time, although what I want them to do most has already begun, for at least some have begun to recognize that there is more to these sessions than simply doing the tasks.

As I return to my office, I think about their comments individually and as a whole. I begin to think to myself, "How much should I debrief on Thursday? Doug brought up something I've never thought to even mention before; that's great. I wonder why the group in the back corner didn't speak in the debriefing? I'll have to watch that next time, I don't think I heard any of the four of them speak." I also begin to think about some of the changes in my own thinking "like a teacher educator" working with new groups of prospective teachers over the past few years. I think about how little I used to bring in to the first session. I remember the first time I did a debriefing like the one I did today. I knew it needed to be done, but we certainly did not delve into as many of the complexities that we considered today. I decide, "I'll have to make sure to keep being explicit about this complexity. Over the last few years, that seems to be one area that takes a long time for them to develop an understanding of. Perhaps, if I keep making that explicit in what they are experiencing, then they will be able to see it in their own teaching." I am excited; another year has begun and it has the potential to be a great learning experience for all of us.

Elaborating our principles of practice

This vignette can now provide a reference point as we explore our five principles of practice in detail. In this section, we explain the ideas embedded in each principle and then provide some of the questions and tensions we grapple with as we use them to guide our practice.

Principle One: Thinking like a teacher involves learning to see teaching from the viewpoint of the learner. Experiencing the role of learner is an important means of developing an understanding of the learner viewpoint

Learning to think like a teacher requires developing an understanding of, and learning to respond to, the learning characteristics of individual learners. Coming to think like a teacher requires an important shift in perspective, away from one's personal concerns as teacher toward an appreciation of the learner's perspective as well as an emphasis on student learning and curriculum. Such a shift in thinking can be facilitated by putting prospective teachers in the role of the learner, to experience the kinds of tasks that teachers might expect their students to engage in and then to analyze these personal experiences of learning, to consider the feelings associated with being a learner in that situation. An example might be dealing with feelings of uncertainty, disinterest, confusion, excitement, and intellectual satisfaction in a learning situation. For the teacher educator, this means setting up experiences that can help to reveal these feelings of being a learner and then facilitating discussion with prospective teachers to articulate and explore the different learner perspectives, so that a genuine appreciation of the diversity of learner responses might be achieved.

As the vignette illustrates, the process of beginning to experience being a student in a more critical manner can begin early. In the vignette, the debriefing aspect of the first class session offers an initial opportunity for the prospective teachers to begin not only to think about how individual activities help them but also to see how the individual activities help or do not help other people in different ways. The prospective teacher is being presented with evidence that a class of seemingly similar people, all future social studies teachers of secondary students, can experience the same physical classroom differently. This will not be the last time the prospective teachers see these differences.

As prospective teachers move from the beginning of their time with us to the end, and as they begin to see from a learner's perspective, the scaffolding, the support, and the activities change. For example, as they begin to plan a unit to be taught to their students in their field site, they are asked to explain how the unit builds on what they already know about the particular students. They are asked about who their students are and how this unit shows their understanding of these students. It is another way to help the prospective teachers begin to move toward thinking of the complexities of a classroom and school.

As they are more able to express these ideas about the learner perspective, we become more confident that there is the level of trust and rapport established (*Principle Five*) so that we can push them further in their thinking like a teacher (*Principle Four*). As the prospective teacher develops, we begin to see this principle that thinking like a teacher involves seeing from the viewpoint of the learner in action in different ways. They begin to recognize that not all learners respond in the same ways and that the way a teacher experiences the classroom is not the same as how the student experiences it. This is a powerful realization and one that takes time and effort to internalize, both for ourselves, as teacher educators, and for prospective teachers thinking about their students.

Principle Two: Prospective teachers need opportunities to see into the thinking like a teacher of experienced others

One way that learning to think like a teacher can be facilitated involves gaining access to the thoughts of experienced teachers as they engage in the process of thinking like a teacher. The teacher educator, as an experienced other and as a member of an environment that the prospective teacher knows well, is ideally placed to offer such insights into thinking to explicitly model the various kinds of decisions that guide the teaching–learning process. Opening up the process of pedagogical reasoning through "thinking aloud" (Loughran, 2006, p. 47) may then serve as a prompt for prospective teachers to begin to consider teaching as an act of decision-making rather than as a series of routinized actions. Our goal is to encourage them to choose to engage in this way of thinking about practice for themselves. For the teacher educator, offering access to the thinking associated with teaching is a complex process that requires more than simply telling prospective teachers what one is thinking. It involves carefully selecting and highlighting particular aspects of one's thinking that might be useful and accessible to prospective teachers, given their particular concerns and interests. This is not an easy task and depends on the teacher educator's ability to discern elements of the pedagogic environment and knowing one's students well, so that what is highlighted for discussion is both personally and pedagogically relevant, and so that expertise in facilitating an environment in which discussing one's thinking about practice is seen as valuable (*Principle Five*).

The prospective teachers in the vignette find that their first opportunity to see into another's thinking comes quickly. During the first class meeting, they are exposed to the thinking of a teacher as they are asked to consider the reasoning for actions of their teacher (the teacher educator) and to hear and discuss some of her reasons for her actions.

Principle Three: Prospective teachers need opportunities to try out thinking like a teacher in order to develop their thinking as a teacher

In addition to providing access to the thinking of others as learners and teachers, prospective teachers need opportunities to explore thinking like a teacher for themselves. This could include creating situations whereby prospective teachers are encouraged to articulate a commentary on the thoughts and feelings they experience within the teaching role. These feelings may be associated with experiences of preparing for teaching, with the act of teaching, or with subsequenct analysis of teaching. Through the experience of talking about their thinking, prospective teachers may then begin to "reframe" (Barnes, 1998) their view of teaching as one that recognizes decision-making as central. However, just as voicing one's responses as a learner (*Principle One*) requires confidence and trust, so too does being willing to think aloud about one's thinking. The role of the teacher educator is vital is creating an atmosphere of trust that might permit such sharing of ideas (*Principle Five*).

Being able to try out thinking like a teacher often manifests itself in the journal entries that we ask our students to write and in the conversations that follow immediately after a prospective teacher teaches. When we ask our students to think about and reconsider their practice, we are setting them on their way toward thinking like a teacher. Of course, the opportunity alone is not enough; there must also be guidance and support (*Principles Four and Five*).

Another time our students can practice thinking like a teacher occurs during post-observation conversations. As these conversations begin, we find that we often ask, "O.K., so what do you think about that class? What was that like for you?" Through the responses offered we can provide other probing questions that help prompt "thinking as a teacher" about the class. For instance, a question such as, "Why did you change the lesson today from what you had planned?" or "I noticed that Jordan [a student] was sitting in the back of the room and drawing a lot. What do you know about him? Was he engaged?" Such questions invite prospective teachers to engage in thinking like a teacher while they have someone to guide them through the process by asking questions that model what to look for or think about. (This clearly connects with *Principle Four*).

Principle Three is also evident when we ask our prospective teachers to be more and more explicit about their thinking as they plan, as they are asked to identify the decision-making associated with themselves as teachers. *Principle Three* is also closely intertwined with *Principles Four and Five*. Without the strong and appropriate scaffolding (*Principle Four*) and relationships (*Principle Five*), giving prospective teachers these opportunities to practice thinking like a teacher could be ineffective or counter-productive.

Principle Four: Prospective teachers need scaffolding (guidelines, questions, structures) to support them in the process as they begin thinking like a teacher

Thinking like a teacher is facilitated through deliberate and appropriate scaffolding, such as providing questions and guidelines that help prospective teachers come to understand what it means to engage in the act of thinking like a teacher. These cognitive supports are different from the emotional and relational supports (*Principle Five*) that facilitate thinking like a teacher, although the two are often closely intertwined. These supports help guide the prospective teachers through their attempts to think like a teacher.

The instance of the post-observation conversation presented in the account of *Principle Three* illustrates another principle in action. It is not only having an opportunity to think like a teacher that matters. We also support our students in this process by asking deliberate and well-placed questions that give guidance on *what* they should be thinking about as new teachers while also providing guidance on *how* to think about them. As the conversation develops, we begin to hear comments that reveal what they see and understand at that point in their developing thinking as a teacher. We use these cues to inform our decisions about the next question to ask. For example, an opening question of "How did you feel about that lesson?" may lead to a response such as, "Oh, it was great," with no further comment. This is where we, as teacher educators, need to be strategic in supporting (rather than closing down) thinking by asking about a specific event in the lesson or about some of the decisions made during the lesson. It is not consistent with our beliefs about teacher education to proceed to tell the prospective teacher our version of the lesson or what we would have done had we taught the lesson. Such transmission approaches represent to us ways of stifling thinking like a teacher because they do not afford any agency to the prospective teacher as one who is capable of analyzing and learning from experience. They can readily suggest that there is only one way (the teacher educator's way) of teaching.

On the other hand, prospective teachers may answer the same question with an elaborate explanation of many areas that went well and others that did not and why. In this instance, we listen closely and consider what to push them towards next. We ask ourselves, "Is he ready for a complex question about the content chosen for today?" or "Is she ready to be asked about the hidden curriculum the students are learning in her classroom?" As we listen, our teacher educator thinking helps us to decide where, how and why to proceed in our conversation.

In the vignette, Alicia begins simply by asking the group to recall the activities of the class. She then elicits possible reasons for the choice and sequence of activities experienced. Throughout this process she is open to questions and comments that can take the conversation further, but at this beginning stage she is not worried if they do not arise or if the group does not yet seem ready to grapple with ideas beyond the what and why of teaching. The process of scaffolding prospective teachers' learning to think like a teacher is important if prospective teachers are to understand the purpose and value of their involvement in the process.

As mentioned in our discussion of *Principle Three*, learning to think like a teacher can be supported through journal writing. Adding specific structure to journal-writing tasks is an example of cognitive scaffolding that can more purposefully direct thinking as a teacher. For example, we may ask prospective teachers to consider a learning experience from the point of view of a student learner (integrating *Principle One*) or to analyze a teaching experience in terms of decisions made and then consider alternatives based on the experience of the lesson. We also may ask further questions in our response to journal entries, questions that help prospective teachers reframe a problem, see alternatives they did not see originally, or consider a new perspective. This is yet another way to add specific, deliberate supports for prospective teachers as they learn to practice their teacher thinking.

Cognitive scaffolding, however, cannot occur without an accompanying understanding of the emotions associated with learning to teach. Teacher educator efforts to support thinking like a teacher require a sensitive understanding of the individual as a whole person, and thus *Principle Four* is intimately associated with *Principle Five*.

Principle Five: Developing responsive relationships is at the heart of learning to think like a teacher and at the heart of supporting our students (relational support)

A teacher needs to know each student well enough to understand the specific needs and concerns of the individual student. As teacher educators, this is no different. We need to know the prospective teachers in our care well and to establish a high level of respect and trust so that we might support them well as they learn to think like teachers. From the very first moments, we need to develop an understanding of our students as learners and as people while developing a relationship of trust with them. We need to be quick to hear, understand, and respond to what happens in and out of class. Sometimes our response might be not to act, but nevertheless these are deliberate decisions that we make based on our developing knowledge of the individuals in our classes.

We need to be able to consider who each student is as we decide what thoughts to share, when to share them, why we share them and with whom we share them. As we learn more and more about prospective teachers and as our relationships with them develop, we gain greater understanding on which we draw when making decisions about what questions to ask, how far to push a prospective teacher at a particular moment, when to offer more direct guidance or less, and when to let a mistake happen because we know that the only way to learn a particular lesson is by living it and then analyzing it. Considerable teacher educator expertise is required to identify and respond to situations that can help move individuals forward in their thinking as teachers without closing them down by posing too great a personal challenge. We see aspects of this in the vignette as Alicia begins establishing a climate of respect and caring through her actions. She chooses her words wisely, makes frequent, deliberate eye contact, and uses individual names when she speaks. Over time, as each of us becomes more familiar with the students in our classes, we are able to make more complex decisions about how we work with individuals.

Challenges and questions with our principles of practice in action

Articulating a list of principles provides insight into our thinking as teacher educators as we prepare to support prospective teachers in their thinking like teachers. However, in preparing this list we encountered two challenges. One is that the principles themselves are not distinct or easily identified as separate in our work. They are closely intertwined, as each draws on and builds on another/others. We hope that we have been able to demonstrate their interrelatedness through the initial vignette and also through our cross-referencing in explaining each principle. A second challenge is that, although we can articulate them neatly in print, these ideas are often difficult to live in our work as teacher educators because the real world of practice continually presents obstacles and raises questions associated with putting our principles into practice. We now describe some of these challenges and questions.

As we act upon *Principle One* (Thinking like a teacher involves learning to see teaching from the viewpoint of the learner), we must be aware that prospective teachers should be able to say honestly how they feel or what they experience as learners. This can be more difficult than it sounds, as learners are not often asked about their feelings or how they experience an activity; it is expected that they simply do a task and the assumption is that feelings do not interfere with learning. Over many years of classroom experience, prospective teachers have learned to hide their real feelings and merely do what is needed to please the teacher. Being able to identify one's personal responses to learning and then having the confidence that it is not only acceptable but necessary to voice these responses, particularly when they may be critical of the teacher educator, requires a high level of trust and respect within the classroom (*Principle Five*).

Another challenge we face as the prospective teachers' guide, especially in relation to enacting *Principle Two*, concerns how to develop our ability to make explicit our thinking about our practice. We question ourselves about our selection of what is important to think aloud. We know that many prospective teachers expect and want their teacher educators to be the expert, so that revealing too much of one's teacher educator thinking may push away some prospective teachers. We recognize that, over time, we have become more experienced in knowing when, where, why and with whom to reveal aspects of our thinking, yet there are always situations in which we struggle to know how to act or what to say that is relevant and meaningful for the particular individuals with whom we are working. We also recognize that it is not just our own thinking as experienced teachers that we want prospective teachers to understand. Mentor teachers in schools are also valuable sources of ways of thinking about practice that prospective teachers can benefit from. Yet there are few mechanisms available for helping mentor teachers recognize ways in which they can offer such access without prescribing how to act or think as a teacher. Thus we continually strive to answer the question: How can we as teacher educators facilitate access to the thinking of experienced others?

As we work to challenge prospective teachers' thinking (*Principle Four*), we must be careful as we provide scaffolding that we do not provide too much structure. Too much structure will never help our students become independent thinkers. Questions that we regularly ask ourselves include, "Has enough been done?," "How might I push further?," or "Should I back down?" Being able to determine appropriate structure for a range of individuals is an important issue that is a constant practical challenge.

Principle Five is a vital principle, yet it is not without its own difficulties as a guide for our practice. As we get to know our students, they do begin to trust us, often divulging information that we might otherwise not hear. When and where do we draw the line in such conversation? Sometimes what we learn might be better handled through counseling, yet is it our place to suggest counseling? Where is the line between teacher educator and therapist? In addition to being teacher and advisor, we also may be important members of the evaluation team with regards to each prospective teacher's progress, and thus conflicts of interest may arise. As we get to know individuals well and guide their learning, we are also the ones to make decisions about continuing along this path. When do we make this call? How do we know what call to make for each student? Questions such as these suggest that knowing each prospective teacher well has implications beyond the pedagogical interactions of the teacher education classroom.

Throughout this chapter we have alluded to the thinking we have developed as teacher educators in supporting our prospective teachers' thinking as teachers. We conclude by turning to this aspect of our learning to highlight both the process of knowledge development and the nature of the knowledge we have developed.

Developing our thinking as teacher educators

"I think my students now are so much better because I've gotten better." During one of our conversations examining our teaching, knowledge, beliefs, and experiences, Alicia shared this statement with Amanda. Looking back over recent years, we see how true this statement is. As we have become more and more focused on our aim of supporting the learning of the prospective teachers in our respective programs, we have developed our professional knowledge as teacher educators (Eraut, 1994) generally and our pedagogy of teacher education (Loughran, 2006) specifically. Through our experiences, analysis, and individual self-study practices, we have been developing our professional knowledge; through our collaborative self-study relationship, we have been able to construct principles of practice. As we continue to develop our thinking as teacher educators, where will our journey take us? The knowledge we have developed does matter. Initially, we had vague notions of what it meant to support the development of beginning teachers. As we continue to develop, we find that our thinking has become both more complex and more refined. In practice, we find that we are better able to support our students' development through specific actions and to recognize their needs. We notice that we are able to respond more quickly to student characteristics expressed in many ways, including evidence from comments in and out of class, assignments, and interactions. Just as teachers of children develop professional knowledge, we have developed professional knowledge of teacher education. The development of knowledge of practice is important for teacher educators in order to improve the quality of our teaching about teaching and the quality of our students' learning about teaching. The development of our pedagogy of teacher education is conceptualized within this chapter as a set of five principles of practice that we believe frame our approach to teacher education that is based on facilitating beginning teachers' learning to think like a teacher. These principles serve as a frame for both the ongoing investigation of our practice and as a signpost for recognizing particular aspects of learning to teach within our classes. We hope that articulating and sharing these principles will encourage others to consider the ways in which their own pedagogy of teacher education is codified and enacted.

References

Barnes, D. (1998) Foreword: Looking forward: The concluding remarks at the castle conference. In M. L. Hamilton (ed.), *Reconceptualizing teaching practice: Self-study in teacher education*. London: Falmer Press, pp. ix–xiv.

Berry, A. (2005, April) Learning to articulate the tensions of practice as a teacher educator. Paper presented at the meeting of the American Educational Research Association, Montreal.

Berry, A. and Crowe, A. R. (2006) Extending our boundaries through self-study: Framing a research agenda through beginning a critical friendship. In L. M. Fitzgerald, M. L. Heston, and D. L. Tidwell (eds.), *Collaboration and community: Pushing boundaries through self-study*. Proceedings of the Sixth International Conference on Self-Study of Teacher Education Practices. Cedar Falls, IA: University of Northern Iowa, pp. 31–35.

Dewey, J. (1933) *How we think: A restatement of the relation of reflective thinking to the educative process*. Boston, MA: D. C. Heath and Company.

Eraut, M. (1994) *Developing professional knowledge and competence*. London: Falmer Press.

Hoban, G. F. (ed.) (2005) *The missing links in teacher education design: Developing a multi-linked conceptual framework*. Dordrecht: Springer.

Korthagen, F. J., Kessels, J., Koster, B., Lagerwerf, B., and Wubbels, T. (2001) *Linking practice and theory: The pedagogy of realistic teacher education*. Mahwah, NJ: Lawrence Erlbaum Associates.

Korthagen, F. J. and Russell, T. (1995) Teachers who teach teachers: Some final considerations. In T. Russell and F. Korthagen (eds.), *Teachers who teach teachers: Reflections on teacher education*. London: Falmer Press, pp. 187–192.

Loughran, J. (2006) *Developing a pedagogy of teacher education*. London: Routledge.

Mason, J. (2002) *Researching your own practice: The discipline of noticing*. London: RoutledgeFalmer.

Myers, C. B. (2002) Can self-study challenge the belief that telling, showing and guided-practice constitute adequate teacher education? In J. Loughran and T. Russell (eds.), *Improving teacher education practices through self-study*. London: RoutledgeFalmer, pp. 130–142.

Perry, W. G. (1988) Different worlds in the same classroom. In P. Ramsden (ed.), *Improving learning: New perspectives*. East Brunswick, NJ: Nicols, pp. 145–161.

Pinnegar, S. (2005) Identity development, moral authority and the teacher educator. In G. F. Hoban (ed.), *The missing links in teacher education design: Developing a multi-linked conceptual framework*. Dordrecht: Springer, pp. 259–279.

Schön, D. A. (1983) *The reflective practitioner: How professionals think in action*. New York: Basic Books.

Wideen, M., Mayer-Smith, J., and Moon, B. (1998) A critical analysis of the research on learning to teach: Making the case for an ecological perspective on inquiry. *Review of Educational Research, 68*, 130–178.

4 Providing the necessary luxuries for teacher reflection

Joseph C. Senese

When actively engaged in reflective dialogue, adults become more complex in their thinking about the world, more tolerant of diverse perspectives, more flexible and open toward new experiences. Personal and professional experiences require an interactive professional culture if adults are to engage with one another in the processes of growth and development.

(Lambert *et al.*, 1995, p. 28)

Those who study teaching as a discipline are well aware of the ironies involved in being a teacher of teachers. The act of teaching anything requires a teacher to balance the complex relationship between what is being taught (subject matter) and how it is being taught (instruction). Both the what of teaching and the how of teaching must be addressed for teachers to be effective. In teaching about teaching there is an even more complex layer that involves understanding how to make explicit this relationship between subject matter and pedagogy and to facilitate learning about this relationship. Simply being aware of this dual nature of teaching is not enough to make someone a good teacher or a good teacher of teachers. If only learning to teach were that simple! Assuming that someone will able to perform well after merely watching another's performance rarely works in any arena. Modeling, as Loughran points out, is not enough to produce good teachers:

> In focusing on our teaching behaviors, it is also important to recognize that simply modeling practice through the use of a range of teaching procedures (e.g. concept maps, Venn diagrams, interpretive discussions), or teaching about teaching by using engaging strategies, is in itself not sufficient in teacher education. There is a clear need to continually go deeper and to address the underlying features of teaching and learning.

(2006, p. 83)

What is missing in the model described above is the preeminence of reflection about how a teacher teaches. Without deep, meaningful reflection about that, teachers have little chance of assuring that "both the subtleties and complexities of practice might be viewed and reviewed in order to shed light on pedagogical reasoning, thoughts and actions" (ibid., pp. 39–40). These underlying subtleties and complexities are the threads that make good teaching and provide actual learning opportunities for both students and teachers. Teachers know why they do what they do because they reflect deeply on their practice and know their students. They continually test the effectiveness of what they do in the classroom and that can only be done while in the process of teaching those students who happen to be in front of them.

The educational community understands the preeminence of critical reflection, but it is not done more routinely in schools. Teacher educators and staff developers alike grapple with how best to support the growth and learning of teachers so that teachers can, in turn, support the growth and learning of their students. This chapter presents the situation from my personal perspective as a practitioner who teaches in a high school, teaches in-service programs for teachers, and also teaches pre-service teachers at a university.

Characteristics of effective teacher reflection

After establishing the importance of reflection in developing teacher practice, Loughran identified six associated assumptions:

> Effective reflective practice emphasizes the importance of reflection for action so that, in the process, deeper understandings of practice might be developed. For that to be the case, effective reflective practice responds to the assumptions that:
>
> - a problem is unlikely to be acted on if it is not viewed as a problem;
> - rationalization may masquerade as reflection;
> - experience alone does not lead to learning – reflection on experience is essential;
> - other ways of seeing problems must be developed;
> - articulation matters;
> - developing professional knowledge is an important outcome of reflection.
>
> (2006, p. 131)

Although Loughran did not intend these assumptions to be used as a sequential list of step-by-step requirements that lead to reflection, I use them here as a list of assumptions to be addressed in order to explore ways to develop deeper reflection in practice.

A problem is unlikely to be acted on if it is not viewed as a problem

In conversations about teaching, whether in a department office, a staff lunchroom, or a parking lot, teachers habitually share successes and, more often than not, difficulties in the classroom. The successes can be self-congratulatory or honest assessments of accomplishment, but the difficulties usually surface as frustrations: "Why is it so difficult for students to do what I say?," "Why are these students so inferior to others I have had?," "Until the administration takes a firm stance on this, nothing can improve," "Students have to be responsible for their own learning." Although identifying difficulties is relatively easy for teachers, taking personal/professional responsibility for addressing those difficulties is another matter. Thinking this way reminds me of the Laurel and Hardy films of the 1930s in which Oliver Hardy often made bonehead mistakes and blamed them on Stan Laurel with a blithe, "See what you made me do?"

Another difficulty here is that a teacher may be unaware that there is a problem at all, either within or without. Ignorance may become bliss. If a teacher does not look for trouble, he won't find any. As Loughran notes,

> in learning about teaching there is a clear need for students of teaching to see *their* own problems in order to choose how to act on them, and this is dramatically different from reflecting on the problems of others or reflecting on the problems that might be pointed out by a (school) supervising teacher or teacher educator.
>
> (2006, pp. 129–130)

If these conflicts, frustrations or difficulties are not framed as problems or not even recognized as problems, they are certainly not addressed.

Rationalization may masquerade as reflection

A standard response to the disclosure of a difficult situation in the classroom is for a teacher to explain it away. Notice that the examples just provided establish the germ of the difficulty outside of the teacher: students, parents, administration, central office, teaching colleagues, government regulations, and so on are the reason each problem exists or endures. If teachers adopt this way of thinking, problems persist. Teachers are absolved from "doing something" about the difficulty because it lies outside their locus of control or influence. Or at least that is the rationalization. Does this happen because teachers are content in their misery or do they not sense their rationalization? Or do they not recognize themselves as agents who have the means to resolve these difficulties, perhaps reframing them as actual problems with solutions? The answer probably consists of a combination of all three.

When I was teaching public speaking, a parent questioned my grading practices. She pointed out that I was manipulating the rubrics to arrive at a grade that I had already determined in my head. At that moment, caught off-guard, I rationalized my logical, mathematical approach to grading student speeches. After one restless night, I called her and admitted that she had uncovered exactly what I was doing. I used the rubrics to protect myself, not to help students. The number of points I assigned each category was arbitrary and I would often determine the grade, then assign points in each category to make it turn out the way I wanted. I had never been forced to explain the way the system worked so I didn't perceive it as a problem. I had rationalized a mathematical-looking format into a protection for me. I could justify any grade by the numbers that I manipulated. I learned a valuable (and difficult) lesson from that parent, but I had to have someone push me into recognizing the problem and my rationalization of it. I also had to be willing to hear the parent and confront the reality of my practice.

Experience alone does not lead to learning—reflection on experience is essential

Adults who address a difficult situation or problem may learn from that experience. But if the problem is perceived as rooted outside of an individual's control (the government, the organization, parents), the problem persists and learning will not occur. What does occur is often a form of endurance, indulgence, or tolerance. The difficult situation remains an unrecognized problem outside of what any individual can address, and a person learns to accept it, embrace it, or tolerate it. Nevertheless, the problem remains.

Teachers can engage in this cycle and act the same way. In schools teachers may even have the added option of separating themselves from the rest of the school, other faculty members, and even their administrators—keeping others at arm's length as they confront perplexity or frustrations but avoid solutions within themselves. Without reflection, these teachers may actually learn a counter-productive response because they disconnect from their problems rather than integrate problem-solving into their teaching. Survival becomes the name of the game.

Consider a teacher who stockpiles these frustrations over time. The more inward the teacher turns, the more isolated the teacher becomes. Unfortunately, recalling an actual teacher who keeps others at a distance is not a difficult feat. Students and parents fear this teacher, colleagues avoid him, and administrators give up on him; dissatisfaction festers. A teacher in this state of existence often feels that the only way to survive is to control the situation. Becoming rigid, unreasonable, demanding, and gruff helps to separate him from the problem as well as from others, and the situation puts this teacher into a limbo of ignorance. The opposite of reflection occurs. To maintain control, this teacher must reject anything that puts him at risk of exposure. This is not a healthy state for someone who should be reflecting deeply on what he does every day and assessing its effectiveness for student learning.

Merely experiencing this state does not lead a teacher to resolve it. It is not enough to experience; a person must do something with that experience in order to integrate it into who he is. The quotation opening this chapter from Lambert (Lambert *et al.*, 1995) was reinforced by Russell who noted, "While experience is powerful, learning from experience is far from automatic, perhaps because all levels of formal schooling pay little attention to learning from experience" (2002, p. 84). It comes down to a person taking control of events or having them control him. This is a fundamental lesson of life that everyone has to learn and relearn at various times and stages of development; it is so common to human experience that many adages address this issue, including these examples:

- If God gives you lemons, make lemonade.
- Every challenge is an opportunity to improve.
- It's not what you have but what you do with it.
- If you are not part of the solution, you are part of the problem.

As familiar as these adages may be, each embodies a truth and is applicable to solving problems, including those encountered in teaching. Strength arises from a teacher believing that she can correct a problem and become a more effective teacher for confronting the problem. Teacher educators and staff developers need to learn how to effect this "can-do" spirit in teachers that helps them to avoid rationalization so they can confront problems in practice.

Other ways of seeing problems must be developed

Once caught in this cycle of difficulty–rationalization–retreat, a teacher cuts off any other ways of seeing a situation as a problem and therefore cannot break the cycle. This critical juncture is when leverage can be applied to assist teachers to break the cycle and enter into a more productive process that includes reflection in action (Schön, 1983).

If a teacher believes that the locus of control is outside of her, the job of teaching merely becomes survival. Entrenched practices, inflexibility, and defensiveness become a way of life. A teacher hopes merely to "get through this day, this week, this year." If any hope remains for a teacher in this bind, the teacher must find some way to get beyond this stagnation in order to continue to learn while teaching. As Loughran put it:

> Framing and reframing (Schön, 1983) are important to reflection for they have to do with coming to see a situation, being able to define it, to describe and account for its features, then to be able to view that situation from different perspectives.
>
> (2006, p. 96)

Thus, every teacher must develop multiple perspectives on problems of practice. Teachers learn to transcend narrow thinking to develop a deeper understanding of the teaching–learning process when they are able to reframe problems, to respond anew, or to adopt another's perspective (perhaps even the perspective of the students or parents). Really listening to another person's perspective on practice offers a teacher the hope of improving through reflection. The key becomes developing ways to help teachers to stay receptive to feedback from a variety of sources.

For example, when I was a new teacher in a private school in Chicago, I assigned a journal-notebook assignment about a current civic problem. One girl, who had difficulties writing coherent sentences, handed in a beautifully constructed project on water pollution. I asked her if she had help and she openly admitted that her sister had handwritten the explanations because she wanted it to look good. I immediately marked her down because it was not her own work. Her mother called me the next day and asked if I had any children. Taken aback by the question, I blurted out, "Not yet." She simply replied that she hoped I better understood students like her daughter after I had had my own. Nothing more. Obviously that comment stuck with me because I am writing about it 30 years later. I learned a valuable lesson about diverse student learning needs that year, but it was not easy for me to hear that parent or that student at the time. I easily could have dismissed that parent's comment, but it spoke to me and eventually improved my practice.

As difficult as some of these lessons have been for me (after all, I am the teacher!), I realize in hindsight that once I invited questions, comments, and responses to my teaching, I became less defensive. Instead, I was forced to think more upfront about why I was doing something a certain way. My best critics have been students and parents. They become partners in my practice, informing me of what works and doesn't work. I invite responses. Feedback is so much easier, enjoyable, and welcome when I ask for it rather than waiting for someone to find something wrong with my practice. Often soliciting honest responses to my practice is paramount to improvement. The section called "My role as a model for others" later in this chapter addresses this professional stance in more detail.

Articulation matters

This assumption emphasizes the need to talk about, investigate, and explore practice in order to understand a problem better in all its complexities. Articulating goals, achievements, frustrations, and actions in honest and insightful ways works hand in hand with developing divergent ways of seeing a problem. Framing and reframing a problem through reflection and articulation distills the problem, clarifies it, and makes it accessible to being resolved.

Throughout my years as a high school administrator, I have seen the need to provide opportunities for teachers to articulate what they think they are doing in the classroom, what they actually are doing, and what they make of it. Teachers have little practice doing this. Most teachers, in my experience, "tell" what they mean by teaching by explaining the steps of a lesson. Describing (and therefore being aware of) the larger purposes, the overarching goals, and the deeper questions involved in teaching and learning require practice and lots of it. Because personal/professional risk is involved in this venture, teachers must practice articulating their work under safe conditions and with trusted colleagues. When they develop confidence through practice and a deeper understanding of what they do and why they do it, teachers are much more willing to take risks, to uncover assumptions, to explore the tacit and make it explicit—all necessary traits for learning about teaching. I made this observation about learning to play the game called school:

The collective structures that we call "school" have infiltrated the way in which students approach learning. We have allowed these structures to condition our responses as learners and as teachers and to influence our behaviors. Consequently, it is unacceptable to not know the answer or to ask questions based on genuine doubt. I am not referring to school-subject ignorance or school-type questions that teachers regularly receive. I am referring to students knowing what they do not know, having their own means to find out, and then discovering the knowledge for themselves. I am referring to students asking genuine questions, ones that have personal meaning and consequences.

(Senese, 2005, p. 51)

Although I was describing student behavior, adults are not exempt from acting in similar ways. As long as everyone in school plays this same game, teachers will continue to be inhibited from expressing genuine doubt about practice and seeking new ways of framing their practice.

Developing professional knowledge is an important outcome of reflection

Out of the opportunity and skill to be able to reframe a problem and to articulate it comes professional knowledge. A problem transforms a frustration that resides in others or in organizations to something that can be seen as multifaceted, complex, and approachable. Diverse perspectives can lead to understanding a problem through its deconstruction. Action becomes possible and the requisite reflection to resolve the problem reduces it to a reasonable challenge. The knowledge that comes from this reflection can be used to avoid or solve future problems. It can be shared with others, and it can direct choices in the future. This is how we, as teachers, learn and grow in our practice. In addition, as practitioners, we develop a body of professional knowledge (episteme) from our collective experiential knowledge (phronesis) (Korthagen *et al.*, 2001) so that our profession benefits from our growth. If the nature of this sequence of events becomes predictable (or at least anticipated), whether during in-service or pre-service work, teacher educators are in a better position to assist teachers to adopt the necessary luxury of reflection in action.

Fostering reflection by addressing shortages and fears

As idyllic as this sequence of steps plays out in theory, there are considerable barriers to teachers achieving it in practice. The barriers generally include shortages (of time, experience, and/or support) and fears (of failure, risk, and/or vulnerability). Without addressing these twin issues, teacher educators have limited effect when helping teachers to grow in their practice. Both the shortages and the fears must be addressed to allow teachers to become truly reflective.

Oftentimes things stay the way they are only because someone cannot envision them otherwise. Why, if knowing that a change would make a situation better, does a person continue with the ineffectual usual? At some time, everyone finds himself in a cycle that perpetuates a bad situation. Those closest to the situation find themselves at a loss to act decisively. Often they cannot see another way to frame the bad situation because they are so close to it or sometimes even because it works (or at least appears to work) for them.

For example, even though we may know that exercise benefits our health, we still may avoid exertion. We may not be in poor health and, although exercising could improve our long-term physical well-being, we may not be motivated (yet) to take another route. The route we currently take seems (and I emphasize that word) to work for us. Unless something either nudges or forces us to change, we may not understand or accept that anything could be better than the current situation. We don't have personal evidence that altering our behavior would actually improve our health. We cannot even envision it. Nothing catastrophic has forced us into changing our current habits so old habits persist.

Given that most people do not respond well to being forced to change, teacher educators and staff developers must discover ways to nudge teachers toward more effective ways to learn about teaching. Teachers must maintain control of a situation (all-important, as we have previously discussed) if the change is to be deep and permanent. There is not any one time in a career when every teacher will be open to being nudged to frame and reframe understanding of practice, but there are naturally occurring opportunities that should be seized. I return to Loughran's six assumptions, as the first two provide a context for identifying the time to enter into this sequence. As long as a teacher does not see a problem, a problem does not exist. Without the irritation of sensing a problem or puzzle and looking inward to solve it, an individual will remain immutable.

Developing a critical reflective stance may take years because many teachers subscribe to a core belief that they are the sole experts in their classrooms. Dislodging that belief or even abridging it is a leap in thinking for most practitioners. One way to provide a nudge to teachers is to engage them in non-threatening conversations about their teaching. These kinds of conversations require that the "other" listens intently and reflects back what the teacher is saying. In this conversation, follow-up questions are preferable to statements or judgments. The teacher must articulate her beliefs and how she enacts those beliefs. As Lambert points out, "Since working with new ideas and information is essential in the meaning-making process, an inquiring stance is essential to constructing change in a school or district" (Lambert *et al.*, 1995, p. 61). Only through guided reflective experiences will a teacher uncover areas that are potential "problems." The colleague must avoid telling, instructing, or even offering suggestions. If a colleague engages in instructive responses rather than invitational responses, the conversation often ends.

As much as people may rail against being told what to do, they find the role of follower easier than the role of creator. As learners, "teachers are no more accustomed to deciding their professional development path than students are used to deciding what to learn and how to learn it" (Senese, 2002, p. 51).

A good example was when teachers at my school were asked to form Learning Teams in order to pursue questions of concern within their own practice. Teachers were given few parameters. They chose their teams, their areas of inquiry, and their means of analysis and reporting out. Yet many responded by saying, "Just tell us what you want us to do and we will do it. It will be easier." Some teachers did not want the challenge or the risks associated with thinking deeply about their practice and maybe uncovering weaknesses in that practice.

Conversations about practice, which provide a venue safe enough for teachers to uncover problems in their own practice, are often easier to have with relative strangers than with close teaching colleagues or supervisors. Within a school, teachers are more at ease talking about practice with teachers who teach disciplines or grade levels other than their own. The preeminence of subject-matter knowledge and content expertise is less likely to be challenged in those situations. The danger of appearing unknowledgeable about what is taught increases when a group of teachers of the same grade level or of the same subject talk about their teaching. But when a teacher is the lone content expert in a group of colleagues, this becomes a relatively unimportant issue.

Similarly, teachers do not feel embarrassed to ask naïve questions when they are not expected to be content experts. I remember a group of teachers from three different disciplines listening to a mathematics teacher complain about the time it took to teach a certain kind of problem. Ignorant about teaching mathematics, the social studies teacher was able to question her about why she taught that content if it was such an irritant. Most mathematics teachers would not have questioned the reasons for teaching that content and might even have feared looking ignorant by asking such a question—a question that was appropriate at that time. A social studies teacher, however, was within his rights to ask the question merely out of ignorance, and neither teacher was threatened or embarrassed by it. Too often, meetings of teachers of the same subject or from the same school or grade-level try to discover areas for improvement in practice but end up in pity parties.

The factor that protects a teacher from feeling threatened while exploring problems or inadequacies in his practice also allows another teacher to ask a non-threatening question: ignorance and a real desire to know. Teachers in mixed groups are required to explain more of what they do and why they do it because their colleagues are honestly unfamiliar with the answers. Questions develop from real points of doubt, not as an exercise. To answer these questions, teachers have to deconstruct their lessons, explain their practice, and reflect on their work. This honest exchange allows teachers a safe way to talk about their own practice and the successes and problems associated with those practices in a non-threatening yet deep way.

Trusted colleagues need to develop a critical ear and a questioning stance. The questions must be framed out of a real need to know, not to lead the teacher's thinking. Naïve questions asked by someone ignorant of the answers can be a valuable way to frame questions about practice. Simply probing to get the teacher to talk and consider his responses will produce some reflection if done over time. So that the teacher does not feel "ganged up on," a group of no more than three should question him. Done sensitively, this kind of dialogue can produce surprising results. The listeners should not feel obligated to "solve" another teacher's problems, but should honestly probe so the teacher develops self-reliance as well as solutions. By listening intently and asking discerning questions about intentions, practices, and outcomes, these critical friends nudge other teachers to reflect on their practice. No one can force anyone else to become reflective, but given favorable circumstances and structures, reflection has an increased chance of occurring.

Developing teachers' reflection in action

I conclude this chapter by describing ways in which my own roles at the high school have helped me to develop reflection in action in teachers. Both as an administrator and as a teacher, I have been fortunate in creating a systemic and personal way to nudge some teachers toward reflection as a way to improve their practice.

Reflection in action

Practicing this reflective stance with trusted colleagues over time helps teachers to grow. One structure that has proven to encourage reflective practitioners at Highland Park High School is a 10-year-old staff development program called the Action Research Laboratory (ARL). The ARL embraces the elements discussed above and provides teachers with a safe environment in which to identify and reframe problems and then take action (Action Research Laboratory, 2006). The design of the Action Research Laboratory is adaptable and evolves, depending on the participants and their needs. Each element detailed below addresses at least one of the shortages or fears that often prevent teachers from critically reflecting on their practices.

Collaborative sessions

Each team of the Action Research Laboratory meets for a full day once a month in order to organize their action research activities and to provide sufficient time for reflection (addressing a shortage of time). At first, teachers are skeptical about taking an entire day to reflect on their work, but, after just one session, they find that they relish this rare opportunity to delve into educational topics with other professionals. Collaborations that develop in these relationships work because,

> If the individuals are becoming different, that is, taking on new assumptions about teaching and learning, this is sustainable development, and it emerges primarily from sustaining conversations. . . . Sustaining is the key element through which polite interactions work themselves into authentic talk about real work.
>
> (Lambert *et al.*, 1995, pp. 92–93)

Balance between content expertise and experimentation

Because the teachers on an ARL team must come from different disciplines, only one teacher per team is a content expert in any given discipline (addressing a fear of vulnerability). Team members are encouraged to think outside of their disciplines. Cross-pollination frequently occurs as the discipline specialists exchange ideas about the learning process and grow in their own understanding of *how* to teach rather than being bogged down in discussions about *what* to teach.

Frequent consultations with a facilitator

Each ARL team has a facilitator (addressing a shortage of experience/support and a fear of risk). During the monthly sessions, the facilitator creates a learning environment for the team, one in which members are comfortable and encouraged to ask questions that are truly meaningful to them, to take risks, to dream of the ideal, to reflect, and to posit solutions (addressing fear of failure/ vulnerability). The teachers are truly in charge of their own learning, a concept that can cause some consternation when teams first form.

The facilitator also provides an agenda, articles for discussion, and a structure in which participants can pursue their own work. During the meetings, the facilitator mostly listens and inserts carefully placed questions (addressing a fear of risk). The facilitator often acts as a resource, applying for funding, cutting through red tape, and suggesting workshops and conferences. Teachers feel that they have an advocate for their work. And they do, both in their team members and in the facilitator (addressing a shortage of support).

Classroom observations of other ARL teachers

Requiring an informal observation of each team member's classes has broadened the perspectives of ARL teachers. They develop not only an understanding of what teachers of other subjects face every day, but also an appreciation of what students encounter as they move from class to class throughout their day (addressing shortage of experience).

Research

Research takes on a dual meaning for ARL teachers. First, they require the latest information from experts in the field of education. Shared readings, membership in a national professional organization, a subscription to an education journal, and attendance at conferences provide many opportunities for discovering and exchanging this information as they create their own understandings and thereby address the shortage of support and the fear of failure. Second, each ARL team is conducting its own collaborative action research that requires them to collect and analyze data from their own classrooms. Teachers experiment with classroom instruction and assessment practices. They have data to reinforce best practices in their own classrooms with their own students and thereby address the fear of vulnerability.

Coordinated conference–workshop–visitation attendance

The ARL supports teacher research over several years (addressing a shortage of support). Therefore, shared experiences at workshops and conferences have extended value. These common experiences, along with periodic readings of the latest thinking and research in education, inform professional discussion, reflection, and further study. They provide a common language and understanding of the theoretical and research bases on which the teams' action research rests (addressing a fear of vulnerability).

Structures in which to share progress with others

Reaching out to other faculty members across disciplines is the key to creating that critical mass of teachers to effect educational change at the school level (Wheatley, 1992). When they agree to participate in the ARL, teachers make a commitment to share with others what they are learning from their action research (addressing a fear of risk). Every ARL team has resisted "reporting out" at the end of their first year of conducting action research, but I insist that they do. They generally offer three reasons: (1) no one would be interested in what we are researching; (2) we have not proven anything yet; and (3) we won't have enough to say. Invariably, after their lunchtime sharing sessions, these same teachers report that (1) they cannot believe how interested *and helpful* their colleagues were; (2) no one expected them to prove anything; they simply related their journey and what they learned; and (3) they had more than enough to share. Through these sharings, ARL teachers take an active stance to spread the word about the results of their own research and about the benefits of participating in action research. In addition to these sessions, each year every ARL team produces something lasting to share with others. Many of these papers, artifacts, web pages, and presentations are published on the high school website at http://www.dist113.org/hphs/action/table_of_contents.htm. Many ARL members have presented their research at conferences and have written articles for education journals. All of these efforts have professionalized their work and provided multiple opportunities for these teachers to articulate their practice, generating additional instances to reflect.

My role as a model for others

During the years that I have been an assistant principal, I have also remained a classroom teacher. My dual roles assist me to appreciate teaching from the inside because "Being part of the experience is crucial to the development of understanding teaching and learning about teaching as something more than a cognitive process" (Loughran, 2006, p. 175). Teaching keeps me real.

Being a classroom teacher informs every aspect of my job as an administrator. I am able to talk to colleagues based on current classroom experience. I face the daily challenges of teaching. I know when the attendance system is down, when there is a surfeit of interruptions in a week, and when the crunch times for grades occur. I am keenly aware of the rhythms of school in a way that I may overlook if I were not teaching. I continue to talk the language of teaching and can relate to what is happening at school; I am able to interact with other teachers in a way that makes sense to them. I truly have many doubts about what I do in the classroom (Senese, 2002, 2005) and I ask other professionals for advice, direction, and guidance. By positioning myself as a fellow learner about teaching, I have created a platform from which I maintain some influence. This is also true of teacher educators who are perceived as teachers by those they teach. Teacher educators perceived as continuous learners about teaching command a respect from teachers. Making practice transparent is equally important as being informed instructors.

This professional stance as a teacher–learner may be considered a type of modeling as defined by Loughran because "it involves unpacking teaching in ways that gives students [pre-service teachers] access to the pedagogical reasoning, uncertainties and dilemmas of practice that are inherent in understanding teaching as being problematic" (2006, p. 6). In order to help me unpack my teaching, I invite many people into my classroom to participate in instruction and to interact with students. The doors are flung open to other administrators, fellow teachers, paraprofessionals, clerical staff, senior citizens from the neighborhood, parents, university professors and students, and even other high school students. My practice is always under scrutiny. I am forced to reflect deeply on what I am doing and why I am doing it because real questions arise that require me to consider and explain what I do and why I do it. My classroom does not always look like a conventional classroom and I welcome questions because, by exhibiting my practice to a wide range of people, I make myself more accountable for everything that happens in class.

> [Structuring learning this way] can mean that students are freer to take their learning outside walls of the classroom. It can mean that teachers are making themselves and their practices accessible to other practitioners. It can mean that teachers admit that they do not have all the "answers." This more open atmosphere can be invigorating for both teachers and students.
>
> (Austin and Senese, 2004, p. 1241)

By simply having a teaching assignment each year as part of my daily routine, I am able to participate in substantive conversations about practice and to cultivate influence (as opposed to control) with fellow teachers. Without that, my contributions would tend to be esoteric or one step removed from teachers' daily lives. Teachers find myriad ways to dismiss the latest trends in education as fads or as the flavor of the month, but when I am enacting pedagogical ideals in the same environment as other teachers, the conversations change. The action research and self-studies that I conduct as the foundation of my own professional learning enrich all my conversations with fellow teachers. For example, when I am considered an administrator, conversations about teaching and learning are generally limited to prearranged conferences in my office, but when I am considered a teacher, I can "talk shop" in the faculty cafeteria with anyone who happens to sit beside me. My position as a fellow teacher provides me with an advantage I otherwise would not have.

Every teacher who is or has ever been a member of the Action Research Laboratory models critical reflection in these same ways. As more and more teachers benefit from participation in the ARL, their collective influence becomes even more formidable. The benefits are doubled because teachers doing action research learn more about themselves by articulating their practice and receiving feedback from fellow teachers; and the teachers hearing about the action research are discovering new ways of teaching and thinking about teaching. The mutual benefits are worth the time and support that schools do not often afford teachers. We certainly believe that "encouraging teacher research then appears as a meaningful option for all those committed to the improvement of professional practice while also being an important strategy for teachers' professional development" (Loughran, 2006, p. 139).

The process of providing ways to support teachers as continuous learners rather than as experts in their profession can yield impressive results on two levels. The history of the Action Research Laboratory at Highland Park High School and the personal interactions I have had with many teachers reinforce my beliefs that "we ourselves engage in change only as we discover that we might be more of who we are by becoming something different" (Wheatley and Kellner-Rogers, 1996, p. 50). We are constantly in the process of becoming better practitioners through critical reflection. What some may see as a luxury is actually vital to continuous professional improvement.

References

Action Research Laboratory (2006) Page titles for ARL articles. Retrieved August 31, 2006, from http://www.dist113.org/hphs/action/table_of_contents.htm

Austin, T. and Senese, J. (2004) Self-study in school teaching: Teachers' perspectives. In J. J. Loughran, M. L. Hamilton, V. K. LaBoskey, and T. Russell (eds.), *International handbook of self-study of teaching and teacher education practices*. Dordrecht: Kluwer Academic Publishers, pp. 1231–1258.

Korthagen, F. A. J., Kessels, J., Koster, B., Langerwarf, B., and Wubbels, T. (2001) *Linking practice and theory: The pedagogy of realistic teacher education*. Mahwah, NJ: Lawrence Erlbaum Associates.

Lambert, L., Walker, D., Zimmerman, D. P., and Cooper, J. E. (1995) *The constructivist leader*. New York: Teachers College Press.

Loughran, J. J. (1996) *Developing reflective practice: Learning about teaching and learning through modelling*. London: Falmer Press.

Loughran, J. (2006) *Developing a pedagogy of teacher education: Understanding teaching and learning about teaching*. London: Routledge.

Russell, T. (2002) Guiding new teachers' learning from classroom experience: Self-study of the faculty liaison role. In J. Loughran and T. Russell (eds.), *Improving teacher education practices through self-study*. London: RoutledgeFalmer, pp. 73–87.

Schön, D. A. (1983) *The reflective practitioner: How professionals think in action*. New York: Basic Books.

Senese, J. (2002) Opposites attract: What I learned about being a classroom teacher by being a teacher-educator. In J. Loughran and T. Russell (eds.), *Improving teacher education practices through self-study*. London: RoutledgeFalmer, pp. 43–55.

Senese, J. (2005) Teach to learn. *Studying Teacher Education*, *1*, 43–54.

Wheatley, M. J. (1992) *Leadership and the new science*. San Francisco, CA: Berrett-Koehler Publishers.

Wheatley, M. and Kellner-Rogers, M. (1996) *A simpler way*. San Francisco, CA: Berrett-Koehler Publishers.

5 From naïve practitioner to teacher educator and researcher

Constructing a personal pedagogy of teacher education

Ruth Kane

I am a teacher educator. With a background in secondary teaching, I have been working in teacher education in universities in Australia, New Zealand and Canada for almost 20 years. I identify myself primarily as a teacher educator responsible (with colleagues both in universities and in schools) for the preparation and support of beginning teachers. In today's terms, I would no longer be considered a secondary teacher, as I have not taught in a secondary classroom in New Zealand since the curriculum reforms of the late 1980s. I am one of those people to whom student teachers (and some classroom teachers) are referring when they say "some of the professors wouldn't know what hit them if they actually had to go back and teach in a secondary classroom!" I do continue to spend time in classrooms and work with teachers, but this is now done predominantly in my capacity of a researcher and sometimes as a partner in the supervision of student teachers during school-based practicum.

When I entered teacher education, I was at first puzzled, and then more deeply troubled, by the apparent lack of coherence between the university-based components of teacher education and the school-based practicum assignments. Most evident in the gaps between on-campus and in-school components, this lack of coherence was also evident between the various on-campus courses as well. Faculty responsible for individual courses within the program were often unaware of the connection of these courses to any other program components. In addition, it was increasingly apparent that student teachers entered teacher education with well-established views on teachers and teaching and many were resistant to changing these views if proposed alternatives were not compatible with their life experiences. Seeking to understand and clarify these challenges provided the impetus for my master's and doctoral research. These and other questions about how best to teach and learn about teaching continue to productively irritate both my practice and research to this day. Fundamental to my work as a teacher educator and as a researcher is the need to understand better the nature of teaching and how best to support students in their preparation as teachers.

This chapter arises from personal interrogation of my development as a teacher educator. It represents an effort to identify and examine the imperatives that underpin my work and that contribute to my current pedagogy of teacher education, which is itself continually under review. My development has been influenced by a range of people and experiences and by my research and writing. Here I examine key stages in my development, both as a teacher educator and as a researcher of teacher education, identifying links with contemporary literature and research on teaching and teacher education and pondering whether, as a teacher educator, I can learn from the experiences of others.

In order to situate my personal and professional development, I first present the context in which I have worked for the past 20 years. Then I chronicle my story of becoming a teacher educator and researcher by exploring three key stages of this development: (1) the naïve practitioner; (2) the novice (naïve) teacher educator; and (3) the teacher educator and researcher. I identify challenges and issues that exemplify each of these stages through my own personal narrative of experience. I seek to make explicit my own learning and how this has influenced my personal pedagogy of teacher education. In an effort to link my story to work that has preceded it, I articulate links with some of the key issues in teaching about teaching discussed by Loughran (2006), including: the challenges of developing coherent teacher education programs, confronting students' preconceived notions of teaching, and making explicit the tacit knowledge of practice. I draw attention to the possibility that, while teacher education has changed in recent years, it has also stayed the same and we remain some distance from enacting a coherent pedagogy of teacher education.

New Zealand teacher education: complex and ambiguous

A review of the history of teacher education faculty in North America reports that the place of teacher education in higher education is "ambiguous, complex and in need of clarification" (Ducharme and Ducharme, 1996, p. 692). The authors contend that the continuous debate about the place of teacher education within higher education affects the role and status of teacher educators and, consequently, the regard for our research. The location of teacher education within university settings, while the rule in the USA, Canada, and Australia, has been highly contested and a subject of ongoing debate in New Zealand.

Until the 1990s, New Zealand elementary and secondary teachers generally completed their teacher preparation in one of six specialist colleges of education, each of which had well established relationships with local schools and offered substantial professional development to teachers within its region (Alcorn, 1999). A New Zealand educational historian reports that the traditional culture of the colleges of education included allegiance to and transmission of government education policy. Staff were, and in most cases continue to be, recruited almost exclusively from elementary and secondary schools and were required to be broadly supportive of departmental and ministerial policies (Openshaw, 1999, p. 329).

Reforms in both the compulsory and post-compulsory sectors through the 1980s were immediately evident in changes in where, how and by whom teachers were to be prepared. Universities lost their monopoly as degree-granting institutions, effectively opening the way for colleges of education and other alternative providers to set up degree and postgraduate teacher education and teacher research programs. The six traditional colleges of education gained approval for degree-level qualifications and formal amalgamations of the six colleges of education with university faculties was completed by the end of 2006. In addition, a range of alternative teacher education providers has emerged, resulting in an internationally atypical pre-service sector where 25 institutions offer teacher education to a population of only 4 million people. These institutions include universities, *wnanga* (Maori tertiary education institutions), polytechnics and private training establishments. Alcorn argues that this diversity is a result of complex factors including:

> the deregulation of higher education; the government's policy of encouraging institutions to compete in an educational market place; policy initiatives hastily put together in response to a teacher shortage that promised to cause considerable political embarrassment; local requests for programmes to be offered in smaller centres remote from existing institutions; and, demand for specialist programmes.
>
> (1999, p. 112)

Each institution offering initial teacher education competes for experienced and qualified teaching staff, most of whom continue to be recruited from primary and secondary schools, although this practice is decreasing in universities, where appointments typically require a doctoral qualification. Quality Assurance Bodies and the New Zealand Teachers Council have requirements related to the qualifications of staff within teacher education programs. Guidelines for Approval of Teacher Education Programs (New Zealand Teachers Council, 2005, p. 13) state: "A clear majority of lecturers will hold a relevant qualification in advance of that being aspired to by the student teachers. Staff who have yet to attain such a qualification will be actively engaged in doing so." A report on initial teacher education policy and practice in New Zealand (Kane *et al.*, 2005) shows that teacher education programs within New Zealand typically remain staffed by ex-classroom practitioners holding (or currently completing) master's qualifications. Most teacher educators in New Zealand have teaching experience and over 70 per cent of staff are tenured (Kane *et al.*, 2005, pp. 181–199). University-based teacher education programs have a higher proportion of staff with doctorates (20–40 per cent), but this is not the norm across departments of teacher education in other types of institutions.

While it is not the purpose of this chapter to re-litigate the historical development of initial teacher education, it is important to present the historical context from which contemporary policy and practice has emerged within New Zealand, especially in so far as it influences the appointment and professional development of teacher educators. This is the context within which prospective teacher educators typically move from their roles as classroom practitioners to being responsible for the preparation of teachers. As reported in the USA (Zeichner, 2005) and the United Kingdom (Murray and Male, 2005), New Zealand teacher educators receive little, if any, induction into their new role. This signals that the transition from teacher to teacher educator is assumed to be unproblematic. In addition, teacher educators in New Zealand (as elsewhere) are faced with the requirements of being effective teachers and of advancing knowledge and practice in their field through active engagement in research and scholarship. This has been brought into focus with the introduction of a national assessment of the research productivity of all academics.

The 2003 Performance Based Research Fund (PBRF) assessment was the first such exercise within New Zealand, as a system for determining the allocation of research funding across tertiary education organisations. The *quality* of research conducted by academic staff was assessed through evaluation of individual research portfolios. The exercise caused considerable anxiety that was particularly evident within faculties of education, and the majority of academics working in teacher education across the country were rated as not having achieved a platform of research activity. The relatively recent adoption within New Zealand of research-based teacher education, the inherent complexity of preparing teachers and the challenge of serving two masters—the teaching profession and the research community—draw attention to the importance of articulating a pedagogy of teacher education. What follows is an analysis of three stages in my own evolution as a teacher educator and of experiences within these stages that caused me to re-examine what it means to teach and learn about teaching.

The naïve practitioner

Prior to my life as a teacher educator I was a secondary teacher, initially in New Zealand and then in Queensland, Australia. As a teacher I was far from remarkable. I enjoyed my work with students but my experiences, like those of many teachers, were limited to specific contexts. I was not someone who excelled as a classroom teacher or who demonstrated leadership or master-teacher qualities that often signal one's potential for moving into teacher education. On reviewing this stage of my professional life, I do see key values that have been significant in my subsequent development of an emerging pedagogy of teacher education.

My work as a teacher in New Zealand led me to question the relative positions of people within society and the forces that determine one's place in society. Amazingly and somewhat shamefully, I had graduated as a secondary teacher in the late 1970s, blissfully unaware of terms such as hegemony, discourse, critical pedagogy, paradigm and poststructuralism, yet I instinctively understood the power of cultural capital. I recognised that some people in society had the language and understanding that enabled doors to be opened and advances to be made, while others did not. Some students advanced quickly at secondary school, while others struggled, and still others appeared to choose not to participate. The classes in my school were streamed and the students in the lower classes were predominantly Maori. While I recognised this to be the case, as a beginning teacher I was caught up in what and how I was teaching and failed to question why classes and achievement were so racially determined.

Upon moving to Queensland, I enrolled in a postgraduate diploma in Aboriginal and Torres Strait Islander education and subsequently taught in two indigenous communities. Unbeknown to me at the time, these were my first steps in seeking to confront and come to terms with the consequences and responsibilities of my own privilege and how these intersect with my role as a teacher and, subsequently, as a teacher educator. It was there that my commitment to equity and social justice in education and schooling began to play a key role in both what and how I taught. While there were syllabi that I was supposed to follow, I found that if one opted to teach the integrated curriculum course for junior secondary English, mathematics and social studies, one had considerable freedom in what and how you taught. At the time I did not name it as such, but here I began my first encounter with co-construction of curriculum with 13- and 14-year-old Torres Strait Islander and Aboriginal students. In seeking to make the curriculum relevant to their worlds, which were so significantly different from my own, I sought their advice and input into constructing learning experiences both inside and outside the classroom. I learned a considerable amount from those students but still had a long way to go to understand the authority of their experience or to ensure provision of meaningful, culturally relevant education that enabled them to have a choice about participating in higher education (Villegas and Lucas, 2002).

Working in Aboriginal and Torres Strait Islander communities within Queensland, I was able to reassure myself that I was making a difference. I enjoyed teaching and working with the students, and I felt that I did a reasonable job. I remained naïve, however, as to the realities of the students' experiences and the forces that affected their worlds. As a child in a large, working-class family, I had been taught both overtly and subtly that if one worked hard enough, one could advance and succeed. While I saw huge potential in the students with whom I worked, I constructed their advancement and success in my own terms and was frustrated by what I interpreted as their lack of aspirations and application. An example of my well-intentioned arrogance appeared in my discussions with one young Aboriginal woman (Anna) in her final years of secondary school:

> Anna was incredibly talented and very smart. She did well academically and excelled in sports and creative performance such as dance and drama. She had an engaging personality and was a passionate defender of what she believed in. I spent hours encouraging her to go to university, to become a teacher, a dancer, whatever . . . anything except stay on the community and waste her life. Anna would not be persuaded. Her mother was elderly, Anna was the baby and she swore she would not leave to study in the city.

I am ashamed to acknowledge that I left that school feeling that Anna had wasted her potential and maybe even let me down; I certainly thought she had let herself down. I was so convinced that I knew what was best for Anna and I interpreted her resistance as lack of motivation. Four years later, I had a call from Anna that both thrilled and humbled me. Her mother had passed away and Anna now treasured the four years they had shared. Anna turned to the steadfast pursuit of her own dreams and went on to become very successful in the Arts; her work is in high demand in Australia and internationally.

If I consider carefully my years as a secondary teacher in New Zealand and Australia, I see two key values that continue to guide my ongoing development as a teacher educator and researcher. Through my work in secondary schools I learned the importance of acknowledging that students have knowledge and experience to contribute to my pedagogical development. It is over 15 years since Delpit (1988, p. 288) suggested that the "teacher cannot be the only expert in the classroom" and since Fullan (1991, p. 70) asked, "What would happen if we treated the student as someone whose opinion mattered?" I learned that by listening to students' voices I could co-construct curriculum that had meaning and value. Students taught me that a meaningful curriculum is one in which they themselves were represented and through which they themselves could participate and grow. They also taught me the value of what they bring to the teaching and learning relationship and their capacity for knowing and articulating their needs when given the opportunity.

My work in schools also heightened my growing awareness of the ways in which access to educational opportunities can be restricted or denied to groups of people and how my own pedagogy can be complicit in or challenge such inequities. Learning about inequality of educational opportunity and my role in challenging or reinforcing it through my own work as a teacher was a key feature of my transition into teacher education.

The novice (naïve) teacher educator

My introduction to teacher education came in a position as a lecturer in the Aboriginal and Torres Strait Islander support unit at the College of Advanced Education, now the Faculty of Education of Griffith University in Queensland. This initial step was motivated both by a desire to leave the classroom and a sense that I could make a contribution to the preparation of Aboriginal teachers, who were sorely needed in Australian schools. I was also motivated by what I presumed to be the high status of working in tertiary education. In hindsight, I should have chosen something other than teacher education! Zeichner (1995) and others have accurately described the low status of teacher education within academic communities.

I viewed teacher education as a career change to a new and challenging role for which I assumed I would receive some level of induction, guidance, and mentoring. However, as others (Loughran, 2006; Murray and Male, 2005; Zeichner, 2005) have described, it was assumed that I could transfer the skills of a classroom teacher to those required to be an effective teacher educator. I still view as a fundamental misconception of teacher education this assumption that expertise in teaching will seamlessly transfer to the new role of teaching teachers. I found it doubly problematic, for I had demonstrated neither excellence nor leadership as a teacher; I was still quite a novice, having taught for less than five years.

The continued practice of recruiting classroom teachers to work in teacher education reinforces the assumption that the preparation of teachers requires no additional preparation beyond experience as a classroom teacher (Zeichner, 2005, p. 118). In and of itself, this practice is fundamentally flawed; classroom teachers are responsible for teaching children or young adults concepts, skills and embedded attitudes, values and dispositions. They are charged with supporting children's learning and advancement in schools. Yet teacher educators are required to work with adults as they prepare to become teachers. As examined comprehensively by Loughran (2006), teacher educators are involved in the practice of teaching and learning about teaching. I am not suggesting that experience as a classroom teacher does not make an important contribution to becoming a teacher educator, but I agree with the arguments of Murray and Male when they conclude that "there is no straightforward 'transfer' of the pedagogical knowledge and experience acquired in and through school teaching to the HE [Higher Education] context" (2005, p. 130).

My early years as a novice teacher educator were fraught with feelings of inadequacy and uncertainty and an ever-present expectancy of being revealed as a fraud. Unlike the teacher educators in the Murray and Male (2005) study, I did not have the security or credibility of excellence or leadership in classroom practice, nor did I hold a higher degree. I also lacked any experience working with student teachers as a classroom-based associate or mentor teacher. My initial experiences as a teacher educator do resonate with the observation by Dinkelman *et al.* (2006, p. 135) that "the initial experience of doing teacher education is a powerful force in shaping the professional practice of teacher educators over their careers." In spite of, or perhaps because of, my limited and somewhat atypical experience prior to entering teacher education, those early years provided a number of sites of resistance that influenced my development as a teacher educator and, in time, led to the genesis of research questions for doctoral study. I turn now to three key issues: (1) challenging student teachers' preconceived notions; (2) developing coherent teacher education programs; and (3) making explicit the tacit knowledge of practice.

Challenging prior assumptions

My knowledge and experience in Aboriginal education and my commitment to equity and social justice, which I viewed as fundamental to the preparation of all teachers, led me to co-teach with an indigenous colleague a course on Aboriginal Education: De-bunking the Myths. This course presented an alternative (and true) account of Australian history with respect to Aboriginal education and deconstructed popular myths surrounding Aboriginal entitlement, handouts and welfare. The resistance and explicit racism we encountered from the student teachers shocked me and then caused me to question how, as teacher educators, we could engage student teachers, who may have had no experience of difference, disadvantage, racism, or inequity, in seeing the world differently. How could we disrupt the robust and tenacious nature of student teachers' preconceptions? How could we enable student teachers to learn from cross-cultural experiences so different from their own life experiences?

Developing program coherence

The next critical influence on my development as a teacher educator manifested itself as a different form of resistance, this time from my colleagues, both school-based and university-based. Unlike most of my colleagues, I entered teacher education with no particular allegiance to a curriculum area. Since 1988, I have identified first and foremost as a teacher educator. What surprised and confused me on arrival in tertiary education was the strong impression that the majority of my colleagues defined themselves in terms of their curriculum area (e.g., as mathematicians) or their discipline (e.g., as sociologists) and clearly did not define themselves as teacher educators. Many seemed to actively resist being termed a teacher educator, yet this was the prime focus of our work—the preparation of teachers. Resistance to identifying with teacher education as a discipline supported the development of teacher education programs that were fragmented and incoherent.

The curriculum of teacher education programs was variously described in the literature of the time as fragmented and lacking in continuity (Bullough and Gitlin, 2001; Levin, 1995) and curriculum-focused (Shulman, 1987). Teacher education programs in the 1990s appeared to be based on what I have previously termed the "immaculate assumption": It was assumed that upon graduation and appointment as beginning teachers, our graduates would somehow miraculously integrate their learning and experience from a range of distinct and disparate courses and practicum experiences in spite of the fact that we, as their professors, had not taken the time to make such links explicit. *The challenge of ensuring coherent teacher education programs is fundamental to enacting a pedagogy of teacher education.* If we, as teacher educators, cannot clearly articulate and defend our practices of teaching and learning about teaching, we will be left to what Shulman has described as "a field where we let a thousand flowers bloom" (Falk, 2006, p. 76).

Connecting theory and practice

A third area of influence as a novice (naïve) teacher educator emerged from my supervision of students on practicum. From the beginning I located myself in what could be called the professional studies component of initial teacher education that includes courses on pedagogy and the practicum. While acknowledging that I was happy to leave the classroom myself, I retained a strong belief in the expertise and wisdom of experienced teachers and saw my role as akin to a triadic partnership with them and their student teachers (Lind, 2004). My reading of teacher education literature and research highlighted the challenge of reconciling what is typically referred to as the theory and the practice of teacher education. In my early years as a teacher educator, this was reinforced in practice in two equally powerful ways by student teachers, classroom teachers and university professors.

First, student teachers repeatedly returned from practicum with stories of how classroom teachers had advised them to forget the theory learned in university classes, for it was in the school classroom where they would really learn to teach. Second, within the initial teacher education program, students reported that individual lecturers seldom explicitly related their course to any other courses and, with the exception of the professional practice course in which the practicum was embedded, few courses explicitly referred to the practicum, thus reinforcing a lack of program coherence. My experience in teaching the cross-cultural course and in teaching professional practice reinforced the notion that student teachers were entering teacher education with conceptions of teachers and teaching that appeared resistant to change. I began to question how, if at all, the teacher education program was influencing the preparation of beginning teachers. In these questions I found my master's and doctoral research focus and began to build a research platform that has progressively contributed to the construction and reconstruction of a pedagogy of teacher education.

The teacher educator and researcher

The focus of my doctoral research emerged from my experiences as a teacher educator. I examined the impact of an intervention in pre-service teacher education in an effort to reconcile the dilemma of the theory–practice nexus by making explicit and examining the typically tacit understandings of both beginning and expert teachers (Ethell, 1997). The intervention brought together the stimulated recall of an expert teacher's thinking and the collegial reflections of a group of novice student teachers. Early opportunities for beginning teachers to make explicit and examine their personal beliefs and preconceptions were provided through the writing of personal histories, repertory-grid interviews, and written reflections on teachers and teaching. The collaborative nature of the group activities demanded that participants examine and justify their beliefs about teachers and teaching in light of their own knowledge and experiences and those of their peers.

The process acknowledged the robust nature of beginning teachers' beliefs and preconceptions, often in the face of new and contradictory knowledge and experiences. The process also allowed student teachers to come to their own new conceptual understandings of teachers and teaching. By being provided access to the typically implicit thinking and reasoning underlying the practice of expert teachers, the student teachers began to view teaching and the role of the teacher in more pedagogically powerful ways. For the participants in the study, gaining access to the thinking underlying the practices of expert practitioners represented a pivotal point in their understanding of the existence and nature of relationships between the theory and practice of learning to teach. It provided the genesis of a pedagogy of teacher education grounded in learning from the experience of others through making explicit the thinking, intentions and beliefs underpinning teaching practice. While the doctorate was the beginning of my research, I soon found that researching teacher education practices was not necessarily regarded in the academic community as real research.

Zeichner (1995, p. 169) explains that, in many research universities, the more closely one is associated with teachers and schools, the lower one's status; furthermore, the lower one's status, the fewer the resources available to support one's research and practice. It is little wonder that so few academics, including those who work within teacher education, choose to identify themselves first and foremost as teacher educators. Teacher education and the related study of teaching and learning to teach do not have a salubrious history within higher education. The study of teaching and teacher education have been variously avoided by education faculty, neglected by university management, and patently ignored by faculty from other disciplines. For those of us who have a passion for, and find intellectual and professional challenge in, the preparation of teachers and the study of teaching and teacher education practice, this historical neglect is confounding and frustrating, with the potential to influence negatively our work and the way we are positioned in the academy.

> Teacher research is tolerated as an interesting and less oppressive form of professional development for teachers, but few treat the knowledge that teachers generate through their inquiries seriously as educational knowledge to be analyzed and discussed.
>
> (Zeichner, 1995, p. 160)

The challenges of choosing to locate my research within the discipline of teacher education has contributed significantly to my personal development as a teacher educator while working in Australian and New Zealand universities. While this decision perhaps had its genesis in an absence of a particular curriculum strength, it was and continues to be fuelled by a drive to understand better how to prepare beginning teachers.

My interest in teacher education as a discipline and as a field of research and scholarship was called into question early in my academic career. In 1998, I submitted a proposal for the university's competitive research grant funding. The proposal described a longitudinal, purposeful inquiry into my personal teaching practices as a key member of the teacher education team. The intention was to problematize and reframe my own teaching practice in an effort to identify explicitly the ways in which my teaching was related to students' learning as beginning teachers. I sought to understand better the process of learning to teach by making explicit the voices of my student teachers. The research design drew heavily on my own doctoral work and was motivated by my passion to understand better how beginning teachers experience and understand the process of learning to teach so that I could continue to re-form my own teaching practice. In due course I was informed that, although my proposal was excellent, the research committee had declined it on the grounds that the project was deemed "operational." What I considered valid and worthwhile research was understood by my colleagues to be purely "operational" and thus inappropriate for the allocation of competitive research funds. I was told it was not research but just part of my work as a university lecturer.

Thus I faced the dilemma of having to establish a research program in order to secure tenure in a context where the nature and value of my research were called into question and not recognised as real research. Was the purposeful, systematic and critical examination of my own work as a teacher educator legitimate research? The challenge can be described as follows:

> The discipline of teacher education holds a unique position within the academy. In teacher education the subject area that is taught or researched (teaching), is also that which is done (teaching). This is not the case for other professional disciplines, such as medicine and law. Typically, the content that is taught, and is the focus of research, be it propositional or procedural in nature, can be separated from the practice of teaching. In no discipline other than teacher education is the content, and the process of teaching and researching that content, so entangled.
>
> (Ham and Kane, 2004, p. 132)

In my quest to assert a place for myself as a teacher educator *and* a researcher of teacher education, I had to defend my area of inquiry, one that sought to take account of the unique complexity of the discipline of teacher education within a political and educational context that clearly favored dominant research traditions. What is important here is the influence this had on my development as a teacher educator and researcher and how these two roles may well be theoretically distinct for the purposes of professional evaluation yet inseparable in practice.

In the next section I demonstrate how what I learned through my experiences as a practitioner, teacher educator and researcher contributed to how I sought to address some of the larger issues surrounding teaching about teaching and learning about teaching (Loughran, 2006). As someone who has more recently had the privilege of influencing the design of teacher education programs, I consider one example of enacting a pedagogy of teacher education by attempting to design a coherent teacher education program.

Coherent teacher education programs: the foundation of teacher education pedagogy

Thus far I have articulated ways in which my own personal development as a teacher educator has served to shape my thinking, research and practice as a teacher educator in relation to three key issues, one of which includes the other two. The imperative to develop coherent teacher education programs encompasses the need for those responsible for teacher education to make explicit the typically tacit knowledge of teaching, learning and learning to teach, and it requires that we take account of the knowledge and preconceptions of students of teaching.

The challenge of developing coherence within teacher education programs has been taken up by a number of researchers and is prominent in current debate. Books edited by Korthagen *et al.* (2001), Hoban (2005), and Darling-Hammond and Bransford (2005) critically examine the ways in which teacher education continues to suffer from a fragmented and incoherent approach to curriculum and pedagogy. There is general agreement on the complexity of teacher education, a complexity that appears not only in addressing questions of *what to teach and how to teach it* within a teacher education program, but also in the conundrum that what we do as teacher educators (teach) is the same as we what we teach as teacher educators (teaching). For some of us, it is also what we research (Ham and Kane, 2004). A review of initial teacher education programs across New Zealand generated evidence of initial teacher education reminiscent more of traditional practices than of coherent programs with clear theoretical and conceptual informants united by a particular vision of teaching and learning (Kane *et al.*, 2005).

Lack of conceptual and structural coherence has long been a frustrating feature of teacher education. Zeichner and Gore (1990) proposed that teacher education programs that lacked a common conception of teaching and learning risked being ineffective at influencing the teaching practice of beginning teachers. Recent research proposes that one of the critical features of strong programs is that they are "particularly well integrated and coherent: they have integrated clinical work with coursework so that it reinforces and reflects key ideas and both aspects of the program build towards a deeper understanding of teaching and learning" (Darling-Hammond *et al.*, 2005, p. 390).

The commitment to a shared vision of teaching and learning and learning to teach articulated through a conceptual framework contributes also to a common practice of pedagogy and assessment across on-campus and school-based elements of the program of study. Put simply, the conceptual framework should include an understanding of "the nature of teaching and how best to learn about it" (Hoban, 2005), both in on-campus and school-based components. In seeking a coherent teacher education program we must simultaneously consider how we make explicit the typically tacit knowledge of the practice of teaching and learning about teaching and how we will challenge student teachers' preconceived notions of teachers and teaching.

Where other researchers and scholars argue for reform of existing teacher education programs, in 2000, I had the privilege of being involved in constructing pre-service programs from initial conception through to eventual practice at a university in New Zealand. In developing the teacher education program, my colleagues and I began with the premise that we needed to make explicit how we understood teaching, learning and learning to teach and what we identified as the critical ethics and assumptions underpinning the preparation of teachers. Working within a group of teachers from university and schools, we articulated big ideas that were continually revised as we worked towards a shared vision of what it means both to teach and to teach teachers. We identified a set of critical themes or ethics that we saw as fundamental to the approaches to planning, instruction, assessment and evaluation. These drew strongly on discourses of social justice and equity and included a commitment to the Treaty of Waitangi, to inclusion, and to lifelong learning. By involving school teachers in the original design of the program, we were able also to articulate clear links between the on-campus and school-based components of the program, both of which drew on our shared vision of teaching and teaching teachers. We acknowledged that the views and conceptions that student teachers hold when they enter teacher education are of critical importance and we designed ways in which we would provide opportunities for student teachers to examine their own beliefs and preconceptions within a context of current research and practice.

The design of our program began not with identifying the content and structure of the qualification, although these clearly were important, but with the conceptual framework and underlying principles that guided the type of pedagogy enacted, modelled for and engaged in by pre-service students, and with the acknowledgement and consideration of the preconceptions and beliefs pre-service students bring with them. While there is not the scope in this chapter to examine the overall effectiveness of this program, there is value in examining more closely one specific area. In particular I draw attention to the commitment within the program and articulated within its conceptual framework to teacher education grounded in social justice.

Underpinning the program was the belief that, as teacher educators, we had an obligation to practise what we preach and to reflect upon our own teaching practice and the understandings supporting that practice (Zeichner, 1995). As related above, I claim a commitment to social justice and equity with respect to education and endeavour to reflect this in my pedagogy as a teacher educator. In the early years of the new program, I had the opportunity to subject my claimed commitment to the scrutiny of myself and of my peers with interesting results.

I was invited to be part of a doctoral research project that required teacher educators to examine ways in which we define and practise social justice (Sandretto, 2004). I participated in an initial interview and in a series of small-group discussions throughout the year that focused on the articulation of my own and other participants' conceptions of social justice, as well as how I enacted this in my pedagogy and practice with student teachers. We shared transcripts and often used these and the researcher's initial analyses as stimuli for subsequent group discussions. The researcher skilfully drew our attention to consistencies and inconsistencies as we revisited previous dialogue.

Participation in this research group revealed to me the complexity not only of discourses surrounding social justice (for example, as fairness, identity, responsibility, ethic of care) but also of the challenges of ensuring that my practice as a teacher educator reflected the rhetoric of the conceptual framework and adherence to critical themes. While I was initially confident that we had designed a coherent program that reflected a commitment to critical ethics, the examination of my own pedagogy within the program was itself a powerful learning experience that forced me, as a teacher educator, to make the tacit explicit and provided an opportunity for me to position myself in some ways as a student and to see inside the practice of myself and of others:

> Making the tacit explicit offers students of teaching opportunities to see into practice so that they can better understand and relate to the deliberations, questions, issues, concerns and dilemmas that impact the pedagogical reasoning underpinning the practice they experience.
>
> (Loughran, 2006, p. 62)

While in many ways my participation in the doctoral study found my practice somewhat wanting, it did call attention to the complexity of teacher education and the importance of being able to articulate and enact a pedagogy of teacher education. In my own case, the existence of a well-articulated conceptual framework and critical themes within the program served as a frame against which I could continually assess my practice. It also served as a guide for subsequent discussions among the teacher educators involved in the program. While it has, since its inception, undergone several iterations, the conceptual framework does enable colleagues to make explicit the assumptions, beliefs, values, ethics and understandings that we identify as critical to the practice of teaching and learning to teach. This is one way that teacher education can articulate systematic ways of preparing teachers.

Toward a coherent teacher education pedagogy

In re-reading this chapter chronicling my past 20 years as an emerging teacher educator and researcher, I am struck by the resilience of the questions that continue to challenge teacher education and I wonder if those of us engaged in teacher education need to examine our own complicity in resisting reform. While I am not suggesting every teacher educator has followed a path similar to mine, I do believe that many of the formative experiences reported here reflect stages in the development of teacher educators who began their careers as classroom teachers. The specifics will be different for each individual, yet I suggest that there are likely to be formative moments from their school teaching experiences that continue to influence their work, including children or young people like Anna who caused them to stop, reflect and listen to the voices of students. Just like a beginning teacher, as a novice (naïve) teacher educator I was preoccupied with survival in my new role, which revealed itself to be fundamentally different from classroom teaching and isolating through its lack of coherence and explicit pedagogy. My initial years of teacher education generated enduring questions that fuelled my research and were a powerful source shaping my subsequent professional practice both as a teacher educator and as a researcher of teacher education. Today I find myself in a new position and still the questions of how best to prepare beginning teachers trouble my daily work.

My current role as a Director of Teacher Education presents me with yet another context for the practice and research of teacher education, a one-year post-degree program leading to a Bachelor of Education degree. Competition for entry to teacher education in Ontario is high and applications exceed places in a ratio of 10 to 1. In many ways I was expecting the relatively high status of teaching to be reflected in a more advanced approach to teacher education. Discussions with students and faculty suggest that, although teacher education has changed in many ways over recent years, its fragmented structure and lack of explicit integration remains. In an exit survey of students, I was disappointed, but not surprised, to find students praising the practicum as the single most valuable component of their preparation while lamenting the lack of connection between on-campus courses and the reality of their practicum experiences. There is clearly a pressing need to examine closely both what and how we teach and how programs of teacher education are organised theoretically, conceptually and pedagogically. Drawing on my experiences in New Zealand, groups of teacher educators from both faculty and partner schools will explore key questions with a view to articulating a conceptual framework for our program that will enable colleagues to make explicit the assumptions, beliefs, values and understandings that we identify as critical to teaching and learning to teach. The goal is to consider first the conceptual framework and underlying assumptions of our program and then develop alternative approaches that will enable partnerships between faculty and teachers to enhance the ways in which we work with student teachers. Questions guiding our discussions include:

- What would it look like if we had a coherent program where professors and associate teachers worked from a coherent conceptual framework and shared underlying assumptions, goals, ethics and a vision of how their work related to the work of others within the program?
- How can we as teacher educators make explicit the typically tacit knowledge of teaching, learning and learning to teach in ways that will enable student teachers to examine the beliefs and preconceptions embedded in their own practices?

These discussions will be driven by our goals to understand better the nature of teaching and how to teach teachers. Discussions will be influenced by the views, beliefs and values colleagues bring with them, and they will be mediated to some degree by university and accreditation agencies requirements, policies and procedures. My hope is that they will be a means to move us closer to articulating and enacting a pedagogy of teacher education that actively and explicitly supports student teachers' transition from student to classroom teacher.

References

Alcorn, N. (1999) Initial teacher education since 1990: Funding and supply as determinants of policy and practice. *New Zealand Journal of Educational Studies*, 34(10), 110–120.

Bullough, R. V., Jr. and Gitlin, A. (2001) *Becoming a student of teaching: Linking knowledge production and practice*, 2nd edn. London: RoutledgeFalmer.

Darling-Hammond, L. and Bransford, J. (eds.) (2005) *Preparing teachers for a changing world: What teachers should learn and be able to do.* San Francisco: John Wiley and Sons.

Darling-Hammond, L., Hammerness, K., Grossman, P., Rust, F., and Shulman, L. (2005) The design of teacher education programs. In L. Darling-Hammond and J. Bransford (eds.), *Preparing teachers for a changing world: What teachers should learn and be able to do.* San Francisco: John Wiley and Sons, pp. 390–441.

Delpit, L. D. (1988) The silenced dialogue: Power and pedagogy in educating other people's children. *Harvard Educational Review, 58,* 280–298.

Dinkelman, T., Margolis, J., and Sikkenga, K. (2006) From teacher to teacher educator: Reframing knowledge in practice. *Studying Teacher Education, 2,* 119–136.

Ducharme, E. R. D. and Ducharme, M. K. (1996) Development of the teacher education professoriate. In F. B. Murray (ed.), *The teacher educator's handbook: Building a knowledge base for the preparation of teachers.* San Francisco: Jossey-Bass, pp. 691–714.

Ethell, R. G. (1997) Reconciling the propositional and procedural knowledge: Beginning teachers' knowledge in action. Unpublished doctoral thesis, Griffith University, Australia.

Falk, B. (2006) A conversation with Lee Shulman — Signature pedagogies for teacher education: Defining our practices and rethinking our preparation. *The New Educator, 2,* 73–82.

Fullan, M. G. (1991) *The new meaning of educational change.* London: Cassell.

Ham, V. and Kane, R. G. (2004) Finding a way through the swamp: A case of self-study as research. In J. J. Loughran, M. L. Hamilton, V. K. LaBoskey, and T. Russell (eds.), *International handbook of self-study of teaching and teacher education practices.* Dordrecht: Kluwer, pp. 103–150.

Hoban, G. F. (ed.) (2005) *The missing links in teacher education design: Developing a multi-linked conceptual framework.* New York: Springer.

Kane, R. G., Burke, P., Cullen, J., Davey, R., Jordan, B., McMurchy-Pilkington, C., *et al.* (2005) *Initial teacher education policy and practice.* Wellington: New Zealand Ministry of Education.

Korthagen, F. J., Kessels, B., Koster, B., Lagerwerf, B., and Wubbels T. (2001) *Linking practice and theory: The pedagogy of realistic teacher education.* Mahwah, NJ: Lawrence Erlbaum Associates.

Levin, B. B. (1995) Using the case method in teacher education: The role of discussion and experience in teachers' thinking about cases. *Teaching and Teacher Education, 11,* 63–79.

Lind, P. (2004) The perceptions of teacher education in relation to the teaching practicum. Unpublished doctoral thesis, Massey University, New Zealand.

Loughran, J. (2006) *Developing a pedagogy of teacher education: Understanding teaching and learning about teaching.* London: Routledge.

Murray, J. and Male, T. (2005) Becoming a teacher educator: Evidence from the field. *Teaching and Teacher Education, 21,* 125–142.

New Zealand Teachers Council (2005) Standards for qualifications that lead to teacher registration: Guidelines for the approval of teacher education programmes. Retrieved August 16, 2006, from http://www.teacherscouncil.govt.nz/pdf/200502-guidelines-for-approval-feb05.pdf

Openshaw, R. (1999) Some twentieth century issues for some twenty-first century teacher educators. *New Zealand Journal of Educational Studies, 34,* 323–334.

Sandretto, S. (2004) Teacher education and social justice: Theorising professional practice. Unpublished doctoral thesis, University of Otago, Dunedin, New Zealand.

Shulman, L. S. (1987) Knowledge and teaching: Foundations of the new reform. *Harvard Educational Review, 57,* 1–22.

Villegas, A. and Lucas, T. (2002) Preparing culturally responsive teachers: Rethinking the curriculum, *Journal of Teacher Education*, 53, 20–33.

Zeichner, K. M. (1995) Beyond the divide of teacher research and academic research. *Teachers and Teaching: Theory and Practice*, 1, 153–172.

Zeichner, K. M. (2005) Becoming a teacher educator: A personal perspective. *Teaching and Teacher Education*, 21, 117–124.

Zeichner, K. M. and Gore, J. M. (1990) Participants in teacher education: Teacher socialization. In W. R. Houston (ed.), *Handbook of research on teacher education*. New York: Macmillan, pp. 329–349.

6 Finding my way from teacher to teacher educator

Valuing innovative pedagogy and inquiry into practice

Shawn Michael Bullock

This chapter is about relationships—between my developing knowledge of teaching and the methods I use to develop that knowledge, between innovative pedagogies and their impact on my teaching practice, and between my long-time critical friend, Tom Russell, and me. In this chapter I trace the development of my interest in using innovative pedagogies that support active learning in students. I also trace the development of my knowledge about teaching through action research and self-study as I strive to develop principles for teaching about teaching.

The purpose of this chapter is to explicate many of the issues raised by Loughran (2006) with a view not only to articulating my existing epistemology of practice, but also to exploring and developing principles of practice that I can enact as a new teacher educator. Thus the chapter focuses on making tacit knowledge explicit, first as a pre-service teacher, then as a teacher and, finally, as a new teacher educator. I document my efforts to challenge traditional pedagogies that centre on teacher talk and I highlight several tensions of practice that I encountered in my journey. An important underlying theme is the professional friendship I formed with an experienced teacher educator, a relationship that modeled reflection, risk-taking, trust and independence in practice.

This chapter is presented in five sections. The first and second sections document my experiences as a pre-service teacher and a secondary school teacher, respectively. Particular attention is given to the influence of both innovative pedagogies and action research on the development of my knowledge of teaching and learning. The remainder of the chapter highlights key moments and turning points in understanding my own values and practices in my early stages as a teacher educator. In the third section, I recount experiences as an in-service teacher educator in a large suburban high school where I worked with experienced teachers to improve their practice. In the fourth section, I describe how self-study helped me to challenge my assumptions about teacher education in my early work as a pre-service teacher educator. Finally, I set an agenda of issues to explore in the road ahead on my journey of learning to teach teachers.

Reflection-in-action as a pre-service teacher

My undergraduate studies in physics were dominated by a transmission-based teaching style familiar to many. The transition from the familiar student experiences of an undergraduate to the unfamiliar, often conflicting, experiences of a pre-service teacher in a B.Ed. program was challenging, particularly as I realized that my default style of teaching was to emulate the successful Socratic lessons that I had seen all my life. Thus my teaching practicum assignments were spent negotiating tensions between my default inner teacher and the new ideas about teaching and learning that I was exposed to both from associate teachers and pre-service courses. The challenge was to confront my default assumption that teaching should focus on transmission of curricular content while forming a pedagogy that I could claim as my own.

Pre-service teaching experiences

My B.Ed. studies in 1997–1998 included a physics curriculum class taught by Tom Russell, with whom I began an extended dialogue about how I was learning and how he was teaching. Not only did this dialogue push me to identify my core pedagogical beliefs and values, but also it provided an early framework for me to pursue my understanding of teaching. Our critical dialogue pushed me to apply the principles of constructivist teaching to my own thinking about teaching and learning. I became particularly interested in the role of experience in shaping students' understanding of science. I also realized that "powerful perspectives on teaching may take years to understand and develop" (Russell and Bullock, 1999, p. 150). Thus I learned to view my pre-service teacher education program as a beginning rather than an end.

Tom taught me to trust my ability to see and learn from my pre-service teaching experiences. I came to see my own professional learning as a process of practice, reframing and consolidation. DeMulder and Rigsby (2003) reported that a newfound professional voice was one of the critical transformational elements of their pre-service teaching program. I developed my teaching voice by establishing positive professional relationships with Tom and my associate teachers. These relationships allowed me to take risks during my teaching practicum placements, and thus I was able to explore my tacit assumptions about teaching and learning. An increase in self-awareness is characteristic of strong teacher education programs (DeMulder and Rigsby, 2003).

Action research

Action research was a critical component of my B.Ed. program, comprising a major portion of the assessment in a course associated with my 12-week practicum assignment. Action research became a powerful structure for developing an authority over my experiences and pushing beyond the technical elements of teaching (Loughran, 2006). My central question concerned whether or not experiments in the classroom should precede or follow instruction on the topic under investigation. The results (Bullock, 1999) suggested that students used the experiences provided through labs as springboards for discussion. Over one-third of the class preferred that experiments precede instruction, a result that encouraged me to further explore the role of experience in learning science.

More importantly, action research provided an early framework for thinking about my teaching. The results of my action research were of secondary import-ance to its power in showing me how to reframe problems that I encountered in my practice. I learned that, even as a new teacher, I could make powerful observa-tions of my own teaching. I found the narrative aspect of writing the action research report to be particularly empowering because it encouraged me to reflect on my practice explicitly. Teachers in the program discussed in DeMulder and Rigsby's (2003) study also mentioned the motivational power of narrative writing when it came to forming new conceptions about teaching and learning. There was an important interaction between the emphasis placed on the action research assignment in my professional studies course and the emphasis on learning from experience in my physics methods course. The action research project made the process of reflection more explicit and helped me see into my teaching experiences in a new way.

Reflection-in-action as a classroom teacher

In September, 2000, I became a physics teacher at a secondary school in Toronto. The school culture seemed to favour traditional approaches to teaching that seemed appropriate to the preparation of students for academic study at uni-versity. As both the youngest member of staff and the most recent graduate of a teacher education program, I initially struggled to find a balance between the school's expectations of my teaching practice and my own pedagogical expect-ations. I used the innovative pedagogies that I began exploring in my pre-service teaching in tandem with action research to further develop my knowledge of teaching and learning. In so doing, I was able both to be true to my developing voice as a young teacher and to make important insights into how to help my students improve the quality of their learning.

Teaching experiences

Acutely aware of my need to construct an alternative to transmission-based teach-ing, I worked to recognize issues and concerns about my practice that would allow me to reframe my professional knowledge. I decided to revisit a teaching strategy from the Project for Enhancing Effective Learning (PEEL) (Baird and Northfield, 1992). This teaching strategy, termed Predict–Observe–Explain (POE), played a critical role in reframing my early practice. POE is an innovative practice because it draws students into the process of identifying their prior know-ledge of science and using that knowledge to make a prediction about what will happen in a given situation. After the observation, which is often designed to be novel or surprising, students attempt to explain their observation. The format of a POE can vary quite a bit depending on the lesson, but the core feature is that students not only express their prior conceptions about science, but also help to develop explanations about science phenomena. By introducing Predict–Observe–Explain activities into my classes in my first year of teaching, I ensured that a teaching strategy that fostered active student learning became routine for the students and for me.

The other innovative pedagogy that I focused on was a series of techniques designed to use writing activities as a way to explore new ideas and consolidate understandings. As a group, these pedagogies are often called Writing-to-Learn, in contrast to passive, familiar writing activities such as note-taking and writing laboratory reports (Hand and Prain, 2002). My use of Writing-to-Learn pedagogies arose naturally out of the Predict–Observe–Explain methods I regularly employed. I felt that the exploratory writing that students engaged in during POEs allowed them to think about the predictions and explanations they offered. By the end of my second year of teaching, students in all of my classes were asked to maintain a separate, bound notebook that served as a forum for engaging in exploratory writing about POEs. I was able to write back to the students individually, thereby extending the discussions we had in the classroom.

During my pre-service program, both Tom and my associate teachers modelled good teaching that often included both reflection and risk-taking. I decided early in my career to model reflection and risk-taking to my students by being explicit about the pedagogies I chose and why I thought they could help them learn. Both Predict–Observe–Explain and Writing-to-Learn pedagogies encouraged my students and me to take an active role in exploring introductory physics topics. It is safe to say that my understanding of the concepts that I learned via transmission-based pedagogy improved dramatically through shared experiences using innovative pedagogies with my students.

Action research

As my third year of teaching drew to a close, I set out to explore my professional knowledge by recording my thoughts, feelings, and observations about my daily teaching for the entire second semester. My motivation to undertake such a task was twofold. First, I knew that my Master's thesis question would revolve around the role of reflective practice in developing conceptual knowledge of physics, and thus I wanted to further explore the role of reflection-in-action in developing my conceptual knowledge of how to teach physics. Second, I wished to revisit the themes that were addressed in Russell and Bullock (1999), with a view to examining how my themes had evolved or changed. Specifically, I was interested in revisiting my pedagogical perspective and "adding links to my map of teaching" (ibid., p. 150). I wanted to examine the role of experience in shaping my conceptual understanding of how I teach physics and further my understanding of the process of reflection-in-action. I used Schön's (1983) epistemology of professional knowledge as the framework for my exploration.

The experience of keeping a daily journal of teaching notes between February and June 2003, was quite different from the experience of exchanging notes about classes and my practicum with Tom in 1997–1998. The most obvious difference was that time had passed and I was a third-year teacher with much more teaching experience. In addition, I was more ambitious in my attempt at journal writing, as I resolved to report on how I attempted to enact my developing principles of practice on a daily, rather than a weekly, basis.

Two main themes emerged from my experiences. First, keeping notes forced me to consider problems I encountered in my practice, and hence I was able to extend and enrich my conceptions of teaching and learning. Second, the process of summarizing the week's events engaged me in considering the tensions, axioms, and assertions about my practice as I worked to develop alternatives to transmission-based teaching. The written notes forced me to examine problems of practice, particularly those concerned with helping my students improve the quality of their learning.

My most critical assertion concerned the importance of teacher–student relationships in developing students' ability to construct a physics world-view. Like most new teachers, I wanted to ensure that I presented the content of the physics curriculum. Although I regularly used innovative pedagogies such as Predict–Observe–Explain and Writing-to-Learn, I often felt the well-known pressure to cover the curriculum. The writing experience of 2003 brought the tension between *how* I teach and *what* I teach into shaper focus than ever before, as I concluded that my pedagogy and the low-risk environment that it requires are far more important for successful teaching than the content of the curriculum.

In hindsight, I find it difficult to believe that I did not see the importance of relationships sooner. My professional relationship with Tom encouraged me to develop a conceptual understanding of how I teach. My attempts to explicate my professional knowledge would not have been very successful without Tom's ability to challenge me to reframe critical issues and to continually point to the bigger picture. He has offered a broad range of experiences from which I have been able to develop my conceptual understanding. The writing experience taught me that it is the relationship that I have with my students that allows me to provide experiences from which they can build a conceptual understanding of physics, just as it is the relationship that I have with Tom that allows me to develop my conceptual knowledge of teaching. Recognizing the primacy of relationships in teaching represented a major development in my thinking.

Reflection-in-action as an in-service teacher educator

In September 2003, I became an in-service teacher educator as part of a school-district pilot project called Learning Plus. The district referred to us as Learning Plus teachers rather than as teacher consultants, although our jobs were similar to those of teacher consultants in the district. The critical difference was that Learning Plus teachers were assigned to a specific secondary school and, although we were often involved in district-wide events, our primary responsibility was to a secondary school and its associated elementary schools.

In a broad sense, Learning Plus referred to a cross-curricular and district-wide initiative designed to improve the quality of students' learning, particularly those students who are labelled at-risk. Within the context of this initiative, at-risk students were defined as those who were struggling to meet the Ontario provincial standards and hence were in danger of dropping out of school. The Learning Plus teacher was initially conceptualized as an on-site teacher consultant. As such, significant professional development opportunities were mandated for Learning Plus teachers, particularly regarding adolescent literacy instruction. One of the reasons for this focus was the district's concern that many of the at-risk students struggled with basic reading and writing skills. Other professional development opportunities were in the areas of change theory, data collection and interpretation, and adolescent literacy. The district outlined two roles for each Learning Plus teacher:

1   Assist in coordinating and providing preparatory activities for the Ontario Secondary School Literacy Test.
2   Help teachers, through co-planning and in-class modelling, to learn how to embed literacy strategies into the teaching of their subjects in order to better support struggling students with the reading and writing tasks that are required to achieve in these subjects.

My early experiences in teacher education were firmly rooted in what Schön (1983) called the swampy lowlands of professional practice. The school board and the training it provided represented a kind of ivory tower that seemed disconnected from the teaching situations that I found myself in on a daily basis. As expected, there was often considerable resistance to the idea of an in-school teacher consultant. I responded by presenting myself as a resource to help teachers work through professional problems rather than as someone who was simply trying to transmit school-board initiatives and policies.

In-service teacher education experiences

My first foray into teacher education was to work with colleagues who often had more classroom experience than I did. I participated in monthly training workshops offered by the school over a two-year period, only to find that the workshops focused on training me in specific content that I was to share with my colleagues. Little or no attention was paid to the pedagogy of teaching teachers.

Although the district provided some guidelines for the role of the Learning Plus teacher, I found myself in the enviable position of being able to define my role within the context of my school. I decided early on that my focus should be on the teachers within my family of schools, rather than on the students. I felt that approaching the position as a kind of resource teacher who withdraws individual students from classes was both outside my area of expertise and unrealistic for a large student population. I chose to focus on supporting the teachers in my school within their subject areas by acting as a critical friend. Thus I returned to the idea of teaching as a relationship that focuses on sensitivity, honesty, and independence in practice (Loughran, 2006).

A major portion of my role involved team-teaching activities that ostensibly supported the development of subject-specific competencies, both with colleagues at my high school and our elementary partner schools. I provided resources and professional development training for staff on issues such as research-based teaching strategies, literacy instruction and assessment. As I worked with teachers, I was mindful of the lesson that I learned from my action research as a physics teacher— relationships are of paramount importance in teaching. In general, teachers tended to be apprehensive about inviting me into conversations about their practice, so I had to work hard at building a trusting professional relationship. Once teachers were comfortable talking to me about their teaching, we often had rich discussions about how to improve the quality of their students' learning. By moving the focus away from their teaching and toward their students' learning, I believe that I was able to engage teachers on a professional level that was non-threatening and highly productive.

Action research

Sarason (2002) has suggested that teachers should begin by knowing both the learners' starting point and the direction that the learner plans to take. Thus, the first place I began as a teacher educator was to get to know my fellow teachers and find out what they needed to improve the quality of learning in their classrooms. I then did my best to address those needs by providing the kinds of resources and support that were requested. The most productive relationships that I had with teachers in my school were those centred on a mutual concern for students' learning. I was careful to emphasize that my role was non-evaluative.

I submit that the most important element of my role as an in-service teacher educator involved the in-school meetings that I created for my colleagues. At these meetings, I encouraged groups of teachers to talk about their teaching and their concerns about students' learning. Rather than pushing a district-sponsored agenda, I noticed that encouraging teachers to talk about their practice addressed most of the external requirements of the school district. In particular, it was useful for teachers to have inter- and intra-departmental conversations about teaching strategies. Often, the results of these conversations were team-teaching collaborations not only between other teachers and me, but also between the teachers themselves.

My experiences as an in-service teacher educator generated the following set of principles as an early framework for my thinking about teacher education:

1   Teachers' professional knowledge is tacit, and professional dialogue is a powerful way to make teacher knowledge explicit (Russell and Bullock, 1999).

2   It is important to provide experiences that encourage teachers to articulate their pedagogy in order for them to realize the characteristics of their default teaching style.

3   It is difficult for teachers to change their default teaching style because there are powerful cognitive and social factors that encourage a transmission-based approach to pedagogy.

When I concluded my time as an in-service teacher educator in June 2005, I anticipated that two years working with experienced teachers to help them reframe their professional practice would give me a strong base of experience that I could draw on in my work with teacher candidates. I learned much about how to help teachers to articulate their teaching style and how to examine the problems of practice encountered in daily teaching. I was surprised to discover that my assumptions about the ways that teachers learn did not readily transfer to my work with pre-service teachers.

Reflection-in-action as a pre-service teacher educator

When I began my Ph.D. program in September 2005, I was excited to share teaching responsibilities with my supervisor, Tom Russell. The team teaching arrangement was both novel and appropriate; in the fall term, Tom and I worked as teacher and teaching assistant, while in the second term I became the teacher while Tom was away on sabbatical leave. As a doctoral candidate teaching pre-service teachers for the first time, I was quick to notice that my experiences leading in-service activities for experienced teachers did not fully prepare me for working with pre-service teachers. Self-study provided a way for me to examine my beliefs and practices in the early stages of developing a personal pedagogy for pre-service teacher education.

Pre-service teacher educator experiences

For the first four months of the school year, I was the teaching assistant for Tom's physics methods course and his practicum supervision course. In early October, shortly after the teacher candidates left for their first four-week practicum, Tom challenged me to write about the differences I had noticed between teacher candidates and experienced teachers. I now summarize those differences in terms of three categories: pedagogical stance, subject-matter knowledge and professional concerns.

• *Pedagogical stance.* Experienced teachers have a well-developed pedagogical stance, although they are often not able to articulate it. The pedagogical stance is shaped by past experiences as a student, and also by professional development experiences, departmental colleagues, and school-district policies and requirements. The justification for making particular choices in the classroom often comes down to statements that begin with the phrase, "In my experience." Attempts to name pedagogies often create misunderstand-ings among teachers, administration, and parents. Experienced teachers are also passionate about their pedagogy, and typically only will discuss it with teachers of the same discipline and grade level. In contrast, teacher candi-dates have a well-developed pedagogical stance that is almost exclusively shaped by their experiences as students. Many candidates seem to be trying to emulate a favourite teacher or trying to avoid the teaching mistakes they endured as a student. I see their pedagogical stances as more malleable than those of experienced teachers, in part because they are consistently looking to acquire new resources to add to their repertoires and in part because they often see themselves as knowing very little. Teacher candidates are generally looking for familiar and comfortable pedagogical approaches, not ones that might feel risky in a classroom.

- *Subject-matter knowledge.* Experienced teachers seem to be self-assured in their knowledge of subject matter, although many rely on textbooks for the acquisition of new knowledge. I found that teachers are proud of their discip-lines and that subject-matter experts have instant credibility with experienced teachers of the same discipline. There is a prevailing belief that a science teacher, for example, is unlikely to say anything about teaching that is relevant to an English teacher. In most cases, teacher candidates are fresh from under-graduate degrees and seem confident in their subject-matter knowledge. Many seem to feel that their primary role is to transmit that knowledge. Much discussion among candidates seems devoted to what they teach rather than to how they teach.

- *Professional concerns.* Experienced teachers are concerned about the structure of the school system. They feel that there are significant system-level struc-tural impediments that need to be removed so they can do their jobs more effectively. Professional development sanctioned by the district is generally scoffed at, whereas subject-based activities provided by professional organ-izations are regarded positively. Teacher candidates often seem obsessed with issues of classroom management. They are understandably concerned with controlling a class and many see management as the first order of business when they step in front of a class. Many candidates seem to take the issue of classroom management personally, as a reflection of their character and of their ability to be a teacher.

These initial assertions about experienced teachers and teacher candidates reveal important differences between the two groups that I needed to consider in devel-oping principles of teacher education. Thus, I was forced to face my first problem of practice as a teacher educator: I was not well prepared by my previous experi-ence as teacher consultant. I did not have much time to dwell on this problem, however, because I immediately began accompanying Tom on his visits to teacher candidates on practicum placements. Although I found the environment of a secondary school to be more familiar than that of a Faculty of Education, I was again confronted with a sense of confusion surrounding my role in the development of pre-service teacher's knowledge about teaching. Again, Tom challenged me to draw comparisons between my work with experienced teachers and my early work observing teacher candidates in their first practicum. I now summarize the differences I noted in terms of three categories: professional questions, critical friendship, and role of the Faculty of Education.

- *Professional questions.* Experienced teachers can be adept at framing questions about their practice and are likely to focus on specific issues pertaining to their subject and to individual students. Subject-matter experts are perceived to be more useful for interpreting problems of practice than teachers from other disciplines. Experienced teachers are able to focus in on one particular element or incident in a lesson for consideration. In sharp contrast, teacher candidates beginning their practica are unlikely to be able to ask questions about how to improve their practice. Success in an early lesson is equated with the ability to get through a class without a major incident such as a discipline issue or a forgotten lesson item. Teacher candidates tend to focus on the lesson as a whole, often feeling that the lesson has finished when the teacher-centred portion is over.

- *Critical friendship.* Teaching is ostensibly a personal endeavour and experienced teachers differ in their comfort with other adults being present in the classroom. A successful critical friendship is one that includes a similar amount of risk for each of the teacher participants with absolutely no evaluative component. Once professional trust is established, experienced teachers are able to consider critically multiple elements of their teaching. Experienced teachers require positive affirmation of their teaching practice, given that they receive so little regular feedback from other teachers.

  Teacher candidates expect to have other teachers and Faculty Liaisons in their classrooms; hence they have an innate predisposition toward the necessity of receiving critical interpretations of their teaching. Teacher candidates are often unable to process more than two or three criticisms of any one element of their teaching and require considerable positive reinforcement from both Faculty and Associate Teachers. In short, they need to know what they are doing well as much as they need to know where they can improve.

- *Role of the Faculty of Education.* The common school perspective on Faculties of Education is dim at best. Experienced teachers are generally unfamiliar with research in education, with the exception of mass-marketed notions such as multiple intelligences. Faculty members are perceived to have little or no role in most experienced teachers' lives, save with those who are enrolled in graduate studies or continuing teacher education.

  Teacher candidates initially believe that their professors should be able to provide lists of best practices to guide them in most teaching situations. Faculties of Education are viewed as places where theory is learned before going into to schools to practice being a teacher. It does not take long for many teacher candidates to avail themselves of the popular notion that a Faculty of Education has little to do with their growth as a teacher.

Self-study of teacher education practices

My interest in self-study of teacher education practices grew naturally from my use of Schön's (1983) epistemology of professional knowledge and the ongoing dialogue I shared with Tom Russell over the years. Tom's critical friendship has frequently encouraged me to reframe my understanding of my practice based on his alternative interpretations of my teaching experiences. Given that Tom and I often discussed problems of practice that we encountered in the classes we shared, it was appropriate to use the critical friendship inherent in the self-study paradigm as a framework for interpreting my early knowledge of teacher education. Thus our team teaching context that uniquely involved both university classes and practicum supervision became a rich context for critical friendship and self-study (Schuck and Russell, 2005).

At the conclusion of the first term I conceptualized my self-study as a series of questions that challenged me not only to minimize the differences between how I taught and what I taught, but also to further explore the differences noted in the previous section. More specifically, I saw the differences between my prior experiences in teacher education and my experiences with pre-service teachers as a series of problems to help me reframe my developing pedagogy of teacher education. The headings in the previous section became a useful organizational framework for my six self-study questions:

1 *Pedagogical stance:* Do I solicit teacher candidates' prior conceptions about their pedagogy?
2 *Subject-matter knowledge:* Do I provide experiences that encourage teacher candidates to think beyond their subject-matter content?
3 *Professional concerns:* Do I make the tacit internal structures of a classroom explicit to teacher candidates?
4 *Professional questions:* Do I provide opportunities for teacher candidates to frame questions about their problems of practice?
5 *Critical friendship:* Do I create an environment of trust so that teacher candidates feel comfortable talking about their pedagogy?
6 *Role of the Faculty:* Do I present an alternative to the standard theory-into-practice dichotomy by providing opportunities for teacher candidates to examine their practice at the Faculty of Education?

My research questions were intended to go beyond yes-or-no answers to serve as a framework for me to think about the characteristics of my pedagogy. My research questions were influenced by Tidwell's (2002) caution against investigating characteristics of practice before finding out if one's practice is enacted in the way it is intended. Instead of asking, for example, *how* I solicit teacher candidates' prior conceptions about their pedagogy, I asked *if* I solicit candidates' prior conceptions of their pedagogy. There is an important distinction between the two questions, namely, that the second question does not involve *a priori* assumptions about the characteristics of my teaching. In this way I hoped to avoid making assumptions about what I was including in my pedagogy of teacher education. I used the six self-study questions to focus my thinking on the dynamics of my interactions with teacher candidates.

The primary source of data for the first three questions was a teaching journal in the form of a web log (blog) that I added to after each pre-service class that I taught. I found that web-log technology allowed me to quickly jot down some thoughts about my practice regardless of where I was, for a blog can be accessed and modified from any computer with internet access. Blogs also have the advantage of allowing me to share my journal with anyone I wish, particularly useful feature given that Tom was away on sabbatical leave during my January teaching. I selected three critical incidents from my blog that helped me explore each of the three focus questions of my self-study.

Blog questions

1. Do I solicit teacher candidates' prior conceptions about their pedagogy?

I noticed in the first term that many of the teacher candidates in our physics class would often discuss what they teach rather than how they teach. I also noticed that a good percentage of the class had a strong interest in astronomy. In the third class of the second term, I decided to do a media-literacy exercise without labelling it as such. I showed the television special, *Conspiracy Theory: Did we really land on the moon?*, that appears from time to time on television. The program presents about 10 ideas that are supposed to convince viewers that the Apollo moon missions never really happened. As expected, the program drew the teacher candidates into an energetic discussion about the veracity of the claims made, to the point that I abandoned my plan for the remainder of class and put the candidates into groups to refute the claims by applying principles of physics. For example, one of the claims made is that the lunar photographs are doctored because there are no stars visible in the sky. The teacher candidates were able to conclude that the reason no stars are visible in the pictures is that film needs to be exposed for a long time to capture dim starlight.

At the end of class I asked the teacher candidates if they would use this activity with high school students. By not taking up the physics content of the activity, I hoped to get them to focus on the pedagogy. The result was somewhat astonishing:

> So What? How and when could a video like this be used pedagogically? The teacher candidates were nearly unanimous in their caution against using the video with grade 9 or 10 students. Their concern seemed to centre on the danger of confusing students with a flashy video. Some candidates suggested that the correct explanations were too difficult for high school students to understand.
>
> (Personal web log, January 12, 2006)

Most of the teacher candidates seemed focused on whether or not students would be able to understand the right answer, namely, that the Apollo missions did land on the moon and that the special was based on flawed reasoning. Most candidates felt that it was safer not to deal with the video, despite the fact that that the program appears regularly on some television stations and students will watch them whether we deal with them in class or not. No one seemed to notice the potential utility of the pedagogy!

2. Do I provide experiences that encourage teacher candidates to think beyond their subject-matter content?

In the middle of January, Tom sent me a file that he had compiled outlining some thoughts from Bain's (2004) *What the best college teachers do*. I decided to use three quotations from the book as an opening activity for one of my physics classes. I asked the teacher candidates to select a quotation that was particularly meaningful to them and write a response. One of the quotations dealt explicitly with the role of subject matter knowledge:

> [The best professors] were no longer high priests, selfishly guarding the doors to the kingdom of knowledge to make themselves look more important . . . A sense of awe at the world and the human condition stood at the center of their relationships with those students. Most important, that humility, that fear, that veneration of the unknown spawned a kind of quiet conviction on the part of the best teachers that they and their students could do great things together.
>
> (Bain, 2004, p. 144)

My account of this to myself reads as follows:

> Our discussion seemed particularly poignant at this moment. One of the complaints that I often heard as a teacher consultant was that teachers live in subject boxes. Indeed, I have often overheard the conversations among teacher candidates as they share war stories about their physics and engineering undergraduate programs. Survival is a badge of honour. I know these discussions well because I have been a frequent participant in them. The risk is, of course, that in our pride we assert ourselves as high priests of the discipline, with knowledge to disseminate to the ignorant masses. Many of the candidates spoke eloquently about the importance of relationships, often sharing anecdotes from their practica. The discussion was an important step in underscoring the importance of how we teach, rather than what we teach.
>
> (Personal web log, January 26, 2006)

*3. Do I make the tacit internal structures of a classroom explicit to
teacher candidates?*

This focus was the least apparent in the physics methods course. There was one
candid moment, however, when I instigated a discussion about unconscious
elements of teaching with some candour about my own challenges in overcoming
tacit behaviours:

> A critical moment came about halfway through the class. I asked the candi-
> dates if anyone would be willing to share an element of teaching that they
> tried to modify upon returning to their placements in December, perhaps as a
> result of an associate teacher's comment. I then told them about my ten-
> dency to cross my arms when I am nervous or trying to project an air of
> authority. I told them about where I acquired the habit and the fact that my
> associate teacher mentioned it to me in discussions in 1997. Finally, I told
> them that Tom had alerted me to the fact that I was folding my arms in this,
> my newest teaching situation. The story was received well and opened
> the floodgates for all kinds of teaching behaviours that they were trying to
> modify (talking to the board while writing, saying "anyone?" when asking
> questions, etc.). I feel like it was a real bonding moment between us.
>
> (Personal web log, January 5, 2006)

The primary source of data for questions 4–6 was a series of personal reflective
pieces that I wrote during the teacher candidates' second major practicum block
in February. During this 5-week block, I spent a significant portion of every week
at the host school, regardless of whether I was scheduled to formally observe a
teacher candidate on a given day. In so doing, I was able to spend a great deal of
time interacting with teacher candidates, associate teachers and other members of
the school community. At the end of the school year, I shared my reflective pieces
with Tom and invited him to comment on my writing. Here I present excerpts
from our dialogue that helped me reframe my practice.

*4. Do I provide opportunities for teacher candidates to frame questions
about their problems of practice?*

SHAWN: One of the most important ways that I reframed my practice as a teacher
educator was to ask teacher candidates to think about the quality of their
students' learning, rather than focusing on their own teaching. By asking
teacher candidates questions about the way their students were learning in
class, I was able to avoid some of the awkwardness associated with the more
standard question: What you think went well in the class that you just saw? In
what ways could you improve? Conversations started with teacher candidates
that focused on improving the learning in the classroom, for both teacher
candidates and students, were far richer and resulted in more spontaneous
follow-up than conversations that began in the more standard way.

TOM: Your first year in our Ph.D. program has been rich in opportunities for you to rethink your assumptions and practices, starting with the early realization that working with teacher candidates is quite different from working with experienced teachers. This entry shows how quickly you picked up on what we were trying to do together in the fall and elaborated that work to keep the focus on learning as a way to provide access to premises and assumptions about teaching practices.

5. Do I create an environment of trust so that teacher candidates feel comfortable talking about their pedagogy?

SHAWN: One of the advantages of the Queen's program is that teacher candidates are placed in large groups in schools. Teacher candidates frequently reported the importance of being able to talk to other candidates not only for support, but also for developing ideas about teaching and learning. Thus my challenge as a teacher educator was not to create an environment of trust among the teacher candidates; rather it was to earn the trust of the candidates themselves. I found that frequent visits to the associate school, particularly around lunch time and the first half hour after school, allowed me to position myself as being available to assist teacher candidates at any time.

TOM: When we taught together in the fall term, we readily agreed on the importance of establishing strong positive relationships as quickly as possible with most, if not all, of the cohort assigned to our school. You must have paid a personal price in time, but being present in the school and eager to begin conversations must be a positive move for both candidates and associate teachers.

6. Do I present an alternative to the standard theory-into-practice dichotomy by providing opportunities for teacher candidates to examine their practice at the Faculty?

SHAWN: There is little agreement as to what the professional studies course that accompanies the practicum supervision should entail. In the first term, Tom created an environment that allowed the teacher candidates to openly discuss what was happening to them, both in other aspects of the program and in their practica. During January classes I endeavoured to provide opportunities for teacher candidates to explore what they felt were critical incidents in their first-term practicum, in order to blur the artificial lines between theory and practice. These practices, initiated by Tom and continued by me, reached their zenith when teacher candidates devoted an entire class at the end of the year unpacking the role that both the faculty and the practicum had in shaping their experiences.

TOM: Here you pick up on a theme in the evolution of my own teaching practices. I have always felt the need for more opportunities for candidates to stand back and look at the bigger picture of what is happening to them during a very busy eight-month program. Practicum periods are so busy that university classes are the obvious place but each course often seems to have a full curriculum. In the last two years I rather accidentally moved in this big-picture direction and have been delighted to see the generally positive responses from candidates. When we continue our collaboration in this course next year, each teaching a group and combining classes at times, I hope we can make further progress on this familiar but very complex dichotomy between theory (at Queen's) and practice (in school).

In retrospect, I could not have picked a better year to begin my Ph.D. studies, for this was the ideal year for me to gain the personal teaching experiences that will guide the development of my own research. Beginning Ph.D. studies in Canada or the USA often seems associated more with courses rather than with opportunities to learn from experience. Working with Tom enabled me to not only challenge my assumptions about teaching teachers, but also use self-study to develop principles of practice and look my future development as a teacher educator. I was able to focus on the problematic in teaching and teacher education by questioning my assumptions about pre-service teacher education and discussing these assumptions with an experienced teacher educator.

The road ahead: still learning to teach

The relationship between my knowledge of teaching and the methods I have used to extend and articulate that knowledge seems critical to my development as a pre-service teacher, teacher, and teacher educator. Throughout my career I have used reflection-in-action to discover what my default teaching style is and to reframe problems of practice to develop principles of teaching. As a pre-service teacher and a secondary school physics teacher, I used innovative pedagogies such as Predict–Observe–Explain and Writing-to-Learn to encourage students to take an active role in their learning. In so doing, I hoped to help my students improve the quality of their learning as I worked to push beyond my default conceptions of teaching and learning.

My journey into teaching and teacher education has been privileged by Tom Russell's critical friendship, which is particularly significant given that he has mentored me throughout my teaching career—as a teacher candidate, teacher, and teacher educator. Tom was often able to broaden my perspectives on teaching both by validating my practice and suggesting ways to reframe my experiences (Loughran and Northfield, 1998). It was more than fortuitous that I had the opportunity to team-teach a physics methods course and a practicum supervision course with Tom in the first year of my Ph.D. studies. Engaging in self-study at this early stage in my career as a teacher educator allowed me to realize that my prior experiences working with experienced teachers were insufficient preparation for working with teacher candidates.

By framing research questions that did not make *a priori* assumptions about how I taught, I was able to investigate the characteristics of my pedagogy. After discovering some of my default pedagogies for teacher education, it is appropriate to reframe the six questions that guided my self-study over the past year. The newly phrased questions encourage me to again focus on how I teach teachers by encouraging me to develop and enact innovative pedagogies of teacher education:

1 *Pedagogical stance:* How do I solicit teacher candidates' prior conceptions about their pedagogy?
2 *Subject-matter knowledge:* How do I provide experiences that encourage teacher candidates to think beyond their subject matter content?
3 *Professional concerns:* How do I make the tacit internal structures of a classroom explicit to teacher candidates?
4 *Professional questions:* How do I provide opportunities for teacher candidates to frame questions about their problems of practice?
5 *Critical friendship:* How do I create an environment of trust so that teacher candidates feel comfortable talking about their pedagogy?
6 *Role of the Faculty:* How do I present an alternative to the standard theory-into-practice dichotomy by providing opportunities for teacher candidates to examine their practice at the Faculty of Education?

Although I am in the early stages of developing a pedagogy of teacher education, the ways in which I teach and research as a teacher educator are defined by what I think is the most important issue in teacher education: teaching teachers. In this chapter I have described my quest to continually put pedagogy above content, largely thanks to an ongoing dialogue with a more experienced teacher educator who helps me to frame problems of practice. I have also described my engagement in simultaneously doing and researching teacher education. Although it is possible to consider the pedagogy of teaching teachers and the research on teacher education separately, they are inevitably intertwined in both practice and scholarship. Finally, I have discussed the differences I observe between teaching experienced teachers and teaching pre-service teachers. The most important consequence of this analysis is that I am now even more committed to both explicating and questioning my tacit assumptions about how teacher education is conducted.

My emerging pedagogy of teacher education is grounded in making my tacit knowledge and assumptions explicit and in exploring my default teaching behaviours. Most importantly, however, my pedagogy of teacher education develops from my desire to offer my knowledge, assumptions, and practices to the critical scrutiny of myself, my students and my critical friends. I am aware of the powerful default teaching behaviours that persist and so I must constantly work to engage and challenge myself, those I teach and those who are my critical friends. I have much to learn on my journey of thinking about teaching and learning and I am confident that self-study of teacher education practices will help me to articulate my teaching practice and also to continue to learn and teach about teaching.

References

Bain, K. (2004) *What the best college teachers do*. Cambridge, MA: Harvard University Press.

Baird, J. R. and Northfield, J. R. (eds.) (1992) *Learning from the PEEL Experience*. Melbourne: Monash University Printery.

Bullock, S. M. (1999) Experiential science: An "experience first" approach to teaching and learning science. *The Ontario Action Researcher*, *2*(2). Retrieved May 20, 2006, from http://www.nipissingu.ca/oar/archive-Vol2No2-V221E.htm

DeMulder, E. K. and Rigsby, L. C. (2003) Teachers' voices on reflective practice. *Reflective Practice*, *4*, 267–290.

Hand, B. and Prain, V. (2002) Teachers implementing writing-to-learn strategies in junior secondary science: A case study. *Science Education*, *86*, 737–755.

Loughran, J. (2006) *Developing a pedagogy of teacher education: Understanding teaching and learning about teaching*. London: Routledge.

Loughran, J. J. and Northfield, J. R. (1998) A framework for the development of self-study practice. In M. L. Hamilton (ed.), *Reconceptualizing teacher practice: Self-study in teacher education*. London: Falmer Press, pp. 7–18.

Russell, T. and Bullock, S. (1999) Discovering our professional knowledge as teachers. In J. Loughran (ed.), *Researching teaching: Methodologies and practices for understanding pedagogy*. London: Falmer Press, pp. 132–157.

Sarason, S. B. (2002) *Educational reform: A self-scrutinizing memoir*. New York: Teachers College Press.

Schön, D. A. (1983) *The reflective practitioner: How professionals think in action*. New York: Basic Books.

Schuck, S. and Russell, T. (2005) Self-study, critical friendship, and the complexities of teacher education. *Studying Teacher Education*, *1*, 107–121.

Tidwell, D. (2002) A balancing act: Self-study in valuing the individual student. In J. Loughran and T. Russell (eds.), *Improving teacher education practices through self-study*. London: Falmer Press, pp. 30–42.

7 Constructing and reconstructing the concepts of development and learning

The central nature of theory in my practice

Linda R. Kroll

Given the complexities and challenges of teaching well, learning to teach is fraught with difficulties. Teaching others to teach well is yet another layer, making teaching about teaching doubly challenging. While I have written before about how student teachers construct their understandings of theory (Kroll, 2004), here I want to step back to look at how I, as a teacher and teacher educator, formed my own personal theories of teaching and learning and how I connected those personal theories with more formal, research-based theories about development and learning. After looking at my own development, I reconsider what that understanding gives me about my students' development of theory and how they connect theory to practice.

A central question for me as a teacher educator has been how my ever-changing understanding of constructivism and developmental theory has affected and influenced my practice. Constructivist theory has in many ways been the framework I have used to understand my work in classrooms with children and with beginning teachers. It has provided multiple lenses through which I can interpret what I observe and experience, and these lenses have changed over the years, as I construct and reconstruct my ideas about how people learn. Therefore, in this chapter, I focus on looking at how my ideas about the theory of constructivism have grown and changed and how these changes are expressed in changes in my teaching.

Meeting constructivist theory

When I was 8 years old, Robert Karplus came to my home to spend the weekend with us in New York City, visiting from Berkeley, California. He had been a colleague of my father's at Princeton (they authored a famous paper together) and he was then in the Physics department at the University of California, Berkeley. We had a standing pole lamp and he asked me if I could figure out the diameter of the pole. I was shocked, for no physicist had ever been particularly interested in what I thought or in how I might address a problem. I was also surprised, because it had never occurred to me to wonder about the diameter of that pole or why it might be an interesting problem to solve. I remember suggesting that one way to figure it out would be to chop off the top of the lamp and measure the diameter directly. Bob told me I could not break the lamp in the process and so asked what else could I do. I suggested a number of possibilities.

This was my first experience with Piaget's perspectives. Karplus later went on to write the Science Curriculum Improvement Study (SCIS) (1967) science curriculum based on Piaget's accounts of how children construct their ideas of science and mathematics. At the time, he was playing around with the clinical method, trying it on every child he met! What strikes me about the incident is that I had no idea what he was doing and yet I remember it vividly. Asking children what they think about something and then really listening to them seems to make a difference. Once I became a teacher and was involved in learning about Piaget's theory, I recalled the experience of being asked and began to realize what it meant.

I had another early, unconscious experience with Piaget and his ideas. When I was 16 years old, we lived in Geneva, Switzerland, for a year. A family friend was about to leave for Paris to study psychology at the Sorbonne. I asked her why she was going off to Paris to study rather than staying to study at the Université de Genève. She replied, "There is nothing but Piaget about psychology here in Geneva. I am interested in psychoanalysis." At that point I had no idea who Piaget was, although I had heard of psychoanalysis. Once I started studying Piaget's ideas myself, I recalled this incident.

I finally met Piaget's ideas officially when I was in my first year of teaching. Margaret Smart came from the University of Southern California to do a series of workshops with the faculty at Loma Vista Elementary School in Vallejo, CA. I was teaching 3rd grade and struggling with the usual challenges that first year teachers encounter, including classroom management and providing instruction for my students that met their needs and moved them forward. While I had many problems, I was also incredibly brave (or foolhardy) as I helped my students put on several full-fledged plays, did cooking in the classroom with everyone at once cooking potato latkes, and other similarly grandiose curricular innovations. Margaret did several Piagetian conservation tasks with our own students, videotaping what she did and then showing the tapes to us for further discussion. I can still hear myself saying, "I don't believe it! How can they not know that the amount stays the same no matter how you pour it?"

Thus began a lifelong interest in Piaget and his ideas about how children learn. What fascinated me about his work was how he managed to get inside children's thinking. He was interested in what and how they understood mathematics and science. As a teacher, those questions were of vital interest to me, but I was also passionate about how children understood reading and writing.

I attended many workshops and summer programs that purported to apply Piagetian theory to children's school subject learning. Much of this work focused on what children could not do because they were not developmentally ready. Piaget's theory was characterized primarily as a stage theory that identified when children would be ready to learn certain basic mathematical and scientific ideas. One challenge a professor set me and some colleagues was to relate Piaget's stages of development to literacy development. While I did not create a set of developmental stages in literacy, I did find it useful to examine children's literacy understanding in terms of the questions *they* might be considering. I continued to be intrigued by the theoretical possibilities and I continued to be puzzled by what my pupils did and did not understand. I began to ask them questions about how they were thinking about their work. While the stages of development were somewhat useful as guideposts, more interesting were the moments of discovery that I began to pay attention to and to see sparking around me. When a child discovered a new word on his own and when another child identified a mathematical pattern she had observed, these moments were noteworthy in my gradual development of personal theory.

In the workshops and summer programs I attended, I learned about the British Infant School Open Classroom model (Rogers, 1970). My principal encouraged me and other interested teachers to experiment with this model, using centers-based learning and mixed-age groups. For several years I taught a group of 32 children aged 5–9 years old in one classroom. The 5-year-olds were there all morning and went home after lunch; the 6–9-year-olds were there all day. Our mornings were devoted to the centers where children were allowed, encouraged, supported to explore a variety of curricula. The afternoons, with ten fewer children, were devoted to direct instruction in language arts, reading, and math. As the teacher, my mornings were devoted to inquiry into children's thinking and learning, as I strove to learn and teach alongside them. I was still reading and thinking about Piaget's ideas, and thus many of my inquiry projects were focused on finding connections between what he had observed in children's thinking and what I might find.

I began by conducting conservation and classification tasks with all my students, who seemed to closely resemble the children Piaget had interviewed. Because I was teaching children between the ages of 5 and 9, most of them seemed to be either transitioning into or firmly located in an early concrete reasoning stage. My youngest students could not conserve number with any consistency, although they did seem to understand one-to-one correspondence. They made graphic collections with the classification materials, just as Piaget's children had done. My 2nd and 3rd grade children (7, 8, and 9 years old), and a few 1st grade children conserved number and grouped objects systematically and exhaustively, demonstrating some understanding of hierarchical reasoning. Many of them understood the simplest class inclusion tasks (the task with beads, Piaget, 1963/1941), but the ones who *did not* were particularly interesting. As I looked at these assessments in relation to my students' understanding of reading, writing, and mathematics, I found that those who were struggling with reading were also the ones unable to answer the class inclusion questions correctly. In retrospect, I do not believe that this relationship was necessarily all that revealing or inspired, but it was an instance of my attempts as a teacher to make connections between theory and practice in understanding children's learning.

This quest led me back to graduate study. Here I met Vygotsky and Piagetian, neo-Piagetian, and sociocultural scholars. In addition, I read a great deal of

Piaget's original work and thought deeply about how these ideas might apply to children becoming literate. On the side, I continually thought about how what I was studying might appear in my classroom. For the first years of graduate school, I remained a classroom teacher. Later I began to work with beginning teachers and taught both a student teaching seminar and classes applying developmental theory to learning to teach, particularly one on learning to teach literacy. During this period I was studying for my qualifying exams and preparing a dissertation that is a neo-Piagetian analysis of children learning to write stories (Kroll, 1985). I became very familiar with Piaget, Vygotsky, and Pascual-Leone (Pascual-Leone, 1972; Pascual-Leone and Goodman, 1979; Pascual-Leone *et al.*, 1979). I found that I dismissed Vygotskiian ideas for two reasons: (1) I did not understand him all that well; and (2) what I did understand seemed not to teach me anything that was different from Piaget's ideas. I now see this dismissal as a good example of how, as learners, we try to assimilate new knowledge to the schemes we have already developed, a very Piagetian idea.

While I was writing my dissertation, and also after I completed it and began further research on children's writing (Kroll, 1987, 1990, 1991, 1993), I read many of the ground-breaking theorists who were connecting developmental theory (Sulzby, Teale), child language acquisition (Wanner and Gleitman, 1982), psycholinguistic theory (Slobin, 1978), and sociocultural theory to learning to read and write (Dyson, Calkins, Graves). In continuing to construct my own personal theories about learning and development, I compared, contrasted and related these ideas to what I understood about Piaget's work. The result was a longitudinal study of 17 children's writing development from kindergarten through 4th grade (Kroll, 1990, 1991, 1993, 1996, 1998). This work was instrumental in helping me to connect Piaget's theory to children's writing development, in particular, using a model of part–whole connections as a way of seeing what children were thinking about as they learned to write. This developmental approach was quite different from the sociocultural perspectives on the process of learning to write taken by other researchers. I recognized, however, that Dyson, Calkins, Graves, Giacobbe and other teachers and researchers were describing real classrooms where children were doing remarkable work in writing. What they were seeing seemed closely related to the part–whole relationships in writing development that I had studied and written about (Kroll, 1998).

In 1988, I moved to Mills College and established a credential and master's program with an early childhood emphasis. I was responsible for teaching classes in development and in the learning and teaching of literacy. My own schooling had prepared me somewhat for these assignments, but, as I taught these classes and as I worked in teacher education, my own understanding of the field kept changing, as did the field itself.

The changing face(s) of constructivism

When I began as a graduate student, there was an ideological divide between the socio-historical-cultural theorists and the cognitive-developmental psychologists.

It was as if they were focusing on different questions and each group expected the other to answer the opposing side's question. Thus the Piagetians and their cohort focused on struggling to apply Piaget's ideas to the classroom. Many books were written with this in mind (e.g., Furth and Wachs, 1975; Schwebel and Raph, 1974) and I read them all very carefully. Like many others, I found them both frustrating and enticing. On the other hand, there was the newly translated work of Vygotsky (*Thought and Language*, 1962, followed by *Mind in Society*, 1978) that also posed interesting questions and answers about the way children learn in school, particularly with regard to the use of language in classrooms. I read all of Vygotsky's work, as well as everything I could find about how language develops and the use of language in the classroom. These too were frustrating and enticing simultaneously. When I began teaching at Mills College, my goal was to help my students learn to connect what we understand about children's development with how we teach them to teach. To me, this meant, in part, as Duckworth (1996, p. 87) puts it, "being Piaget."

As a new faculty member, I tried to help my students understand what I understood. I tried to set up constructive situations for them to learn to watch children and work out what the children were learning, for them to closely observe children constructing literacy (both reading and writing) and simultaneously understand how they themselves learned and continued to learn to read and write. Asking them to consider both children's development within specific domains of knowledge and their own learning and development within these same domains proved to be both disequilibrating and eye-opening (Kroll, 2004). This parallel observation of development on the part of my students and on my part was my way of trying to apply what I had learned about Piagetian theory. To a certain extent it was successful. My students were definitely "kid watchers" by the time they left Mills College. This reflected what I had learned from all my study and in particular the ideas of Duckworth (1996) with regard to Piaget's theory and the ideas of Yetta Goodman (1990) with regard to literacy development. I had yet to make sense of the sociocultural aspects of learning, although Goodman's work certainly drew heavily on sociocultural theory.

In 1994, I had the opportunity to invent a new course for the early childhood master's students, a course that would focus on developmental theory and constructivism. This was my opportunity to both read and teach about constructivist theory in a different way. While I continued to teach the other courses on development and learning to read and write, I now added a full course on learning to read about constructivist theory and its applications to teaching and learning. We focused on constructivist theory as applied to classroom teaching; required readings included Duckworth (1996), Fosnot (2005), and Rogoff (2003). Here I had both opportunity and time to consider both aspects of constructivist theory with my students. There is nothing like teaching about something to help one learn it. The more I tried to make it clear for my students, the more I myself learned about both Piagetian theory and sociocultural theory.

For the past ten years I have taught about constructivist theory to master's and doctoral students. The master's students are becoming teachers, but the doctoral students are already credentialed and experienced teachers who are studying to be educational leaders of some kind (principals, curriculum developers, professional development specialists). A glance at the syllabi demonstrates how my thinking about constructivism and my questions about constructivist theory have developed. While all of the syllabi juxtapose Piagetian theory with sociocultural theory, they do so in a progressive way. I began with Duckworth (1996) and Tharp and Gallimore (1988). From the outset, the contrasting questions of these two theoretical perspectives were evident. Duckworth writes about student and teacher learning, using Piagetian theory to understand what students are doing and to think about how to help teachers do the same. Tharp and Gallimore write about teaching and the school context. They invite you into teacher and student interactions, while Duckworth invites you into teacher or student thinking. For my students, both questions were burning questions. Being enrolled in a teacher education program that focuses on urban schools meant that the context of school was an essential element to consider in thinking about teaching. In many ways it was easier for them to think about the questions that dealt with school and the interactions that occurred within classrooms because they were observing these interactions at the same time as they participated in my class. Looking closely at both their own learning and the learning of the children they were teaching was more difficult, although, for many of them, asking the question of how they learned something was a particularly revealing activity.

By juxtaposing sociocultural theory and cognitive constructivist theory, we came to understand together how these two related theoretical viewpoints could help us understand learning and teaching. "Where is the mind?" (Cobb, 1996) was a particularly helpful reading that helped us all to see the different questions and the different lenses that these two perspectives offered on classrooms, teaching and children's learning. Cobb speaks of the two as foreground and background. If you put the children's learning and understanding in the foreground, as sometimes you must, then the context of the school and community is essential background for interpreting what you are seeing in the foreground. On the other hand, if you put the context of classrooms, schools and communities in the foreground, what children learn is essential background for interpreting what you see. This is where I found myself for the past five years in terms of understanding constructivism. I continued to challenge myself and my students with further readings in both perspectives and with readings such as Saxe's (1995, 1999) work on mathematical reasoning in different sociological contexts that crossed these perspectives

New ideas about constructivist theory

Recently I have found myself asking new questions. Research into my own teaching practice and into the learning of my students, as well as further reading in the field of cultural psychology (Cole, 1996; Rogoff, 2003) continues to challenge my ideas about the very nature of development. As Rogoff so ably points out, the very nature and path of development are up for question when we examine development in a variety of community contexts. As a developmental psychologist, I find these conclusions fascinating for the light they shed on the purposefulness of human society. Repeatedly in her text, Rogoff (2003) gives examples that raise serious questions about the relationship between human development and the context in which it occurs. While there are undoubtedly some biological commonalities that limit the possible developmental paths children take, within those constraints there are many paths along which a child may develop and learn in order to become a productive member of the society into which he or she is born. Rogoff's work helped me to see more clearly the interaction between individual human development and the goals and needs of the larger society. She made me aware of the wonder of the richness and varieties of human developmental possibilities.

My students, on the other hand, tend to use Rogoff's work to condemn or approve particular practices, somehow missing the point that what is interesting is the differences and the reasons for the differences, not that one way is better than another. They also tend to miss the difficulty of examining their own experiences and practices. Given that I have just begun to teach this material, my own experience tells me that it will be a few more years before I am really able to help them grapple with these questions of what is different and what the consequences of these differences are. Further complicating the issue is the burning question of how we prepare children in our own society for success, children whose background has not necessarily prepared them for the same developmental path as that of mainstream America. While Rogoff's work helps us to see the differences, it is only at the very end of her book that she begins to address what these findings can mean for practitioners.

There are still cognitive constructivists who look for the common factors in human development, as opposed to the cultural differences (e.g., Turiel, 2002). They maintain that, despite vast cultural differences, there are human needs and aspirations shared across the species and appearing in every culture; these include the basic need for autonomy and independence from the control of others. While this may manifest itself differently in each culture, Turiel maintains that it is there. This tension between sociocultural and cognitive constructivism is still present, in my mind, although the basis of the tension has changed. Rather than having to accept one view as the correct view, as practitioners, we need to draw on different theoretical perspectives to understand the different problems confronting us in educating teachers and helping beginning teachers to teach all children well.

So where am I now as a teacher educator? Piaget describes human learning as a dynamic balance that is constantly changing. I certainly feel that this is true for me in my own learning to be a teacher educator. I grapple constantly with the tensions of understanding the relationship between individuals and their communities. By confronting this question, I can think about how to help my students make sense of what they are trying to do in classrooms on an everyday, every minute basis. I feel the same is true for me. As I introduce new readings and at the same time feel my own balance become shaky again, my teaching changes. Each time I step back to look at what is happening, I am surprised anew to see that my students' thinking and my own can be so in concert. Cobb's (1996) notion of foreground and background is useful, but recently the socioculturalists and the cognitive constructivists are coming together to show how each body of work can inform the other. I am trying to use this same perspective with my own students as we think about the different aspects of understanding children's learning, teaching, classrooms, schools and communities. It is not just a matter of teaching them to use the two lenses, but also a matter of teaching them to look for the links between the lenses. As I use these lenses in my own teaching, and as I continue to read and think about the influences of context on development and development on context, my own ideas undergo constant reconstruction.

What about the students?

I have written before about how student teachers connect theory and practice and about the difficulties they have in doing so (Kroll, 2004). Part of this difficulty lies in the nature of the connections that student teachers are expected to make. Often student teachers are taught theory and then proceed to go into classrooms where what they learn is very much tied to the daily practice and problem-solving of on-the-spot teaching. Even when they are instructed to make connections (through journal writing, through course assignments, or through class discussions), they have difficulty making the connections in any but the most awkward and inauthentic ways. Kessels and Korthagen's (2001) constructs about the different kinds of knowledge that teachers use help clarify the theory–practice gap (Loughran, 2006), through considering the constructs of *episteme* and *phronesis*. *Episteme* is experimental, scientific, propositional knowledge, probably closely related to what I have termed conceptual knowledge (Ammon and Kroll, 2002) and what Fenstermacher (1994) referred to as "knowing that." *Phronesis* is related to what I called procedural knowledge, "knowing how," but it is more than knowing what to do about something. It is what Kessels and Korthagen (2001) call practical wisdom. *Phronesis* is related to what one might call one's own personal theories, developed through experience, although I would argue that it also incorporates a third sort of knowing, *metacognitive knowledge* (Ammon and Kroll, 2002; Chang-Wells and Wells, 1993), that not only determines what knowledge is to be used where, but also what knowledge is to be learned.

By studying constructivist theories, how can my students connect these ideas to what they are doing in their practice? In the college classroom they learn theoretical perspectives and they read what other people have done to connect theory with practice. Here is the *episteme* that Kessels and Korthagen discuss. Making sense of others' theoretical ideas requires that one inquire into one's own practice to see if what one understands about that practice reflects what theoreticians are identifying. As the students become more experienced in teaching, through their assignments and their practicum teaching, they pose questions about their practice, begin to inquire into their practice, and thus begin to articulate their own theories of teaching and learning (*phronesis*). What seems to be key in relating the *episteme* to the *phronesis* is the use they make of *metacognitive knowledge*, controlling both what they want to learn and how they want to apply it. This process of consciously applying and connecting research-based theory to personal theories is unique and individual. How I was able to do it will not necessarily reflect what my students need or do. Nonetheless, I am their guide. I choose what they begin to read and I assign the structure of the problems they investigate; I ask the questions that hopefully promote connections. Ultimately, however, they must make the connections themselves.

In thinking about how my students learn about constructivism and developmental theory and about how they make sense of them in their own practice, I must remind myself that my path to understanding probably will not reflect their paths. While I can provide them with numerous opportunities and scaffolds to consider these theories and their usefulness in creating their own beliefs and theories, it is unlikely that their histories of understanding will reflect mine. The contexts, the readings and the teaching are all different. Reviewing the history of my own theoretical development and looking at this development in relation to my students' learning and development serves to remind me of the uniqueness of each person's path and, simultaneously, of the effects of community on what we learn and how we learn it.

This constant reviewing and reconstruction are what makes teaching and learning so interesting. It keeps alive the purpose of what we do and allows us to stay focused on our mission of making schools a better place for everyone who participates in them—children, teachers, families, administrators, teacher educators. The educational community is wide. Despite the political pressures of "having to get it right *right now*," there is still scope for learning about why it does or does not work and for using theoretical perspectives to help us see what is or is not working.

References

Ammon, P. and Kroll, L. R. (2002) Learning and development in constructivist teacher education. In J. D. Rainer (ed.), *Reframing teacher education: Dimensions of a constructivist approach*. Dubuque, IA: Kendall/Hunt, pp. 193–241.

Chang-Wells, G. L. M. and Wells, G. (1993) Dynamics of discourse: Literacy and the construction of knowledge. In E. A. Forman, N. Minick, and C. Addison Stone (eds.), *Contexts for learning: Sociocultural dynamics in children's development*. New York: Oxford University Press, pp. 58–90.

Cobb, P. (1996) Where is the mind? In C. T. Fosnot (ed.), *Constructivism: Theory, perspectives and practice*. New York: Teachers College Press, pp. 39–60.

Cole, M. (1996) *Cultural psychology: A once and future discipline*. Cambridge, MA: Harvard University Press.

Duckworth, E. (1996) *"The having of wonderful ideas" and other essays on teaching and learning*. New York: Teachers College Press.

Fenstermacher, G. D. (1994) The knower and the known: The nature of knowledge in research on teaching. In L. Darling-Hammond (ed.), *Review of research in education 20*. Washington, DC: American Educational Research Association, pp. 3–56.

Fosnot, C. T. (2005) *Constructivism: Theory, perspectives and practice*, 2nd edn. New York: Teachers College Press.

104   *Linda R. Kroll*

Furth, H. and Wachs, H. (1975) *Thinking goes to school.* New York: Oxford University Press.

Goodman, Y. (1990) *How children construct literacy: Piagetian perspectives.* Newark, DE: International Reading Association.

Karplus, R. (1967) *A new look at elementary school science: Science Curriculum Improvement Study.* New York: Rand McNally.

Kessels, J. and Korthagan, F. A. J. (2001) The relation between theory and practice: Back to the classics. In F. A. J. Korthagen, with J. Kessels, B. Koster, B. Langerwarf, and T. Wubbels (eds.), *Linking practice and theory: The pedagogy of realistic teacher education.* Mahwah, NJ: Lawrence Erlbaum Associates, pp. 20–31.

Kroll, L. R. (1985) The relationship between information processing capacity and text-level planning in the stories children write. Unpublished dissertation, Stanford University.

Kroll, L. R. (1987) The relationship between information processing capacity and text-level planning in the stories children write. Paper presented at the meeting of the American Educational Research Association, Washington, DC, April.

Kroll, L. R. (1990) Making meaning in writing: A longitudinal study of young children's writing development. Paper presented at the meeting of the American Educational Research Association, Boston, MA, April.

Kroll, L. R. (1991) Making meaning: Longitudinal aspects of learning to write. In J. Campione (Chair), *Developmental and cognitive psychology contributions to learning basic school subjects.* Symposium conducted at the Mini-Convention, Contributions of Psychology to Learning and Education, at the meeting of the American Psychological Association, San Francisco, August.

Kroll, L. R. (1993) "Who did I write this for?" Social aspects of learning to write: A longitudinal study of young children's writing development. Paper presented at the meeting of the American Educational Research Association. Atlanta, GA, April.

Kroll, L.R. (1996) Applying Piaget's theory to understanding the development and teaching of literacy. In L. R. Kroll (Chair), *Applying Piaget's theory to understanding school-based domains of knowledge and teacher education.* Symposium conducted at The Growing Mind/La Pensée en Évolution conference at the University of Geneva, Geneva, Switzerland, September.

Kroll, L. R. (1998) Cognitive principles applied to the development of literacy. In B. McCombs and N. Lambert (eds.), *How students learn: Reforming schools through learner-centered education.* Washington, DC: American Psychological Association.

Kroll, L. R. (2004) Constructing constructivism: How student teachers construct ideas of development, knowledge, learning, and teaching. *Teachers and Teaching: Theory and Practice, 10,* 199–221.

Loughran, J. (2006) *Developing a pedagogy of teacher education: Understanding teaching and learning about teaching.* London: Routledge.

Pascual-Leone, J. (1972) A theory of constructive operators: A neo-Piagetian model of conservation, and the problem of horizontal decalage. Paper presented at the meeting of the Canadian Psychological Association, Montréal, June.

Pascual-Leone, J. and Goodman, D. (1979) Intelligence and experience: A neo-Piagetian approach. *Instructional Science, 8,* 301–367.

Pascual-Leone, J., Goodman, D., Ammon, P., and Subelman, I. (1979) Piagetian theory and neo-Piagetian analysis as psychological guides in education. In J. M. Gallagher and J. A. Easley (eds.), *Knowledge and development,* Vol. 2: *Piaget and education.* New York: Plenum Press, pp. 243–289.

Piaget, J. (1963/1941) *The child's conception of number.* New York: W. W. Norton.

Rogers, V. R. (1970) *Teaching in the British primary school: Ways to manage child-centered, experience-based programs and practices for responsible, individual learning.* London: Macmillan.

Rogoff, B. (2003) *The cultural nature of human development.* New York: Oxford University Press.

Saxe, G. B. (1995) From the field to the classroom: Studies in mathematical understanding. In Steffe, L. P. and Gale, J. (1995) *Constructivism in education.* Hillsdale, NJ: Lawrence Erlbaum Associates, pp. 287–311.

Saxe, G. B. (1999) Sources of concepts: A cultural-developmental perspective. In E. K. Scholnick, K. Nelson, S. A. Gelman, and P. H. Miller (eds.), *Conceptual development: Piaget's legacy.* Mahwah, NJ: Lawrence Erlbaum Associates, pp. 253–267.

Schwebel, M. and Raph, J. (eds.) (1974) *Piaget in the classroom.* New York: Basic Books.

Slobin, D. (1978) *Psycholinguistics.* New York: Scott Foresman and Co.

Tharp, R. and Gallimore, R. (1988) *Rousing minds to life: Teaching, learning and schooling in social context.* Cambridge: Cambridge University Press.

Turiel, E. (2002) *The culture of morality: Social development, context, and conflict.* Cambridge: Cambridge University Press.

Vygotsky, L. (1962) *Thought and language.* Cambridge, MA: MIT Press.

Vygotsky, L. (1978) *Mind in society.* Cambridge, MA: MIT Press.

Wanner, E. and Gleitman, L. R. (1982) *Language acquisition: The state of the art.* Cambridge: Cambridge University Press.

8 Do you encounter your students or yourself?

The search for inspiration as an essential component of teacher education

Fred Korthagen and Hildelien S. Verkuyl

> Learning about teaching is a very personal experience. Helping students of teaching to capitalize on that learning is an essential aspect of teacher education.
> (Loughran, 2006, p. 118)

As we have worked in teacher education for more than 25 years, we have been fascinated by promoting reflection in teachers. Over those years we also started to worry about the fact that reflection in teacher education often does not seem to touch the deeper layers in our student teachers' thinking, layers that seem to be important to their identity as a teacher. Most teacher educators restrict themselves to promoting reflection on behavior, competencies and perhaps beliefs about teaching and learning. We saw many of our student teachers, who were often fairly competent on these levels, struggle within themselves, especially in their final teaching practice where they had full responsibility for teaching a limited number of classes. Their struggles seemed to be related to their personal motivation for the profession and the gap between this motivation and the realities of teaching.

Authors such as Allender (2001), Bullough (1997), Loughran (2006), and Palmer (1998) support our belief that these people were confronted by what is called the teacher's self, and that these student teachers need to become more aware of their inner selves in order to contribute in an adequate way to children's learning, growth and well-being. One aspect of this process involves reflecting on one's own patterns of survival behavior as a teacher, patterns that often surface when tensions in the classroom grow. Awareness of these patterns can be a starting point for further understanding of the teacher self.

The aim of our collaborative study was to find out whether we could help those student teachers who, during the last stage of their preparation for the profession, often struggled with their role as a teacher and who sometimes wondered whether they would be able to realize the ideals they had in mind when they enrolled in teacher education. Our goal was to offer these student teachers insight into their own professional identity and a renewed sense of mission and inspiration.

From the outset it was clear to us that we could not undertake this enterprise without questioning our own professional identities and missions as teacher educators (see Loughran, 2006, p. 18). One cannot help others look more closely at their own inner selves if one has not done this oneself and become acquainted with the fears, obstacles and joys inherent to such a quest. For that reason we engaged in an intensive joint self-study process during which we promoted each other's reflection on our behavior as teacher educators and our own inner potentials, as they surfaced during the preparation and presentation of the workshop. Moreover, we decided that it was necessary to also share with the student teachers elements of our own professional struggles, past and present. We kept track of our own journey and repeatedly questioned each other, especially on issues such as our own ideals in education and the deeper sources of our ways of functioning as teacher educators. We also asked the students to record their learning processes during the workshop. Finally, we evaluated the whole enterprise with them, both orally and by means of a questionnaire. Here we report our study, which began with clarifying our theoretical starting points and own philosophy of teacher education.

Theoretical framework and philosophy of education

A view of reflection

Reflection is generally acknowledged to be an important instrument in teacher development (Korthagen *et al.*, 2001). However, in many teacher education programs the emphasis is often placed on a fairly instrumental interpretation of reflection that stresses the initial steps along the professional path and the need to survive in the midst of a multitude of intensive experiences. This approach can lead the student teacher to concentrate on the problem of how to handle tomorrow's lesson. Moreover, those student teachers who do tend to think deeply about their lessons may have a narrow view of their profession. The "restricted professional" (Hoyle, 1980) is often oriented towards the content and pedagogy of his subject, giving insufficient thought to the moral aspects of education and the moral culture of the school, i.e., the values, standards and belief systems that are propagated on an individual level and within the school as an institution.

Klaassen (2002) maintains that such teachers are failing to fulfil their social-pedagogical task, and we concur. In our view there is no longer any doubt that as a teacher one does indeed have a moral task to fulfill (Hansen, 2001; Willemse *et al.*, 2005). The moral task is there, whether one acknowledges it or not (Fenstermacher, 1994). Hence we see it as the responsibility of teacher educators to create conditions that help student teachers develop a view of the moral aspects of the teaching profession and of their own social-pedagogical task. In this context, a major role must be reserved for reflection on one's own professional identity and one's social-pedagogical goals and responsibility. Moreover, assistance and guidance must be provided as, step by step, students strive to flesh out their social-pedagogical ideas and ideals. In this way, initially vague concepts can take on form and content, as student teachers refine and differentiate their ideas and come to their own personal interpretation of the profession.

In this light, it is encouraging to see that many educators do focus on helping their students to think more deeply about the way they function with respect to the goals and values they are striving for in their teaching, and with respect to the social, political, economic, and cultural context in which that teaching takes place. The focus of this chapter is the promotion of such reflection among student teachers, reflection on their personal interpretation of the goals of the profession and on their own professional mission. We consider this of particular importance in view of the highly socializing influence of the school context (Zeichner and Gore, 1990). The question is whether it is possible to counterbalance this influence and to help teachers to develop a truly personal professional identity.

When studying our own practice as teacher educators in a one-year, post-graduate teacher education program at a Dutch university, we had to ask ourselves to what extent we, as teacher educators, succeed in doing what has long been expected of student teachers:

> Student teachers can be armed against socialization into established patterns of school practice. The student teacher must first gain some idea of who he or she is, of what he or she wants and, above all, of the ways in which one can take responsibility for one's own learning.
>
> (Korthagen, 1988, p. 39)

The teacher education program, preparing teachers for secondary education, places great emphasis on developing the capacity for reflection; students are encouraged to reflect in various ways (Korthagen *et al.*, 2001). And yet we kept asking ourselves whether we had actually reached the core of the matter. In our view, the crux lies at the point where the development of one's own identity as a human being intersects with one's professional development (Allender, 2001; Nias, 1989a, 1989b). For example, we believe that it is important for teachers to become aware of their own strong points, or core qualities, and the personal values and ideals (Newman, 2000) they are striving for. It is also important to consider how to give shape to one's values and ideals by using their core qualities when confronted with obstacles,. We call the kind of reflection that incorporates such issues *core reflection* (Korthagen, 2004; Korthagen and Vasalos, 2005).

The actualization of core qualities

Our focus on personal core qualities is linked to a recent development in psychology, advocated by people such as Seligman and termed *positive psychology*. Seligman and Csikszentmihalyi (2000, p. 7) state that this movement is a reaction to the fact that for too long psychology has focused on pathology, weakness and damage done to people, and hence on treatments. They emphasize that "treatment is not just fixing what is broken; it is nurturing what is best." Hence they point to the importance of positive traits in individuals, which they call *character strengths*. They mention as examples traits such as creativity, courage, kindness, and fairness (Peterson and Seligman, 2000). A central issue in positive psychology is how these strengths mediate between external events and the quality of experience, something that is directly relevant to teacher education.

Peterson and Seligman emphasize that, although character strengths can and do produce desirable outcomes, they are morally valued in their own right, even in the absence of obvious beneficial outcomes: They state that, although strengths and virtues no doubt determine how an individual copes with adversity, the focus is on how they fulfill an individual. Peterson and Seligman add that when people are referring to their strengths, this correlates with a feeling of this is the real me, that they show a feeling of excitement when displaying a strength, and, importantly for our discussion, a rapid learning curve.

The way Seligman and other psychologists within this new field write about strengths clarifies that they are synonymous with what Ofman (2000) calls *core qualities*. He states that such core qualities are always potentially present. He maintains that the distinction between qualities and competencies lies primarily in the fact that qualities come from inside, while competencies are acquired from outside. Almaas (1986, p. 148) talks about *essential aspects*, which he considers absolute in the sense that they cannot be further reduced to something else or analyzed into simpler constituents.

It should be stressed that, when a student teacher comes into touch with a core quality, it is important for teacher educators to help him or her take the step towards actualization of that quality in terms of behavior. Only then it can influence the environment (for example, students in school). Hence it is crucial that the teacher is not only cognitively aware of a core quality, but that he or she is emotionally in touch with that quality, makes a conscious decision to mobilize it, and then carries out that decision (Korthagen and Vasalos, 2005). This is a process that in our experience often needs support from the teacher educator.

This focus on core qualities may have strong implications for teaching children. One of the central aims of education is, in our view, to ensure that students of every race, social class, sex, and age are aware of, and give shape to, their own inner potential, strength, talents, value, and dignity, whereby others, including teachers, can provide support and guidance. Hence, in our view, teacher educators should take the lead in translating the ideas of positive psychology to education.

Individuation

The process by which human beings become aware of their own unique personal qualities, learn to handle those qualities in their contact with the outside world, and ultimately become an individual distinguishable from other human beings is what Jung (1964) called *individuation*. Maslow (1968) employs the related concept of *self-actualization*. This concept has occasionally been criticized for being too individualistic and failing to do justice to the relationship between individuals and their environment (Jansen and Wildemeersch, 1998). In our view, the process of individuation or self-actualization will not lead to isolation as long as the relationship with others is the point of departure. This is in line with the views of Dewey (1908), who stated that it is above all in their relationship with others that human beings come to what Maslow later called self-actualization, a process Dewey describes as a development of the person that is in keeping with his capacities and potential.

We see no room for individuation or self-actualization until the individual has succeeded in internalizing the norms of the environment in such a way that a frame of reference is first formed. In the course of development from birth onwards, we see that the necessary foundation is provided by imitation of and identification with others. In adolescence, young people often experience how the need to belong and to be part of a community conflicts with the need to be yourself and to develop an identity of your own (Erikson, 1964). There is a temptation, which continues throughout one's later life, to turn away from the individual path and opt instead for adaptation. Independent of the degree to which people choose the road less traveled or adaptation, they cannot be themselves without others. For example, it is precisely in the meeting with others that we realize that we are different, become aware of our uniqueness, and acquire the capacity for further development (Taylor, 1989). At the same time, without a sense of self, there can be no true meeting, no meaningful collaboration. In order to discover yourself and to meet others, you have to put yourself on the line (Korthagen, 2004).

The way to self-knowledge: identity and self-understanding

In the process of individuation, a person develops a realization of his individuality. This is what Erikson (1964) means when he speaks of *a sense of identity*, which "focuses on the meanings constituting the self as an object, gives structure and content to the self-concept, and anchors the self to social systems" (Gecas, 1985, p. 739; see also Beijaard, 1995). According to Erikson, identity is a concept that refers to unity of being. Despite the processes of change a person undergoes, he or she remains the same person and becomes increasingly aware of his or her self. Some authors speak of the importance of *self-understanding* (Heschel, 1965; Kelchtermans and Vandenberghe, 1994).

Professional identity

A major part of a person's development and identity is the choice of career and the manner in which one behaves in a profession, particularly in relation to the aims, values and norms guiding professional actions. Student teachers, especially those who start teacher education after completing a degree course at university, usually face relatively late the questions and choices related to their profession and the practice of that profession. Within a period of just one year, our students go from being a student to being a teacher. In that year the foundation is laid for that part of the identity that has to do with one's profession. What kind of teacher am I? What kind of teacher do I want to be, given who I am and what I stand for? Because one's professional identity is inextricably bound up with other aspects and components of a person's identity (Lipka and Brinthaupt, 1999; Nias, 1989a, 1989b), the development of professional identity will affect all aspects of the student teacher's personality. Through the confrontations inherent in teaching, questions related to the person's self-knowledge and self-esteem, as well as personal norms and values, will again be relevant and have to be answered. Teaching and guiding children offers a valuable mirror for anyone who takes the time and effort to hold it up and look within. It makes possible the next essential developmental step: dealing with the question "Who am I and how do I express who I am?" We believe that these are essential questions for teachers and, as Clandinin and Huber (2005) indicate, these questions interweave the personal and the professional.

Tickle (1999, p. 123) notes that, both in policy and practice, the connection between "personhood and teacherhood" has had scant attention. An exception is the work of Kelchtermans, who emphasizes the importance of professional *self-understanding* of teachers (Kelchtermans and Vandenberghe, 1994, p. 89) and the role of *critical incidents, phases and individuals* in the professional development of teachers. Another recent exception is Allender (2001), who shows how teacher educators can help student teachers to explore issues related to the teacher's self. Taking a step along the path leading to a professional identity of your own means being able to interpret your behavior, analyze situations and acquire insight into the reciprocal processes that take place between you and your students (Korthagen *et al.*, 2001, pp. 108–130). For a student teacher, such advanced reflection requires, for example, that you have the courage to examine your own survival patterns, patterns that come into play when the tension in the classroom increases. This is the moment when the question arises of who you are in addition to those patterns, or who you really are. It will be clear that such a question goes beyond the field of professional development. In some cases the individual discovers the central role that mere survival has come to play in his or her own life. Examining your professional identity has everything to do with the ability to acknowledge your own vulnerability (Kelchtermans, 1996; Palmer, 1998).

We see our perspective concurring with that of Loughran (2006, p. 136), who states that "professional learning is not developed through simply gaining more knowledge, rather professional learning is enhanced by one becoming more perceptive to the complexities, possibilities and nuances of teaching contexts." We add that it is important to also become more perceptive of the complexities, possibilities and nuances of one's own personal and professional being.

The workshop

Here we describe how the themes sketched above affected our own practice as teacher educators and also affected our own professional identities. We developed a workshop consisting of 4 half-day sessions (plus homework) to be held at the end of the one-year teacher education program, after the independent final teaching practice period. During this three-month period, each student teacher had full responsibility for a number of classes in secondary education (a 40 percent weekly teaching load) and was supervised at a distance by a co-operating teacher who did not attend the student teacher's lessons. Our workshop was one of 21 offered in our program, from which students were required to choose two. This meant that we were able to work with student teachers who had expressed a certain affinity with the theme, a pre-condition that we felt was important. One cannot force people to become actively involved in their own development. The point at which people are prepared to address questions about their own identity, including their professional identity, varies considerably.

The title of the workshop, "Do you encounter your students or yourself?", apparently hit the nail on the head, for many student teachers said it was precisely the question they had been wrestling with. In the workshop we took this as our point of departure for a reflective process. We made it clear that a crisis is an opportunity, an opportunity to find out more about who you actually are and what you should be doing in the classroom. Fifteen students registered for the workshop.

Elements of the workshop

We now describe some parts of the workshop to show how we worked together and to illustrate the reflection put forward by the student teachers. At the start of the first session we asked the participants the following questions:

1   What made you sign up for the workshop? Did the text of the announcement appeal to you?
2   What do you want to get out of the workshop?
3   How are you planning to ensure that you succeed?

The participants worked in groups of two, helping each other to come to a clear formulation of their answers. After they finished, a fourth question was added:

4   How will you know when what you wrote under question 2 has actually been achieved? What is the criterion?

One-third of the participants reported that they were attracted by the title of the workshop; during the independent final teaching practice period, in particular, they increasingly felt that they were indeed part of the problem. In the first round, participants reported the following statements on their wish lists:

• How do I turn unexpected situations to my advantage?
• What are the alternatives and what kind of teacher do I want to be? Who am I, how do I want to function, and once I know that, how do I go about doing it?

- I want to do something, but it turns out differently than I expected. Is it my fault, or the fault of my students? I want to be able realize in time that things are going wrong.
- I want to feel positive about myself.
- I need more certainty about the choices I make.
- I'd like to get out of the vicious circle: the same aspects of my character keep surfacing. I don't seem to be able to break the pattern.
- Fundamental doubts: why do I do things? Is this what I want, or have I made the wrong choice? How do I handle this?
- I take things too seriously. I wish I could see things in perspective.
- I have to behave in a certain way—I can do it, but I don't feel comfortable with it. That means making choices. It also means looking deep inside myself.
- Being myself in the classroom, instead of playing a role. The latter doesn't suit me. Am I going to be asked to do things that I'm not comfortable with? Can I be myself?
- I want clearer limits, and I want to be able to define them more clearly.
- I can't allow myself to have doubts, I'm afraid to have doubts. I want to be able to give classroom experiences and my own behavior a place. Now I spend too much time brooding about things that went wrong.
- In the class I see myself as a kind of policeman, and that's something I don't want to be.

We believe that this list mirrors the student teachers' struggles to find and express the self in teaching, something that we made explicit in the workshop. The list led to an intense discussion of the purpose of teaching, including issues such as inspiration and dealing with obstacles to one's inner mission.

The next assignment, named *discrepancy analysis,* is simple but highly effective for promoting core reflection: *Think about one positive and one negative experience during your practice teaching. What is the difference between these two experiences?* During their teacher education program, all the participants have become familiar with having conversations with their peers that promote reflection (*peer-based reflection*). Thus they have experience in active listening and responding empathetically, asking open follow-up questions and summarizing, all of which are intended to help the person who raised the point to arrive at a clearer formulation of his or her own thoughts and feelings. We made use of this background by dividing the participants into groups and giving them an assignment to further clarify the difference between the positive and the negative experience. At the end of the exercise they are asked to complete one of the following statements:

I am someone who needs . . .

I am someone who considers . . . important.

I am someone who strives for . . .

To give the exercise additional depth and promote core reflection, we introduced a model of levels of reflection that is an adaptation of the Bateson model (Dilts, 1990). Korthagen (2004) calls it the onion model, as he visualizes it with circular layers (see also Loughran, 2006, pp. 118–119). The following levels are distinguished and are considered to range from outer to inner, as in Figure 8.1: (1) *Environment* (What do I encounter?), (2) *Behavior* (What do I do?), (3) *Competencies* (What am I competent at?), (4) *Beliefs* (What do I believe?), (5) *Identity* (Who am I?), and (6) *Mission (or spirituality)* (What inspires me?). Loughran (2006, p. 121) states that reflection at all these levels helps to shape the development of the professional self.

In groups of three, the participants helped each other to determine at which level or levels their questions and dilemmas were located. During this exercise it also became clear that the inner levels influence the outer levels. For example, the resolve not to act as a policeman in the classroom will determine the characteristics you want to develop and your subsequent behavior, and thus your environment. By contrast, the confrontation with the environment (such as a difficult class) will make it clear that you are not at liberty to display the behavior you want to; you may then have a desire to develop certain competencies. This, in turn, can lead you to ask yourself to what extent you can be yourself in the classroom, and

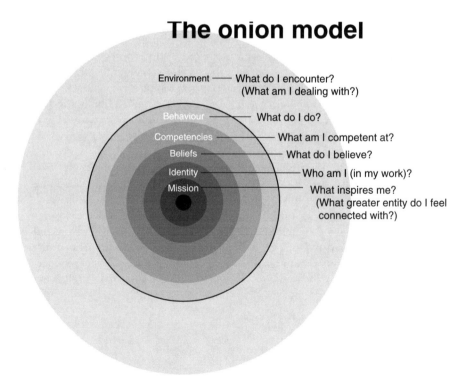

Figure 8.1 Layers in the onion model

who that self actually is. Through confrontation with the environment, the process can continue right up to the most inner level, touching on such questions as how to give meaning to one's work (level of mission). A number of participants later mentioned that the level schema provided new insight, because it helped them to place their experiences within the big picture, as in the following example:

> I want to learn how to be clear and maintain classroom order. This is a point that came up in the "environment." It was related to "competencies." I had to expand my behavioral repertoire in dealing with a group. It's not so much about my identity, since in day-to-day environments people often say that I'm bossy and strict. The classroom setting itself demanded strictness and clarity.

> Positive thinking and learning to cope with the unexpected have to do with identity. Often I'm restless or I try to do a lot in a short time. And I've never been that sure of myself. I tend to be intimidated by people who have a lot of self-confidence. Often a whole class draws its self-confidence from sheer numbers.

> Trying to find—and keep—some peace and quiet (in myself) also has to do with "competencies." I have to learn certain forms of behavior in a group that up to now I've had difficulty mastering.

Against the background of the Markings image (Hammarskjöld, 1966), the participants were given an opportunity to record in their logbooks their impressions of the results of the exercises, the insight achieved, and the new questions and dilemmas raised.

Their homework consisted of a pack of cards with illustrations of animals and, underneath, some behavioral characteristics of each animal. The assignment was as follows:

How do you deal with situations in your work where it is difficult or even impossible to function in keeping with your own values?

Take the situation from the previous exercise that you experienced as negative.

- How did you react in that situation?
- Which of the animals (one or more) is the best example of your reaction? Alternatively, you can create an animal metaphor of your own.
- Which quality of that animal is most characteristic of your reaction in that situation?
- Does the way you reacted help you to realize the values you are trying to bring about, or does it have the opposite effect?
- Can you think of an alternative way of responding which you would be

more comfortable with (because it would help you to achieve what you really want)?

- What keeps you from putting this alternative response into practice?

The participants wrote responses to these questions and handed them in. They all received a detailed written reply and, in some cases, they were given an article to read or a particular book was recommended. The notes in the logbook also played a role in the third session, where the participants worked in small groups. They were also asked to make a collage focusing on the theme: "What do I consider important in education? If I start from my ideals: where am I? What do I do? What am I capable of? What do I believe in? Who am I?" (Compare the reflection levels mentioned above.)

In the second session the answers to the above questions were discussed in groups of three. Some of the participants' comments were as follows:

Self-reflection is difficult, because you don't always allow yourself to put a name to the underlying reasons. And in the reflection towards others you always show your vulnerable side, you give yourself away. So you try to hide, avoiding direct questions. The image of the owl suits me best: intellectualization of feelings.

I reacted like an elephant: I kept my cool, and continued to be friendly, pretending it didn't bother me.

When asked whether this response helped her to master the method of working that she was striving for, this participant answered:

No, not really. I consider it important to be myself and to get into touch with the students. I wasn't myself because I didn't show my true feelings, and that's why there was no contact.

Another participant used an animal metaphor of her own:

I reacted like a seven-headed dragon. I want to do everything at once, but I ended up not doing anything. All the heads contradicted each other.

For the plenary session, each group was asked to summarize the most important aspects that had occurred and to make note of any questions that had arisen. Against this background, we also discussed some of the more theoretical aspects of the workshop, which the participants were given in written form to take home. First, we looked at the theory behind growing as a human being, which is related to the development of personality (together with the accompanying survival patterns), and then at the question of how you can use crises to find the way back to yourself. We placed the students' own reflections within a theoretical framework, using a number of concepts from developmental psychology related to the development of personal identity. These theories were presented because they benefit the students' development and their present experiences. We believe they are also of fundamental importance for a better understanding of the developmental processes that secondary school students undergo, and as such we consider them essential equipment for teachers. We deliberately illustrated the theories with examples from our own careers in education. For some students it was a revelation that the people who were giving the workshop had wrestled with just such confrontations in their own work, that they still did so, and that the quest apparently never ends.

The collages on the theme of "What I consider important in education" were discussed in pairs, with participants helping each other to put the images into words and to record the essence of their findings. The activities were rounded off with a guided meditation, during which the students used the power of imagination to get in touch with their own power. Each of them was then asked to come up with one word or one core principle that expressed his or her own strength or quality as a teacher. They then wrote that word under their collage.

Evaluation of the workshop

How successful was the experimental workshop? We evaluated the workshop carefully, both orally and by means of a questionnaire. The 15 student teachers were enthusiastic about the workshop, especially about the fact that it touched on aspects of their professional development that they experienced as fundamental but that had not been dealt with in their preparation program. The theme of the workshop focused on the very aspects they struggled with and helped them to learn from these struggles. Some reactions were:

- The workshop hit the core: we talked about the essence of being a teacher.
- This should be a standard element in the teacher education program.
- This stimulates your professional growth, as you are forced to look at the essentials of what happened during your teaching practice.

On a 5-point scale 77 percent of the students scored the workshop a 4 (good) and 23 percent scored a 5 (very good). They also indicated that the timing of this workshop (at the end of independent final teaching practice period) was essential for its success, and that it added something important to the guidance they had had before during the teacher education program. We conclude that indeed a more fundamental process, which we promoted during the workshop, is needed when encounters with students in school cause feelings of crisis in student teachers. As one student teacher said: "When I can see clearly again, I have more courage to face the confrontation and I can feel my feet on the ground."

Final thoughts about the workshop

In our Western world, individuals who have reached the age of 18 or 21 are legally adults and thus responsible for their own actions. Becoming an adult is a transitional process that may take many years, depending on the person, his or her activities, and the responsibilities he or she faces. Most student teachers have already made certain choices related to searching for and finding a partner; almost all of them have lived on their own for a number of years and have seen quite a bit of the world. Many have considerable work experience, if only in the form of part-time jobs designed to provide some financial flexibility. Life has not left them untouched. Judging by their stories, the transition from the status of student to that of teacher, with all the accompanying responsibilities, is a large step indeed. They realize that theirs is a pedagogical responsibility, one that cannot be shirked.

During this phase, students and beginning teachers have considerable doubts about their own abilities. These doubts arise during the teaching practice period, in particular during the independent final teaching practice period, and they continue in the initial months or years of their teaching career. These doubts are concerned with their own limitations, uncertainty about the image that students and colleagues have of them, and uncertainty about their own beliefs. These doubts are well founded and this uncertainty is justified, given that freedom of choice, certainty, and self-confidence are only achieved on the basis of experience and the learning process those experiences provide.

> In the negative experience that I had in mind for this session, I was obsessed with the need for clarity. What were the limits I wanted to accept, and within which the students would feel comfortable? I ignored disturbances and failed to deal with troublemakers because I wanted to finish a test. The result was loss of interest in the class, run-of-the-mill teaching, and students who were just "sitting it out" (i.e., saved by the bell).

Contact with students can confront beginning teachers with existing feelings of uncertainty and lack of self-confidence, leading to worry that they may never become a good teacher, and even that they are unsuited to the profession.

Developing an identity of one's own with respect to the profession one has chosen is a process that has only just begun for the majority of student teachers and beginning teachers. That is why it is so important to promote core reflection, which implies reflection on identity and mission, and to provide the space student teachers need to explore their experiences in more depth (see Korthagen and Vasalos, 2005).

> Via the question of how I can be myself in class, I started thinking about whether I really belong in the classroom. My uncertainty about that last point makes it more difficult to answer the first question.

One participant described the snares and traps that lie along the "winding path leading to self-understanding" as follows:

> For me it's important to learn how not to let people walk all over me in the class. It doesn't take students long to realize that that's what I do, and then there's no stopping them. During teaching practice several students were extremely insolent to me, and I let them get away with it. In the workshop I want to find out what it is that goes on inside me when a student walks all over me and I just let it happen, instead of standing up for myself.
>
> Some students have made disparaging remarks about my teaching skills. I really took that to heart. It's clear that this is a problem on the level of competencies. But that's not all. Am I actually someone? Or am I nobody?

After expressing her confidence in her own capacity for growth, this same student teacher said:

> I believe that teaching is something you learn by making mistakes; in fact, the more mistakes you make, the more you learn. Maybe things don't go well right from the start. But that doesn't mean that you have to go through a kind of identity crisis if you don't perform well.

If we proceed on the assumption that every new aspect of adulthood has to be integrated into one's sense of identity, then having to settle into the profession in such a short time may well generate a sense of crisis. Apparent certainties disappear, questions raised by classroom situations go unanswered, qualities you were accustomed to rely on are no longer sufficient. Have you come to a dead end? Would it be better to just give up? A crisis creates new possibilities and room for development, but it is not until a crisis is over that you can say anything meaningful about your own crisis experiences and, more cautiously, about those of others. Throughout a lifetime, even in the moment of crisis, it is possible to retain the trust that this, too, will come to an end and that it is one of those experiences necessary to give meaning to your life. The majority of young people are not yet receptive to these words of wisdom. It is a difficult and trying period, one that requires guidance if beginning teacher are to get through it, perhaps not unscathed but enriched by a deeper realization of their own identity. Diamond (1991) believes that such a learning process represents the highest level of teacher development, as does James (1996), because it involves a fundamental change of perspective (Mezirow, 1981). One participant in the workshop wrote that, in difficult confrontations with students, she tended to just give in because she finds such confrontations so threatening. She is prepared to go to any length to restore calm, and she tries to please everyone: "When I'm seeing things clearly, I'm not afraid of a confrontation and am better able to stand my ground." Often more is needed to achieve this than can be provided during a teaching practice period. In the words of Jung (as cited in Pipes and Davenport, 1990), "In the great crises of life, in the supreme moments when to be or not to be is the question, little tricks of suggestion do not help" (Hammarskjöld, 1966).

Our own quest

As teacher educators, we learned a great deal from this workshop. First, a it has brought us to a deeper level of contact with our own ideals concerning the promotion of core qualities in both teachers and students. This concurs with Loughran's (2006, pp. 119–120) point that in order to work with student teachers on the deeper levels of the onion (such as the level of mission), teacher educators themselves need to be in touch with their mission. A deeper awareness of our own missions was stimulated by confrontations with our own struggles and fears. After all, we were doing something completely new—new to ourselves and also to our institute, and perhaps even to the larger community of teacher educators. This made us feel vulnerable, a feeling further enhanced by the reactions of some colleagues. Even before the workshop began, some reacted negatively, suggesting that what we intended to do represented a form of therapy. In their view, we should stick to our roles as teacher educators, roles that apparently have little to do with conceptions at the identity level. In terms of the onion model, the message seemed to be "confine yourselves to student teachers' behaviors, competencies, and perhaps beliefs, but stay away from discussing underlying personal struggles. That's none of your business!" Apparently, people tend to connect going deeper with therapy, and consider it dangerous, whereas to us therapy is something completely different from what we were attempting in the workshop (Korthagen and Vasalos, 2005). In fact, we viewed *not* going deeper as dangerous, because many student teachers seem lost in their encounters with students in schools, with little support for such significant struggles.

We had to obtain permission to offer the workshop, and the program coordinator even asked us to organize small group meetings with the entire staff in order to explain in more detail what we intended to do. Although the request seemed bizarre because other colleagues had never been asked to follow such a procedure after developing new approaches, we did organize the small-group conversations. Surprisingly, they appeared to result in an unexpected incentive for the program as a whole. Our entire staff became more aware of the professional choices we were all making, often without being aware of them. Moreover, our own awareness of our roles and missions as teacher educators was enhanced by presenting our ideas and answering the questions. Permission to proceed was granted and, in retrospect, most colleagues seem somewhat amazed that they initially wanted to stop us.

The insight that our workshop would fall into a sensitive area certainly added to our sense of vulnerability. We had to question and support each other intensively to be able to proceed under this pressure and deal with the insecurity that it created. In other words, we encountered ourselves. The positive outcome was that we became even more aware of the hidden, or even forbidden, areas of teacher education, and of our wish and potential to fill this gap. To both of us, this crisis was a powerful boost in our own professional development. For Fred, it has led to the development of a new approach to supervision, the so-called *multi-level* approach, which is grounded in the concept of core reflection. It has been successful in promoting the further professional growth of in-service teachers in the Netherlands (Korthagen and Vasalos, 2005). Hildelien has recently abandoned her job as a teacher educator in order to devote herself completely to the intensive support of children (and their parents and teachers) struggling with the core conflict of adjustment versus being oneself.

Both developments illustrate how an encounter with a threatening environment may ultimately help to express more fully one's personal mission. As Loughran (2006, pp. 18–19, 116) describes it, teachers also must be willing to use their experiences for an encounter with themselves, as an opportunity to gain a deeper understanding of oneself. Thus, even before the workshop began, we embarked on a quest for the essence of our professional and personal selves. The workshop itself contributed to another important aspect of this quest— authenticity. The workshop almost forced us to show our own genuine inner selves to student teachers, particularly in those moments when the students came face to face with parts of themselves they had long tried to avoid becoming aware of. In trying to stay close to these students in such moments, we as teacher educators were faced with the question, "Do we encounter our students or ourselves?" Like the student teachers, we were in a process of constant change, as we were continuously confronted with situations that forced us to look in the mirror and ask ourselves questions such as "Who are you?," "What do you stand for?" and "Are you willing to be completely true to yourself?" These are precisely the questions that our student teachers struggle with. We were fairly open to them about our own struggles, and we linked this not only to their experiences but also to supporting children who are struggling to find their own identities. For student teachers and children alike, providing such support requires an attitude of openness, respect and humility in order to support the other self in finding his or her own answers. Providing support also demands the willingness to accept one's own vulnerability. As Loughran (2006, p. 123) states: "Learning and teaching about teaching is a risky business." To this we add that it is also a rewarding business.

References

Allender, J. S. (2001) *Teacher self, the practice of humanistic education.* Lanham, MD: Rowman and Littlefield.

Almaas, A. H. (1986) *Essence: The diamond approach to inner realization.* York Beach, ME: Samuel Weiser.

Beijaard, D. (1995) Teachers' prior experiences and actual perceptions of professional identity. *Teachers and Teaching: Theory and Practice, 1,* 281–294.

Bullough, R. V. (1997) Practicing theory and theorizing practice in teacher education. In J. Loughran and T. Russell (eds.), *Purpose, passion and pedagogy in teacher education.* London: Falmer Press, pp. 13–31.

Calderhead, J. (1989) Reflective teaching and teacher education. *Teaching and Teacher Education 5,* 43–51.

Clandinin, D. J. and Huber, M. (2005) Shifting stories to live by: Interweaving the personal and professional in teachers' lives. In D. Beijaard, P. C. Meijer, G. Morine-Dershimer, and H. Tillema (eds.), *Teacher professional development in changing conditions*. Dordrecht: Springer, pp. 43–59.

Dewey, J. (1908) Ethics. In J. A. Boydston (ed.), *John Dewey: The middle works, 1899–1924*, Vol. 5. Carbondale, IL: Southern Illinois University Press.

Diamond, P. C. T. (1991) *Teacher education as transformation. A psychological perspective.* Philadelphia, PA: Open University Press.

Dilts, R. (1990) *Changing belief systems with NLP.* Cupertino, CA: Meta Publications.

Erikson, E. H. (1964) *Childhood and society.* New York: Norton.

Fenstermacher, G. D. (1994) The knower and the known: The nature of knowledge in research on teaching. *Review of Research in Education 20*, 3–56.

Gecas, V. (1985) Self-concept. In A. Kuper and J. Kuper (eds.), *The social science encyclopedia*. London: Routledge, pp. 739–741.

Hammarskjöld, D. (1966) *Markings.* London: Faber and Faber.

Hansen, D. T. (2001) Teaching as a moral activity. In V. Richardson (ed.), *Handbook of Research on Teaching*, 4th edn. Washington, DC: American Educational Research Association, pp. 826–857.

Heschel, A. J. (1965) *Who is man?* Stanford, CA: Stanford University Press.

Hoyle, E. (1980) Professionalization and deprofessionalization in education. In E. Hoyle and J. Megarry (eds.), *World yearbook of education 1980: Professional development of teachers*. London: Kogan Page, pp. 42–56.

James, P. (1996) *Learning to reflect: A story of empowerment.* Melbourne: Hawthorn Institute of Education.

Jansen, T. and Wildemeersch, D. (1998) Beyond the myth of self-actualization: reinventing the community perspective of adult education. *Adult Education Quarterly 48*(4), 216–226.

Jung, C. G. (1964) *The development of personality.* New York: Bollingen Foundation.

Kelchtermans, G. (1996) Teacher vulnerability: Understanding its moral and political roots. *Cambridge Journal of Education, 26*(3), 307–323.

Kelchtermans, G. and Vandenberghe, R. (1994) Teachers' professional development: A biographical perspective. *Journal of Curriculum Studies, 26*, 45–62.

Klaassen, C. (2002) Teacher pedagogical competence and sensibility. *Teaching and Teacher Education 18*(2), 151–158.

Korthagen, F. A. J. (1988) The influence of learning orientations on the development of reflective teaching. In J. Calderhead (ed.), *Teachers' professional learning*. London: Falmer Press, pp. 35–50.

Korthagen, F. A. J. (2004) In search of the essence of a good teacher: Towards a more holistic approach in teacher education. *Teaching and Teacher Education, 20*(1), 77–97.

Korthagen, F. A. J., Kessels, J., Koster, B., Lagerwerf, B., and Wubbels, T. (2001) *Linking practice and theory: The pedagogy of realistic teacher education.* Mahwah, NJ: Lawrence Erlbaum Associates.

Korthagen, F. A. J. and Vasalos, A. (2005) Levels in reflection: Core reflection as a means to enhance professional development. *Teachers and Teaching: Theory and Practice, 11*(1), 47–71.

Lipka, R. P. and Brinthaupt, T. M. (1999) How can the balance between the personal and the professional be achieved? In R. P. Lipka and T. M. Brinthaupt (eds.), *The role of self in teacher development*. Albany, NY: State University of New York Press, pp. 225–228.

Loughran, J. (2006) *Developing a pedagogy of teacher education.* London: Routledge.

Maslow, A. H. (1968) *Toward a psychology of being*, 2nd edn. Princeton, NJ: Van Nostrand.

Mezirow, J. (1981) *Transformative dimensions of adult learning*. San Francisco: Jossey-Bass.

Newman, C. S. (2000) Seeds of professional development in pre-service teachers: A study of their dreams and goals. *International Journal of Educational Research, 33*(2), 125–217.

Nias, J. (1989a) Teaching at the self. In M. L. Holly and C. S. McLoughlin (eds.), *Perspectives on teacher professional development*. London: Falmer Press, pp. 155–171.

Nias, J. (1989b) *Primary teachers talking: a study of teachers at work*. London: Routledge.

Ofman, D. (2000) *Core qualities: A gateway to human resources*. Schiedam: Scriptum.

Palmer, P. J. (1998) *The courage to teach*. San Francisco: Jossey-Bass.

Peterson, C. and Seligman, M. E. P. (2000) *Values in action (VIA) classification of strengths*. Philadelphia, PA: Values In Action Institute. Retrieved August 31, 2006, from http://www.ppc.sas.upenn.edu/viamanualjustice.pdf

Pipes, R. B. and Davenport, D. S. (1990) *Introduction to psychotherapy*. Englewood Cliffs, NJ: Prentice-Hall.

Seligman, M. E. P. and Csikszentmihalyi, M. (2000) Positive psychology: An introduction. *American Psychologist, 55*(1), 5–14.

Taylor, C. (1989) *Sources of the self: the making of the modern identity*. Cambridge, MA: Harvard University Press.

Tickle, L. (1999) Teacher self-appraisal and appraisal of self. In R. P. Lipka and T. M. Brinthaupt (eds.), *The role of self in teacher development*. Albany, NY: State University of New York Press, pp. 121–141.

Willemse, M., Lunenberg, M., and Korthagen, F. (2005) Values in education: A challenge for teacher educators. *Teaching and Teacher Education, 21*, 205–217.

Zeichner, K. M. and Gore, J. M. (1990) Teacher socialization. In W. R. Houston (ed.), *Handbook of research on teacher education*. New York: Macmillan, pp. 329–348.

9   A teacher of teachers

Cristy L. Kessler

I am a teacher, and the term *teacher* conjures up many familiar images and stereo-types of what a teacher is and what a teacher does. I am a teacher educator—a teacher of teachers. Again, many images come to mind, but not all center on the synergies associated with being a teacher and doing teaching. In many instances, the differences between being a school teacher and a teacher educator are per-ceived to be so great that the distinction is exacerbated, often to the detriment of the teacher educator. Perhaps it is partly as a result of these differences that there was a push in late 1980s and early 1990s for teacher educators to be more in touch with teaching, leading to a call for teacher educators to have recent, relevant and successful classroom experience (Boxall and Burrage, 1989). At the heart of this debate is the ever-present gap between theory and practice (Korthagen and Kessels, 1999; Korthagen *et al.*, 2001) and the issues, problems and concerns associated with any such discussion: "In educational discourse, there has been for many years an extensive, though perhaps not very fruitful, discussion of the relations between 'theory' and 'practice,' the 'foundations of education' and actual teaching" (Brandon, 1995, p. 69).

I can state confidently that I now better understand how issues associated with thinking about the theory–practice gap can grow and take on a life of their own because, for a brief period of time after I moved to the university arena, I forgot what it was to be a teacher. In so doing, difficult questions quickly arose, includ-ing "Did I choose to escape the K–12 ranks to avoid the pitfalls associated with No Child Left Behind?" and "Was I really prepared to become an educator of pre-service teachers and be challenged to investigate my own teaching?" For me, the only way to respond to these questions was to do what I could to "practice what I preach" and become a highly qualified teacher as mandated under *No Child Left Behind*. On November 18, 2005, I was awarded National Board Certification in Adolescence and Young Adulthood/Social Studies-History (see National Board for Professional Teaching Standards, 1998). As a university professor with a doc-toral degree, I am now deemed to be highly qualified as measured by the National Standards, but what does all of that mean for me as a teacher of pre-service teachers? What does it mean for my student teachers?

Loughran (2006) suggests that teacher educators' teaching about teaching should be explicit, articulated, meaningful and immediately evident in what he described as a pedagogy of teacher education. In this chapter I explain how my experience in gaining National Board certification has not only enhanced my knowledge of a pedagogy of teacher education but also helped me to develop the ways in which I enact that pedagogy. What I experienced through National Board certification goes well beyond more common and superficial understandings of recent and relevant experience and captures deeper intentions that highlight the importance of the interaction, as opposed to the often-maligned gap, between theory and practice. This is a crucial learning outcome in enacting my pedagogy of teacher education.

Challenges faced when moving into the university

Professors are often described as living in an ivory tower. As both a pre-service teacher and as a university student, I observed professors who projected this image. I also experienced this image while pursuing my two graduate degrees. Hanna (2003, p. 26) describes the ivory tower as "a time when knowledge was to be awarded in order to be preserved, when it served to separate those with 'class' from those without, and when the primary medium for storing knowledge was physically and geographically bound books." This image of the ivory tower became even more apparent to me as I walked through the door into university life.

Prior to my first academic appointment, I had taught social studies for 11 years in a middle school and a high school. Making the change in title from teacher to professor appeared to earn a little more respect from the general public, and I believe is related to the ivory tower image. Not only did I change my title, but also there was a major shift in my teaching style. With so much more freedom at the university level, a huge burden was lifted from my shoulders; I realized that there were no standardized tests to which I would be held accountable. The ivory tower allowed me to set my own office hours while the university determined my class schedule. If a student missed one class, it was easy for me to make it their issue and tell them to stop by during office hours to discuss matters with me.

In moving from being a school teacher to a university professor, the most noticeable change was in my approach to teaching. When I first joined the university, I relied heavily on the tenured professors who previously taught the classes I had been assigned. I asked for copies of their syllabi and asked them to share with me their pedagogy related to teaching pre-service teachers. Because I was the rookie, I adopted many of their ideas and, to some extent, modeled my own syllabi after those provided by tenured faculty members. I soon came to see that what I was doing was abandoning my own knowledge of teaching, gained as a classroom teacher, in favor of the practices of my new academic colleagues. By the end of my first semester of university teaching, I found myself disappointed in my newly adopted teaching style; I felt that I had let down these soon-to-be teachers who were my students. I began to see that I needed to do much more to give them a better idea of what it really meant to teach in the K–12 setting.

During this period of adjustment, I began to question and challenge my own beliefs as a teacher of teachers. These challenges were partially driven by components of No Child Left Behind (NCLB) legislation. In 2002, NCLB was "the most sweeping reform of the Elementary and Secondary Education Act (ESEA) since it was first enacted in 1965" (US Department of Education, 2005). Most of my university colleagues were opposed to many aspects of NCLB. I struggled with this because I believed it was my job to prepare future teachers to be successful in their classrooms. To be successful, I believed that they needed to be prepared to meet the requirements set forth by NCLB. This federal legislation requires all classroom teachers to be highly qualified in the subject areas in which they teach. No Child Left Behind "required local school districts to ensure that all teachers hired to teach core academic subjects be highly qualified by the end of school year 2005–2006" (US Department of Education, 2005). NCLB defined a highly qualified teacher as someone who must possess the following qualifications: (1) a bachelor's degree; (2) full state certification or licensure; and (3) prove they know each subject they teach (US Department of Education, 2005).

I assumed I would be deemed highly qualified on the basis of the advanced degrees I had earned. Reality was that, by NCLB's definition, I was not highly qualified. My advanced degrees were in the fields of education and educational leadership, and I lacked advanced coursework in my subject area. Because I was certified as a social studies teacher and taught subjects such as world history, US history, law, economics, sociology, and psychology, I needed graduate courses in each of these subject areas or successful completion of the Praxis exam in these subject areas to be considered a highly qualified teacher. As my first semester of university teaching was nearing its end, I began to question the impact of NCLB on me as a university professor: "How could I ensure that my pre-service teachers would be highly qualified when they entered the teaching profession?" More importantly, as I continued to grow dissatisfied with my own teaching at the university level, I questioned how I could practice what I preach and be a highly qualified teacher.

National Board Certification: the idea, the process

I interviewed for my academic position with the University of Hawaii at Manoa in March, 2004. The Dean of the College of Education questioned me over breakfast. As we talked, I believe he came to the realization that I was, in fact, a teacher. It was at this moment, when he confirmed that I still held a valid teaching license from the state of Maryland, that he posed the question: "Would you consider going through the process of National Board Certification (NBC) as a professor?" Knowing that this job was my dream job, I responded very positively. I recognized from the expression on the his face that, if I were successful, this would be a highly acclaimed accomplishment for his college of education. I also knew that, had I stayed in the high school classroom, I would have also chosen to undertake this process. At this time, I had no sense of how the journey through NBC would profoundly change me as a university professor, nor did I recognize the impact it would have on my university career, as some colleagues embraced my pursuit while others critiqued me every step of the way. Nonetheless, I became a candidate for the Adolescence and Young Adulthood/Social Studies-History Certificate. If the question was "How will I be highly qualified and demonstrate those skills to pre-service teachers?", then one answer was to pursue National Board Certification from the National Board for Professional Teaching Standards (NBPTS).

The purpose of NBPTS is to establish high, rigorous standards for what accomplished teachers should know and be able to do, in order to develop and operate a national, voluntary system to assess and certify teachers who meet these standards and to advance related education reforms for the purpose of improving student learning in American schools (NBPTS, 2005). NBPTS identifies five core propositions for accomplished teaching:

1   Teachers are committed to students and their learning.
2   Teachers know the subjects they teach and how to teach these subjects to students.
3   Teachers are responsible for managing and monitoring student learning.
4   Teachers think systematically about their practice and learn from experience.
5   Teachers are members of the learning communities.

(NBPTS, 2005, p. iii)

It was through these core propositions that I began to revisit what good teaching is all about. I thought that if I could achieve National Board Certification and be considered highly qualified, then I could .model quality teaching for my own pre-service teachers. What better way for them to learn about teaching?

The process associated with NBC changed my entire outlook on teaching teachers. Prior to my pursuit of NBC, while working on my graduate degrees, I was trained to do research on education and write from an analytic and descriptive standpoint. The NBC process required me to be a reflective writer. By going through the process myself, I developed new insights into the ways I perceived my university students. I began to see the need to develop them as reflective practitioners for their entry into the teaching profession.

The NBC process was rigorous. A candidate must collect data and submit a portfolio based on four separate entries. Each entry includes several artifacts and requires the candidate to use descriptive, analytical, and reflective writing practices to tie the artifacts to key components associated with each entry. Portfolio Entry 1 for the Adolescence and Young Adulthood/Social Studies-History certificate requires the teacher to "select three writing assignments/prompts from three different points in time in an instructional sequence" (NBPTS, 2005). In this entry, the teacher must show how she teaches reasoning through writing assignments. Entry 2 must showcase a videotaped segment of how the teacher engages the students in a whole-class lesson. The discussion needs to showcase how civic competence is fostered in the classroom. Entry 3 must be a videotape submitted to highlight the teacher effectively engaging students in small-group work that should be based on the idea of promoting social understanding in a social studies classroom. The fourth and final entry is based on the teacher's documented accomplishments. This entry may include accomplishments for the prior five years of teaching, but a major focus must demonstrate two-way communication with parents during the year in which the portfolio is being completed.

Once the portfolio is submitted, the second part of the NBC process requires the candidate to provide evidence of content knowledge across the entire developmental age range of his or her certificate area, as outlined in the standards set forth by NBPTS. The assessment consists of six exercises, each allowing up to 30 minutes for a response. These exercises, developed and designed by practicing teachers in each certificate area, are designed to assess a candidate's fundamental content knowledge that supports quality instruction in their classroom on a daily basis, not the textbooks or resource materials that they might acquire. An exercise may consist of one or more prompts or questions that may present a scenario or student profile for one to consider before responding (NBPTS, 2005).

To complete the entire NBC process I needed to find a classroom where I could teach for a sufficient length of time to collect all of my evidence, and I felt anxious about the process because I had left the public school arena. I wondered how many other university professors had tried to do this certification. I knew other candidates had borrowed classrooms to fulfill the requirements for National Board Certification, but most, if not all, still worked in the K–12 setting and had easy access to classrooms. Additionally, most of them were familiar with their schools and the surrounding communities. I had just moved 6,000 miles from my home in Maryland to Hawaii and I was not familiar with the public schools in Hawaii. I did not know the name of a single student, nor did I know the parents or school community. To ease the difficulty of the process, I borrowed two 10th grade world history classes in a public charter school; world history had been my specialty as a high school teacher in Maryland. I borrowed the classroom for a total of eight weeks, two weeks observing the classes with their regular teacher and six weeks teaching classes to collect data for the portfolio.

What does the process of National Board Certification mean?

Initially, I thought I would go through the NBC process on its own, not realizing that the process could generate a research agenda in my new role as a university professor. Fortunately, I decided to keep a journal to highlight my accomplishments and struggles through the process. The journal served two purposes, helping me to construct my written responses for the portfolio entries and, later, helping me to revisit and analyze my own teaching practices. It was through this reflective process that two themes—flexibility and planning—emerged, propelling me to revisit my own teaching techniques as I worked with pre-service teachers. In order to understand how the NBC process could influence my college courses, I also needed to analyze several dimensions of my return to the high school classroom.

Flexibility

The first major theme I identified was flexibility. After moving to the university ranks, I became somewhat rigid in my teaching practice. My classes were scheduled for the same day and time every week, and if a student missed a class, class still moved forward. There were no assemblies, field trips, fire drills, or personal issues to disrupt class. It was my time, my class, my agenda, and my inflexibility. Students with issues could always stop by during office hours to discuss their concerns, and the reality was that my office hours were created for my convenience, not the students'.

This same philosophy followed me into the 10th grade classes I prepared to teach. Although I had only been away from the public high school setting for 18 months, I was amazed at what I learned by again walking through the doors of a public high school: "The bell rings, class is ready to start, my heartbeat is off the charts, and I am developing sweaty palms and shaky hands; class is ready to begin."

There I was, an 11-year teaching veteran now with a doctorate, returning to the work of a classroom teacher. Once the bell finished sounding, students started to charge to the front of the room, full of questions: "What was for homework?"; "Can I please go to the bathroom?"; "I need make-up work now." I had forgotten how these concerns can seem so paramount to the student, and I had not prepared for this. I wanted to be in control and I was trying to find my footing, and all the while my mind was saying to just tell them what I would tell my university students: "Stop by during office hours and we will take care of it then." Then my heart kicked in and reminded me of my passion for kids and teaching and learning. Thankfully, I was able to find my footing.

In the high school I reverted to a mode of flexibility that compelled me to create and support a safe learning environment for my new 10th grade students. Once I remembered what flexibility was all about, I was able to get myself under control and out of panic mode, maintain my composure, and deal with each individual student in a way that was acceptable to all of us. The most important thing to come out of this experience was the way my students felt about being in my classroom. As I became more flexible, I demonstrated to students how much I valued them as individuals. I was able to honor each of their concerns and still engage them in meaningful learning. This raised major questions about what I had been doing with my students at university.

Planning

The second major theme centered on the idea of planning. As a professor of preservice teachers, I established certain requirements associated with the development of lesson planning. When I returned to teach in the high school, I had to take these expectations, apply them to myself, and then explore these self-imposed expectations. Surely this would determine whether or not they were valid.

Almost two months prior to my return to the high school classroom, I finished outlining the units I would teach. In addition to preparing to teach 10th grade, I was doing a full workload for the University of Hawaii College of Education. I did not give a second thought to the amount of planning time. After all, I was a veteran of the high school classroom and now a professor who teaches teachers. How much did I really need to plan? I see now that the lack of time I spent planning and preparing for my 10th grade world history classes would eventually lead me to restructure how I taught my university methods courses.

I had required my pre-service teachers to create two lesson plans as well as a unit plan. I asked them: (1) to address national and state standards for content; (2) to establish learner outcomes that would be assessed; (3) to develop an essential question for the unit/lesson taught; and (4) to construct summative and formative assessment pieces that related directly back to the learner outcomes. As I embarked on my return to K–12 teaching, I was compelled to look at whether or not I practiced what I was preaching to my pre-service teachers, and the answer was no. I was too pompous, believing that I was already a good teacher. I had only completed a skeletal outline for my teaching units, and it resembled nothing like the work I ask my pre-service teachers to do. Given that I was an 11-year veteran of the classroom, did I really need to write everything down?

How did my planning look when put into practice on my first day back in the high school classroom? My first lesson was a disaster. Lesson plan; what lesson plan? I was so arrogant that I really believed I could use my skeletal unit outlines and make up the rest on the fly. On my first day, in front of 50 students over two class periods, my timing was off. I completely forgot to do my closing activity, which was also my assessment piece for the lesson. But the real eye opener came when I looked back at that first lesson and realized that I never identified my learner outcomes. How could I have let this happen? I am a teaching professional who spends at least half a semester working with pre-service teachers doing the things I forgot to do in my own teaching. In my own defense, after talking with a colleague who observed my first day, it was difficult for my students to tell that I was unprepared. My prior teaching experiences did allow me to cover up for my lack of planning, but I knew that this was unacceptable.

Feeling like a complete failure on my very first day teaching 10th grade world history, I decided to rectify the situation by putting more effort into my teaching preparation. I headed for home with the intention of sitting down and constructing a formal lesson plan, just as I ask my pre-service teachers to do. I spent five hours doing one lesson plan for the next day of teaching, struggling to find the best way to teach concepts of Imperial China so that it would be relevant and interesting for my students. I struggled to find connections between Imperial China and things my students were familiar with, to build on their prior knowledge and make concepts meaningful for them. I recognized the value of a planning process by forcing myself to revisit content and clearly identify what students needed to know, be able to do, and care about to achieve quality learning.

Constructing daily lesson plans is not a requirement for National Board Certification; however, this planning process was essential for me to be an effective classroom teacher and to guide the learning process. While preparing my lesson plans, I also was reminded of another critical issue—flexibility. Until that first day of teaching, I had no idea of the class structure, the school and classroom schedule, the personality of the class and, most importantly, the needs of the learners in each of my two classes. I now found myself sitting down every night to revisit my lesson plans to ensure that I used instructional strategies to help all of my students be successful.

How the themes influenced my university teaching

The two themes of planning and flexibility are, in a sense, paradoxical; a carefully constructed plan could interfere with efforts to be flexible. In preparing pre-service teachers, I found it extremely important to get my students to understand the value of preparation for teaching on a daily basis as well as the need to be flexible to address unforeseen events and the diverse needs of the learner that can arise on any given day within the structure of the school setting. In order to best prepare my students for this paradox in education, I came to see the need to restructure my teaching of lesson and unit planning and to demonstrate for them the impact of flexibility on student outcomes.

As a rookie professor I established a set of requirements for the social studies methods course, including rigorous guidelines for lesson plans and a unit plan. I expected my future teachers to generate these detailed lesson plans in less than nine weeks and to have their unit plans completed two weeks later. The guidelines for these lesson plans needed to include the elements of:

- Introduction/rationale;
- time required for teaching the lesson;
- generalization/content area(s)/Department of Education Content Standards/National Council for Social Studies Themes;
- concepts of the lesson;
- materials required;
- instructional objectives/learner outcomes;
- procedures;
- evaluation/assessment;
- closure.

My students were required: (1) to select a unit or theme that can be taught within a five- to ten-day period in any history class—world history, US history, or Hawaiian history; (2) to integrate the major generalizations from a minimum of three social studies disciplines; and (3) to incorporate the major components used for the lesson plans. Just two weeks after the pre-service teachers finished their second lesson plan, the unit plan was due at the end of the semester. There was little discussion of their lesson and unit plans, as I only provided written feedback and then returned them. There was no time built into the course for students to act on the feedback and rework their plans. Although this process was considered sufficient for preparing students for their student teaching, based on advice from university colleagues, my personal experience in returning to the high school arena now revealed otherwise.

My course syllabus might look rigorous and essential to support quality teachers. Was this type of rigor promoting realistic outcomes? When I looked in the mirror and walked the daily walk of a teacher, I easily identified with the learning process of a student teacher. I was expecting pre-service teachers to construct lesson plans and unit plans that only accomplished teachers could create. I was expecting them to create their plans with minimal guidance and feedback. Although I taught concepts associated with teaching secondary social studies, I expected the pre-service teachers to know how to take these concepts and to apply them to their plans, even though they had spent little time in a real classroom. They had no experience, from a teacher's perspective, of classroom dynamics, student learning styles, classroom time limits, or real curricula.

I was compelled to change how I taught lesson and unit planning to my pre-service teachers and I began using the concept of chunking to teach planning and preparation. I began my discussion of lesson planning by setting the stage for my pre-service teachers with a class profile describing the students in a real class. For example:

> You are teaching a 7th grade world history class to 32 students. The class is 45 minutes in length. It is scheduled for 2nd period, and the school schedule does not rotate. Of the 32 students, 14 are boys and 18 are girls. They are of average ability. Three students have been identified as ADD.

After distributing the profile, we discuss the elements that must be considered when deciding how and what to teach. Then I ask them to select any topic that fits within 7th grade world history. Once their topics are selected, they construct the first part of the lesson, including backward mapping. They identify learner outcomes, standards being taught, and assessments. During the next class, we break into small groups to discuss these elements. I ask my students to make sure the learner outcomes relate to the selected topic and to make sure the assessment connects directly to the outcomes. Once we have clarity on these aspects of lesson planning, we move into the development of strategies to engage all students. These are shared in small groups, again making sure that the pre-service teachers are able to link to the learner outcomes and remain consistent with the topic and assessment.

After enough class time has been spent on identifying and understanding teacher-directed and student-directed activities, I ask my students to create one of each and add it to their lesson plan. We then talk about transitioning between activities and I always remind them to make sure they connect to the learner outcomes and assessment. Again, in class, we share and discuss each pre-service teacher's ideas. We critically evaluate where we are and make necessary changes. The last part of the lesson development is the closing. We also discuss pros and cons of how homework should look and how it should be used.

Once we have discussed, revised, and sometimes re-vamped our individual lesson plans, we might then also address another class profile and change the lesson plan to fit the dynamics of the new classroom. A new profile might read as follows:

> You are teaching a 10th grade world history class consisting of 30 students. This class is an advanced-placement course with 17 boys and 13 girls. The total class time each day is a 75-minute block.

I want my pre-service teachers to understand that one size does not fit all when it comes to teaching. As a teacher, they will need to adjust their plans to meet the diverse needs of their students and classes. This new process for creating lesson plans takes half a semester in my university methods course. We develop the lessons in conjunction with our learning of instructional strategies, classroom management, and student diversity. Instead of teaching planning in isolation, it is woven into each class session to incorporate all the major concepts associated with research-based best practices.

My experience with Board certification also highlighted for me the need to fundamentally change my approach to the unit-planning process in my methods course. Using the lesson development process described above, we now focus on how to expand one of their lessons into a ten-day unit. My students are given the choice of taking one of their lessons (either the middle-level or the high school lesson) and use the backward mapping design process to construct a multi-lesson unit plan. Student teachers identify the unit, develop learner outcomes and the standards to be used in the entire unit, and construct summative assessment pieces. During our next class session, we move into small groups to discuss and align the assessment piece with the learner outcomes and standards. Over the last half of the semester, my students use the same process to develop individual lesson plans for their unit. During each class, time is devoted to discussion and refinement of lessons. By the time the unit plans are turned in, they have learnt much more about teaching, learning and planning for teaching and learning through the collaboration and feedback received during the process. In short, they are no longer just doing a task. As Kellough and Carjuzaa (2006, p. 14) state: "Students need teachers who are well organized and who know how to establish and manage an active and supportive learning environment." This environment has now become a primary focus in my teaching about teaching and I aim explicitly to develop these characteristics in my pre-service teachers.

As noted earlier, linking flexibility and planning seems somewhat paradoxical, yet the two ideas really do fit together. My revised approach to lesson and unit plan processes now incorporates major ideas associated with the need for flexibility. As each classroom scenario is changed, and as we work together to discuss and develop our understanding of lessons and units, pre-service teachers come to see the need to adjust their plans to accommodate all learners. With a focus on flexibility, I am now more easily able to teach differentiated instruction and provide concrete examples of how it can be employed in the classroom.

Just as I came to see the critical importance of flexibility to my success as a high school teacher, I have also come to realize how much I need to adopt this concept in my university teaching. By remembering how I set the stage with my high school students on the first day of class by addressing their needs, I am reminded of the need to do likewise with my university classes. "Students respond best to teachers who provide leadership and who enjoy their function as role models, advisors, mentors, and reflective decision makers" (Kellough and Carjuzaa, 2006, p. 14). If this is to hold true for students in the K–12 setting, should it not also apply to pre-service teachers at the university level? Being a flexible teacher matters in meeting the needs of students in the classroom.

My experiences in completing National Board certification helped me to better understand the development of my pedagogy of teacher education. The notion of flexibility highlighted for me that when I practiced flexibility, I also displayed compassion for my students. I began to see how my practice as a teacher educator was being informed by my knowledge of practice. I no longer responded to my students by saying, "Stop by during office hours"; rather, I deliberately stepped down from the ivory tower to model for my pre-service teachers how being flexible demonstrated compassion. As I enacted a new pedagogy of teacher education, I came to purposefully build time into my lesson plans to address the needs of my students. I became more open to their ideas and we worked together to solve problems. My pre-service teachers could see, first hand through my own teaching about teaching, how flexibility and compassion support the development of a positive and caring learning environment.

What does it mean to be a teacher of teaching?

How do teaching and learning really improve? It's as simple as this: I cannot improve my practice in isolation from others. To improve, I must have formats, structures, and plans reflecting on, changing, and assessing my practice.

(Glickman, 2002, p. 4)

Although I did not realize it at the time, when I embarked on National Board Certification, the parallels between teaching and teaching about teaching made it almost inevitable that the process would be a catalyst for me to study my own practice and to do so through a self-study methodology (Hamilton *et al.*, 1998). Self-study highlighted the importance of applying the same intentions inherent in my high school teaching to my teaching of pre-service teachers. As a teacher of future teachers, the process of National Board Certification reminded me of my mission: To prepare highly qualified teachers for their own classrooms. The process has now changed the essence of my university teaching and allowed me to survive and thrive in my profession as a teacher of teaching.

Returning to the hallowed hallways of high school in my quest for National Board Certification forced me to question how I prepared my pre-service teachers for their careers. To work in the ivory tower does not mean abandoning what I knew as an accomplished high school teacher, but it does mean developing and extending that practice to purposefully bridge the gap between the university (or the world of theory) and public school classrooms (the world of practice).

At the university level I became more aware of the importance of modeling good teaching practices and dispositions. When I recognized the connection between flexibility and compassion and then employed such dispositions in my university classroom, my students seemed better prepared to create positive learning environments for their future students and classrooms. Compassion is certainly a disposition associated with the profession of teaching. Wenzlaff (1998, p. 566) states that colleges of teacher education should help pre-service teachers "realize their beliefs about teaching and dispositions desired for effective teaching." Richardson and Onwuegbuzie (2003, p. 14) go on to say that "by understanding the beliefs, skills, and dispositions of teacher candidates, teacher educators are able to guide the candidates through the teacher education program and foster positive dispositions that will be productive in teaching and learning." In my quest for National Board Certification, I was forced to revisit good teaching dispositions. By making use of these dispositions and modeling them in my university courses, my pre-service teachers could experience how flexibility and compassion can create and sustain a positive classroom environment.

In developing and then enacting my pedagogy of teacher education, I and my pre-service teachers were able to see how integral the concepts of planning and flexibility were to successful teaching. "Those institutions that focus on helping students know how to learn and how to apply what they learn to real situations will be increasingly valued" (Hanna, 2003, p. 27). Such learning surely begins with the teacher educator.

Conclusion

Once it was announced to the College of Education faculty that I had indeed passed the National Board Certification process, I found that my university life immediately began to change. I changed the teaching process in my own courses because I had gone back to the classroom and actually tried to implement what I had been expecting my student teachers to do. I saw the need to explicitly model being a reflective practitioner so that my student teachers could see into this process and think about how to change and develop they way they might teach.

Some of my teacher education colleagues found value in what I had learnt and the way in which I had begun to develop and enact my pedagogy of teacher education. As a consequence, I am now involved in the Master of Education in Teaching (MEdT) program in the College of Education, and this has allowed me to combine the two things I most love to do in my professional life: work with pre-service teachers in our partnership schools and integrate professional development activities for the in-service teachers in those schools.

When I was teaching in the borrowed high school classroom to do my National

Board certification, I realized how much I really missed school teaching. I missed the energy generated by teenagers, I missed the ability to connect with these students every day, and I missed the life of being a classroom teacher. As others (Dinkelman *et al.*, 2006; Murray and Male, 2005) have noted, beginning teacher educators often feel a sense of loss as they move from being a school teacher to being an academic. I too felt better prepared to be a classroom teacher than to be a professor. Perhaps this was partly associated with the fact that I had very limited understanding of what is required to develop and enact a pedagogy of teacher education.

I now work with two partnership schools, a middle school and a high school, where all of my pre-service teachers are housed for an intensive two-year teacher preparation program. Because of our close relationship, I have found tremendous support from the administrators and faculties at both schools. I see my teacher education work involving purposeful ways of developing learning communities and building relationships between the university and our partnership schools. My experience has taught me new ways of challenging strongly held perceptions embedded in views of theory, practice, and their relationship. My experience has also taught me ways of posing challenges so that we better appreciated knowledge about teaching and learning about teaching, a result that is crucial to the work of teacher education.

References

Boxall, W. and Burrage, H. (1989) "Recent, relevant experience": CATE's narrow definitions. *Journal of Further and Higher Education, 13*, 30–45.

Brandon, E. P. (1995) "Relevant experience" for teaching the foundations of education. *Caribbean Curriculum, 5*, 69–85.

Dinkelman, T., Margolis, J., and Sikkenga, K. (2006) From teacher to teacher educator: Experiences, expectations and expatriation. *Studying Teacher Education, 2*, 5–23.

Glickman, C. (2002) *Leadership for learning: How to help teachers succeed.* Alexandria, VA: ASCD.

Hamilton, M. L. (ed.) (1998) *Reconceptualizing teaching practice: Self-study in teacher education.* London: Falmer Press.

Hanna, D. E. (2003) Building a leadership vision: Eleven strategic challenges for higher education. *Educause Review, 38*(4), 25–34.

Kellough, R. D. and Carjuzzaa, J. (2006) *Teaching in the middle and secondary schools*, 8th edn. Upper Saddle River, NJ: Pearson Education.

Korthagen, F. A. J. and Kessels, J. (1999) Linking theory and practice: Changing the pedagogy of teacher education. *Educational Researcher, 28*(4), 4–17.

Korthagen, F. A. J., Kessels, J., Koster, B., Langerwarf, B., and Wubbels, T. (2001) *Linking practice and theory: The pedagogy of realistic teacher education.* Mahwah, NJ: Lawrence Erlbaum Associates.

Loughran, J. J. (2006) *Developing a pedagogy of teacher education: Understanding teaching and learning about teaching.* London: Routledge.

Murray, J. and Male, T. (2005) Becoming a teacher educator: Evidence from the field. *Teaching and Teacher Education, 21*, 125–142.

National Board for Professional Teaching Standards (1998) *NBPTS standards: Social studies/History for teachers of students ages 7–18+*. Retrieved August 25, 2006, from http://www.nbpts.org/for_candidates/certificate_areas?ID=5&x=63&y=12

Richardson, D. and Onwuegbuzie, A. (2003) Attitudes toward dispositions related to teaching of pre-service teachers, in-service teachers, administrators, and college/university professors. Paper presented at the meeting of the Mid-South Educational Research Association, Biloxi, MS, November.

US Department of Education (2005) No Child Left Behind (NCLB). Retrieved August 25, 2006, from http://www.ed.gov/nclb/landing.jhtml

Wenzlaff, T. L. (1998) Dispositions and portfolio development: Is there a connection? *Education*, *118*, 564–572.

10 Enacting a pedagogy of practicum supervision

One student teacher's experiences of powerful differences

Matthew Olmstead

> I can't believe how difficult that practicum was. I never slept and hardly ate because I was so stressed out and over-worked. It seemed like nothing I did went the way I hoped and the harder I tried, the worse things got! I don't know if I'm cut out to be a teacher.
>
> (First practicum experience of eight weeks)

> I can't believe how enjoyable that practicum was. I got to try lots of new things that were established in the school and take new ideas to the classroom! The workload was huge, but it wasn't so bad because I had help when I needed it and space when I didn't. I can't wait to teach again.
>
> (Second practicum experience of five weeks)

Research literature suggests that the pre-service practicum is not only the most memorable part of pre-service teacher education, but also the most critical in terms of the formation of professional identity (Clift and Brady, 2005). Tabachnick and Zeichner (1999) have suggested that practicum experiences often have a greater influence than methods courses on the development of teacher candidates' professional knowledge. The relationship between associate teachers and teacher candidates is of paramount importance from a pedagogical perspective. Tobin, Roth, and Zimmerman (2001) reported that this relationship is complex and multi-layered. My own experiences as a teacher candidate confirm that the practicum plays a critical role in learning to teach.

The reader might conclude that the two opening quotations are from different teacher candidates, perhaps from different pre-service programs. In fact, both are quotations from my journal, written during two very different practicum experiences with two very different associate teachers in my pre-service year. Some of the emotion expressed in the quotations may seem familiar to those who have gone through a pre-service teacher education program. The purpose of this chapter is to explicate some of the issues explored by Loughran (2006) that arose during my experiences of two very different pedagogies of practicum supervision. As Loughran points out, learning about teaching is difficult business and it is important that teacher educators understand and respond appropriately to teacher candidates' interpretations of their practicum experiences, just as teachers work to understand and respond to their students.

An issue of particular importance to this chapter is the primacy of the relationship between teachers and learners (from both a teacher educator's and a teacher candidate's perspective). My experiences recounted here illustrate the overarching importance of relationships in a pedagogy for productive practicum learning. My goal is to illustrate how the nature of the relationship between an associate teacher and a teacher candidate actually mediates the candidate's ability to learn from his or her own practicum experiences. It is through these professional relationships that challenges to the traditional apprenticeship of observation during practicum experiences can be productively encouraged to enhance learning about teaching. My experience of profound differences between two associate teachers was instrumental in my highlighting and exploring different elements of my growing professional knowledge of practice. My goal is to offer insights into ways of enacting a pedagogy of teacher education.

I begin this chapter by setting the contexts for my two practicum placements, based on my first-day experiences at each school. After setting the contexts, I describe my first teaching experiences in both practicum assignments and my reflections on those experiences. I then describe how powerful differences in my associate teachers' pedagogies of practicum supervision affected the contexts in which I learned to teach. Finally, I offer some conclusions about the importance of communication and professional trust in the relationship between associate teachers and teacher candidates. My intention is not to criticize or praise either of my associate teachers. I learned much from each of them, even as I found the quality of my learning to be much higher with one than with the other.

Setting the stage: the first practicum

I telephoned my first associate teacher several weeks before the practicum began to find out what I could do to prepare for my first classroom teaching experience. I was disappointed to learn that my associate teacher did not want to meet in advance. I was advised to read through the science and mathematics curriculum documents. On the first day of the practicum, the vice-principal greeted the group of us assigned to the school and we subsequently paired up with our associate teachers. My associate teacher led me to the classroom and handed me a stack of paper—a computer printout of timetable, class lists, identified students in the school, and a detailed schedule for my lessons based on the chapter in the text and a copy of each of the three textbooks used by the classes.

I felt overwhelmed. The pile of paper held little contextual meaning for me. The schedule was full of codes I did not understand and misaligned times, rooms and courses. The list of identified students offered no indication of what their identifications were, much less any indication of how I should modify my teaching to accommodate these students. I voiced my concerns about the students who were identified and my associate teacher suggested that I go to the main office to look at each student's individual education plan (IEP). I had little or no idea of how to interpret an IEP.

Just before class began, my associate teacher directed me to sit at a table at the back of the classroom. I was informed that the table could be used as a desk by up to 3 students in any given class, given the cramped conditions of the classrooms. My associate teacher told me to circulate around the room when students were working, to field questions and generally provide assistance wherever required. I was introduced to only one of the five classes that day—the mathematics class that, I later learned, I was to begin teaching almost immediately. In the other four classes I was introduced as "our student teacher."

I did not have much time to engage in productive conversations with my associate teacher on that first day. We had 10 minutes to talk during the preparatory period. I requested some extra textbooks to take home for the practicum and some resource materials that would give me an idea of what had been done with the mathematics class in previous years. My associate teacher pointed me to a bookcase and invited me to look through several binders, provided that I did not misplace any handouts. At lunch time, I sat with my associate teacher, who spent most of the time speaking with colleagues. When we did speak to each other, the conversation focused on students who were at risk of failing.

At the end of the first day I assisted my associate teacher by providing extra mathematics and science help to some of our students. After our extra-help session, I was told that I would begin teaching the mathematics class in two days' time. I was asked to follow the lesson schedules I had been given earlier in the day. The lesson schedule consisted of the date, class number, and textbook chapter section to be covered on a particular day.

Setting the stage: the second practicum

A week before I started my second practicum assignment, I met with my associate teacher. My second associate felt that it was important for me to have a sense of the teaching environment that I was going to be a part of. I was welcomed into the classroom during a preparation period, and together we set out to tour both the classroom and the school. I was introduced to office staff and to several members of the science department. We spoke at length about my teaching and learning experiences, both as a student and as a teacher candidate. I was asked about the classes I might be interested in teaching and aspects of the school schedule and course timetables were explained. At the end of the meeting my second associate teacher provided me with desk space to use, keys to the photocopy room and classroom, and copies of the course textbooks to keep at home. I was told that computer access and photocopy codes would be ready for me upon my return.

The first day of my second practicum was just as welcoming as our preliminary meeting. Again, my associate teacher greeted me in the classroom and spent time explaining lesson plans for the day. The computer account and photocopy codes promised at the preliminary meeting were provided. Before classes began, I was invited to choose a place in the classroom where I would be comfortable observing the lesson.

I spent the rest of my first day observing my associate teacher's teaching style. I took particular notice of how students were welcomed to the first class of a new semester. I was introduced to each class as Mr. Olmstead and my associate teacher explained to the students that we would be sharing teaching responsibilities for the duration of my five-week placement. After each class this second associate teacher made a point of speaking to me about students with special needs and made it clear that certain students required a "bit more effort from us."

At the end of the day my associate teacher and I met for 30 minutes to discuss the plan for my practicum. We decided that I would start to teach a physics class in a few days, with the option of teaching additional classes as we both felt appropriate. I was offered a CD-ROM of material used in the past with classes; it included old tests, projects, student work, marking schemes, and a full course outline for the term (including subject matter, text chapter references and homework). Additionally, I was given a DVD of past class presentations so that I could become familiar with an assignment planned for another group of students. Finally, my associate teacher made it clear that the resources were to serve as a guide for my planning, and the personal touch I could bring to the course were welcomed.

The stages are set: two very different learning environments

I was unsure what to expect from an associate teacher when I began my pre-service program, and thus I was willing to accept just about any kind of help in the first few days of my first practicum. Initially, I accepted the approach taken by my first associate teacher. I felt that I received an appropriate amount of initial information. Yet I had a general sense of discomfort about my first practicum almost immediately. I felt that I was intruding on the privacy of another teacher's classroom and I sensed that it was up to me to justify my place in the host school. After observing the lessons on that first day, I sensed that my vision of teaching and my associate teacher's were very different. I could only wonder how this would play out once I began to teach.

My experience on the first day of my first practicum understandably contributed to the anxiety I felt when meeting my second associate teacher. Clearly, the first day experiences were very different. My second associate teacher seemed genuinely concerned with creating a productive learning experience for both of us. Immediately, I felt like a member of the staff because my second associate provided me with a workspace and ensured that I had access not only to textbooks, but also to keys, passwords, copy codes and phone numbers. In short, I felt fully integrated into the classroom from day one.

Bain (2004) has explored the importance of classroom environment for student learning. As a student of teaching, the very different learning environments created by my two associate teachers had profound implications not only for the way I enacted my pedagogy, but also for how I learned from my teaching experiences in these two practicum placements. Sarason (1996) has argued that learning can only be productive for students if their teachers also work in a productive learning environment. The quality of my learning on teaching placements is explored in the following discussion of my first teaching experiences at each school.

Enacting my pedagogy: the first practicum

My first pre-service teaching experience was in a mathematics class that I took over from my associate teacher in the middle of a unit. My associate teacher expected me to give the students a quiz as a part of my first lesson. In addition, I was asked to take attendance, to check that students had completed their homework, and to record the names of students who had not completed their homework and of students who did not have their day-planners.

At the 3-minute warning bell before my first class, my associate teacher moved to the back of the class with a pad of paper and seemed to write non-stop throughout that first lesson; I could not help but feel concerned about what observations were being recorded. At the same time, however, I anticipated that the notes would be invaluable. My plan for the class included taking attendance, checking homework, administering the quiz, giving a short writing assignment to help me learn about the students, teaching the class how to solve an equation algebraically, taking students through two examples, and assigning homework. I hoped to allow class time to work on homework, with opportunities for help from peers, myself, or my associate teacher.

My first lesson was a powerful learning experience, particularly regarding my inability to manage class time. The school's complex attendance system was my first stumbling block. Because school policy was not to penalize students if absent for a legitimate school-related activity, I had to cross-reference each missing student with several lists of sports and field trips. By the time I finished taking attendance, I was already far behind in my lesson plan. I asked the students to have their homework out and their day planners open to the correct day. I also announced the quiz. Again, an apparently simple task became complex, as checking homework seemed to take forever as I juggled both my associate teacher's mark book and the seating plan that I had hastily sketched the day before by listening as my associate teacher called the students by name in class to answer questions. The quiz was then distributed, written and collected. I felt some relief after collecting the quiz, because it meant that I had finally addressed the initial requirements and could begin to teach. To my horror, a quick glance at my watch revealed that I had 14 minutes to complete my lesson plan.

I quickly decided that getting to know the students was a priority. I thought that the writing assignment would not only assist me in remembering students' names, but also help me to design lessons that built on students' interests. After the writing assignment was completed, I set out to teach as much of my lesson as possible. As the period came to a close, I felt that my brief explanation of algebraic expressions had been clear. I was pleased to have drawn an analogy between weights and algebraic expressions. I explained that anything done to one side of a scale must be done to the other side of the scale to keep it balanced, just like an algebraic expression or equation. At the sound of the bell, I hurriedly assigned homework and dismissed the class.

Overall, I felt pretty good about the lesson. Although I had run out of time, I felt that I had done a decent job with my very first formal teaching experience. The students seemed to enjoy the class discussion that I led and, perhaps most importantly, students seemed to understand more about algebraic expressions than when they started the lesson.

Enacting my pedagogy: the second practicum

My second practicum began in a physics class and the start of the second practicum coincided with the beginning of the school's second semester. I was in the enviable position of starting the second semester with the class, so I was able to introduce the course and the first unit on electricity. I was pleased to have the opportunity not only to introduce the first unit and help to set the tone for the class, but also to teach a challenging unit.

I did not begin teaching the physics course with a full lesson. Instead, my associate teacher and I negotiated shared teaching arrangements on the third day of the semester. My associate teacher taught for the first half of the third class and then turned things over to me. I was encouraged me to use the Predict–Observe–Explain (POE) teaching procedure (Baird and Northfield, 1992) to introduce the electricity unit. In addition, I prepared a handout to assess students' prior conceptions of electricity. I was particularly pleased to have the opportunity to use two teaching procedures that I had experienced in my education classes. I felt that using these active learning approaches would give me a chance to experience how they are enacted from a teacher's perspective.

The first POE sequence went smoothly as I demonstrated a static electricity device, encouraging students to generate questions about the apparatus and the physics behind it. The class participated in a discussion of the physics of electricity and ended up posing more predictions of the effects of the apparatus under different circumstances. I tried out their suggestions, and the students seemed surprised and intrigued with the results. By choosing to test students' predictions, however, I was unable to use the diagnostic assessment handout that I had prepared.

My associate teacher let me plan my first full lesson on my own and indicated that no comments would be offered during the class unless I asked for input. My second associate teacher seemed to trust me as a young professional to come up with an appropriate lesson plan. I was encouraged to enjoy planning the lesson and challenging my practical skills.

Attendance at my second school proved to be much simpler than at my first school. Armed with the seating plan that my associate teacher and I had created together on the first day, I quickly took attendance and noticed that my associate teacher had moved to the back of the room without any paper. Whenever I looked at my associate teacher during the lesson, I noticed that my teaching behaviours and the students' reactions were being observed. My lesson started with the diagnostic handout I had planned to use the day before. After going through the questions with the class and clarifying a few terms, the students filled in sheets designed to solicit their prior conceptions and added them to their notebooks to be reviewed as the unit continued. The handout seemed to be well received both by the students and my associate teacher.

I immediately moved to another POE in which I demonstrated the attractive quality of electrical charge, first by sticking a balloon to the wall, and then by using the static electricity generator to bend a stream of water flowing a tap on the front desk. I then introduced Coulomb's law of electrical attraction and repulsion together with the underlying principles of static electricity. The students asked many thoughtful questions and the ensuing class discussion took a fair bit of time. At the end of class I assigned homework as outlined in the unit plan, omitting a few questions that we had not yet covered. I felt good about the lesson, but with some teaching experience behind me from the first practicum, I expected more of myself. In addition, I worried that an incorrect definition that I had presented would be difficult to explain to students the next day. I also noticed that I was still struggling to fit my lesson plan into the time available.

Enacting my pedagogy: preliminary thoughts

After my very first lesson as a teacher, I was full of confidence. Although there was obviously much room for improvement, I felt that I had taught an acceptable first lesson. I was generally pleased with the response of the class and my recovery from some awkward moments at the beginning of the class. Teaching felt good and I was excited about the possibilities for the remainder of my first placement.

In contrast, I was much less confident after my first lesson in my second practicum. Although the lesson seemed to proceed smoothly, my thoughts were focused on the incorrect definition that I had given. I felt that I had let down both my students and my associate teacher, and I resolved to regain everyone's trust the following day.

Talking about teaching: first lesson, first practicum

> Matt, you forgot to take up the homework questions on the board. You took too long to do attendance. The homework check took too long. The quiz was too easy. You forgot to stamp one student's planner. You misspelled "coefficient" on the board. The writing thing you had them do took up a lot of time and had no value to the students.

I was taken aback by the barrage of criticism leveled at me by my first associate teacher after my first lesson. I tried to explain the reason for the writing assignment, which I developed from a recommendation from my aunt who had taught for 30 years. I told my associate teacher that I wanted to show interest in the students and build a positive relationship. My associate teacher felt that the writing assignment took too long and offered several more criticisms of my lesson: I did not spread out questions evenly to the class, I dismissed the class late, and I did not give the students enough homework.

I was understandably surprised when, at the end of the meeting, my associate teacher asked when I would take over two more mathematics classes. Although I had initially felt good about my lesson, I was no longer confident in my ability to teach one, let alone three classes of mathematics. My associate teacher told me that I should add classes as soon as possible to keep pace with previous student teachers. Before I could respond, my associate rushed out the door.

Talking about teaching: first lesson, second practicum

> Yes, your definition was off a little bit, just correct it tomorrow and it'll be fine. They'll love that you admit to being wrong. It is probably a good thing in the long run.

My second associate teacher gave no other feedback on my first lesson, explaining a preference for observing for a few days before making any substantial comments, although I was complimented on the handout I used to solicit students' prior conceptions. To my surprise, my associate teacher produced a personal version of the handout for use in a different physics class the next day. My second associate added to my idea by asking students to vote on their prior conceptions. Additionally, students were asked to vote on which questions they found most interesting and my associate teacher promised to take time to focus on the physics behind the high-interest questions. It was a powerful opportunity for me to reframe my own practice by observing my associate teacher use a teaching procedure that I had introduced, and this quickly created confidence in our relationship.

When feedback on the first few lessons finally did come, my second associate teacher was brief and supportive:

> You've got good presence in the class. The POEs are great, I like the amount of time that you take to give the students time to think about that, that's good. You could give them a bit more in class work on the problems, especially with the quiz coming up. The students are really engaged, and you're handling well the ones who are trying to trip you up with tough questions. Would you mind if I use that activity that you did with them for electric fields? I thought that was really smart and the students loved it.

We then chatted about the next few days of the class and the pacing of the unit in general. I had concerns that I was behind in the unit plan; I was assured that I would be able to catch up with diligence. The atmosphere seemed supportive and respectful.

Reflections on my feedback: challenging the authority of my experience

I was shaken by my first feedback session with my first associate teacher. I felt demoralized and doubted my ability to make sense of my experiences. I felt that I completely failed both my associate teacher and my class. It was made clear to me that my impressions of the lesson were less important than my associate teacher's interpretations of the lesson. I inferred from the tone of my associate teacher that my mistakes were inexcusable. I wondered how I would ever be able to teach in that classroom again.

This approach to providing me with daily feedback turned out to be a predictable pattern in my efforts to learn from my first associate teacher. I would feel confident that I had made some improvements to a lesson; my associate teacher would then provide a list of increasingly minor failures on my part. For example, although I managed to encourage two students who had difficulty in mathematics to feel confident enough to work at the blackboard, my associate teacher's feedback focused on my failure to discipline a boy for chewing gum during class.

I approached my first feedback session in my second practicum with caution, and I was pleasantly surprised by how my second associate teacher provided feedback, focusing on the positive things that had happened in the classroom and bolstering my confidence. My second associate teacher also took an active interest in what I was doing in class and encouraged me to discuss my developing philosophy of education. Suggestions for improvement were made constructively, and I was particularly struck by my second associate teacher's modification of lesson plans so that I could observe a lesson similar to my own with some added features or techniques. My second associate teacher seemed to believe in both the power of modeling teaching practices and the importance of mutual respect. This commitment to my learning seemed to increase my commitment to the students' learning. I worked to use the same positive reinforcement and constructive criticism techniques with my students that my associate teacher used with me.

My professional learning in these two practicum assignments were markedly different because my learning environment was shaped by the pedagogy of teacher education enacted by both of my associates. Table 10.1 illustrates the messages that I took from each of the two learning environments. I sense a negative learning approach from my associate teacher in the first practicum assignment and that approach made me seriously doubt my abilities as an educator. Despite the pedagogical approach, I did learn a great deal from that first experience. I was able to compare my teaching philosophy with someone who had a very different style and philosophy. Some of my first associate teacher's comments were valid and provided me with clear, painfully-stated ways to improve.

There was almost no effort by my first associate teacher to affirm any positive traits that I might have as a teacher. I felt that I had to comply with a teaching style that did not feel natural to me. I was exhausted for much of my first practicum as I spent considerable time and effort battling my emotional responses to highly critical feedback. I felt neither respected nor cared about. There were many

Table 10.1 Messages conveyed in two practicum environments

Messages from my first practicum	Messages from my second practicum
"You didn't . . ."	"Let's work on . . ."
"You forgot to . . ."	"How's it going so far?"
"You should have . . ."	"I really liked . . ."
"Why didn't you . . .?"	"Have you considered . . .?"
"It's not that I don't trust you. I just didn't want you to give them the answers to the test! That's why I took your text away."	"I don't know how the students will react to that, but I'm excited to see how it turns out."
"In both my personal and professional life I am just not a very positive person. Anyway you don't need positive reinforcement, you're not a student, you're a grown man with a Master's degree!"	"How are you feeling today? You look a bit tired. Is there anything I can do to help you out?"
"Wow, the students really loved that science game, how long did you work on that? . . . Yes, that's why I don't do things like that."	"That was great! Do you mind if I try using an expanded version of that for my other class?"

times during my first placement when I seriously considered leaving the teacher education program.

In contrast, I had a rich and productive learning experience in the second practicum. I learned the value of a professional relationship built on trust and mutual respect. My second associate teacher realized that it was not necessary to point out my every shortcoming in order to motivate me to change and grow. The power of that associate teacher's enthusiasm for students' learning and for my learning was more than enough to make me want to bring out the best in myself and the students. I developed a sense of authority over my experiences and I also enjoyed the experience. The workload was comparable to that of the first practicum placement, yet the classroom environment and my relationship with the second associate teacher made the work far more enjoyable. My personal life improved because I was able to sleep well and have more recreational time to myself. Buoyed by the success of the second practicum, I was once again excited to become a teacher.

Learning to teach: the importance of relationships

Teachers who accept teacher candidates into their classrooms have enormous power to influence the learning processes of a future teacher. Practicum experiences are, hands down, the most important and influential part of any pre-service teacher education program. As such, emotionally-laden practicum experiences have the ability to powerfully shape a new teacher's pedagogy. I offer the following conclusions based on my experiences.

1   It seems crucial that associate teachers foster teacher candidates' ability to see and learn from their own practice.

2 Effective associate teachers model good practice for their teacher candidates.
3 Learning to teach is more than an apprenticeship of observation; it is a relationship between associate teacher and teacher candidate built on mutual respect and trust.

At a basic level, pre-service programs should strive to ensure that there are well-established guidelines for the practicum experiences. These guidelines should include a well-constructed assessment form that is applied consistently by associate teachers. The hiring process for new teachers puts considerable emphasis on practicum evaluations, and this reality creates real possibilities for tensions and unproductive learning for new teachers.

Although associate teachers will necessarily differ in pedagogical approaches, it should be clear to both teacher candidates and their hosts that learning to teach is not about learning how to mimic. An associate teacher's pedagogical approach to a new teacher's professional learning has profound potential to shape the candidate's developing stance toward professional learning. Learning to teach is about learning to reframe one's own practices based on professional conversations that build on shared evidence of students' responses. When associate teachers view teacher candidates as capable of offering insights into the analysis of teaching and learning experience, they help to launch a career of constructive professional learning. When teacher candidates experience their associate teachers as guides providing alternative perspectives on problems of practice, they experience a pedagogy of teacher education that is both powerful and productive.

References

Bain, K. (2004) *What the best college teachers do.* Cambridge, MA: Harvard University Press.

Baird, J. R. and Northfield, J. R. (eds.) (1992) *Learning from the PEEL experience.* Melbourne: Monash University Printery.

Clift, R. T. and Brady, P. (2005) Research on methods courses and field experiences. In M. Cochran-Smith and K. Zeichner (eds.), *Studying teacher education: The report of the AERA panel on research and teacher education.* Mahwah, NJ: Lawrence Erlbaum Associates, pp. 309–424.

Loughran, J. (2006) *Developing a pedagogy of teacher education: Understanding teaching and learning about teaching.* London: Routledge.

Sarason, S. (1996) *Revisiting "The culture of the school and the problem of change."* New York: Teachers College Press.

Tabachnick, B. R. and Zeichner, K. M. (1999) Idea and action: Action research and the development of conceptual change teaching of science. *Science Education, 83,* 309–322.

Tobin, K., Roth, W. M., and Zimmerman, A. (2001) Learning to teach science in urban schools. *Journal of Research in Science Teaching, 38,* 941–964.

11 Program restructuring and reconceptualizing practice

An epiphany

Andrea K. Martin

I would like to believe that I would have reconceptualized my practice as a teacher educator without the catapult of a dramatically restructured teacher education program. In truth, living through a dramatic restructuring compelled me to focus on how I and my colleagues enact a pedagogy of teacher education. One of the most notable features of our restructured program was an extended fall practicum that began on the first day of the school year. When teacher candidates returned to the Faculty for two on-campus weeks midway through the fall semester, it quickly became apparent that traditional, transmission models of teaching were both inadequate and inappropriate. Teaching experience-rich pre-service teachers would require us to develop a new pedagogy of teacher education (Loughran, 2006). Thus began my journey to reconceptualize my practice, to enact new pedagogical strategies and to reconsider and reframe my goals and purposes.

In this chapter, I identify notable markers along the way and particular challenges that I confronted and continue to confront, such as provoking candidates to question their assumptions about teaching and learning and working to induce conceptual change. I have had to learn how to listen harder and to hear better the voices of all of the stakeholders in the becoming-a-teacher enterprise, including teachers and administrators as well as our candidates. Putting theory into practice has taught me to attend far more closely to the voices of teacher candidates, to honour their perspectives and experiences, to challenge their beliefs and values, and to work to thread these more openly into the fabric of the teacher education classroom. It has also taught me that this is an intensely important and demanding enterprise.

Program reform and restructuring

Teacher education reform is a complex business. Cole and Knowles (1998, p. 18) highlight some of the "overwhelming volume of conflicting, confusing analyses of the condition of teacher and general education, and subsequent proposals and programs for achieving reforms." These include appraisals, such as Zeichner and Liston's (1991), that identify four traditions tied to reform efforts: academic, social efficiency, developmentalist, and social reconstructionist. Other assessments focus on teacher education curriculum as the cornerstone of reform efforts: Knowles and Cole (1996) emphasize the personal and sociocultural aspects of teaching and the systemic pressures imposed by the university milieu, Giroux and McLaren (1986) approach curriculum through critical analysis, while the Holmes Group (1995) promotes concentrating on specific areas of educational knowledge and skills. Another approach to reform centres on pre-service program structure and supports extending the practicum component so that candidates spend more time in schools (Knowles and Cole, 1998; Upitis, 2000a) or anchoring the entire program on site within schools rather than within the university (Wilmore, 1996). Yet another thrust to calls for reform considers the calibre of prospective teachers, requisite selection criteria, and program length (Darling-Hammond, 1997, 2000).

The 1997–1998 academic year saw the full implementation of a dramatically restructured pre-service teacher education program at the Faculty of Education of Queen's University at Kingston. In the preceding year, 60 teacher candidates had volunteered to participate in a pilot program for an all-encompassing reform endeavour. Not merely were all of the curriculum courses overhauled, but the methods courses were entirely redrawn and new courses were introduced, including two compulsory field-based courses—Critical Issues: Equity and Exceptionality, and Theory and Professional Practice. Further, the practicum component of the program was completely recast; and the entire structure of the academic year was reconfigured. Embedded within this reform initiative was what our then dean described as the possibility for a "new model for teacher education" (Upitis, 2000b, p. 9). It was a heady time. There was anticipation and excitement, as well as trepidation and, not surprisingly, considerable resistance.

Noteworthy among the features of the restructured program was the extended 14-week fall practicum that began on the first day of the school year on the first Tuesday in September. This was preceded by an intensive orientation week in August immediately prior to the practicum. Teacher candidates were placed in Associate Schools, typically in cohorts of 5 to 12, with a Faculty Liaison assigned to the Associate School for support and supervision. This required an intense commitment on the part of the school, as candidates would continue at the same Associate School for each of their required practicum periods, including the extended 14-week fall practicum and a three-week practicum in the winter. What would change were their associate teachers. Approximately halfway through the fall semester, candidates returned to the Faculty for two weeks of on-campus classes and then returned to their Associate Schools. The majority of their campus-based courses occurred in the winter term, along with two other shorter, 3-week practicum placements, one in their Associate School and the other, an Alternate Practicum, in a setting that could offer a view of education and schooling other than that seen within their Associate School classrooms. The Alternate Practicum was tied to a full year, on-campus Program Focus course that allowed for more in-depth exploration of an area of personal interest (for faculty as well as candidates), such as exceptional learners.

Irony and paradox

Bullough and Pinnegar (2001) provide a thoughtful and concise set of "Guide-lines for quality in autobiographical forms of self-study research." They use Frye's (1957) discussion of the four heroic modes and suggest that the ironic hero story is particularly apt as a narrative form for teacher educators because it "allows a focus on the failed, the difficult, and the problematic and does not require the tragic end or the heroic romantic return" (Bullough and Pinnegar, 2001, p. 18). Moving into full-time teaching at the Faculty in 1997–1998, having successfully taught—or so end-of-term course evaluations indicated—a variety of courses on a part-time basis, including foundations and methods courses, I blithely assumed that I could continue teaching as I had been teaching and as I had been taught, what Russell (2000) calls "default" teaching strategies. But the catapult was launched in August of that year and my real journey as a teacher educator began.

Bullough, Knowles, and Crow (1992) draw attention to the daunting problem of the beginning teacher, using Schön's account of the paradox of learning a new competence:

> The paradox . . . is this: that a student cannot at first understand what he needs to learn, can only learn it by educating himself through self-discovery, and can only educate himself by beginning to do what he does not yet understand.
>
> (Schön, 1987, p. 85)

The consequence is that new teachers are highly "vulnerable to criticism and to feelings of failure; and even the best educated and most able and emotionally secure . . . face moments of frustration and self-doubt" (Bullough *et al.*, p. 79). The paradox is further sharpened and deepened "as at every turn the beginning teacher is reminded in various and powerful ways by students, other teachers, and by small private and personal disappointments, of what she cannot do or does not understand" (ibid., p. 79). This sense of vulnerability, inadequacy, and inability is equally applicable to teacher educators confronted with the challenges of a radically altered pre-service B.Ed. program.

When candidates returned to the Faculty for the two on-campus weeks, I was forced to confront my growing awareness and ever-increasing discomfiture that I had no real idea how to proceed in my teaching. The on-campus weeks had been designed to thread field experiences with coursework and to work towards unpacking and contextualizing dilemmas of practice. Because candidates had already experienced 4–6 weeks of practicum work, it was self-evident that they needed opportunities to debrief those experiences. My dilemma was how to ensure that they would also receive sufficient content to complement and buttress those in-school experiences. Alas, my interpretation of content at that time was more in keeping with Korthagen's and Kessels (1999, p. 7) description of *epi-stemic* knowledge, "Theory with a big T," rather than on *phronesis* or "theory with a small t" (see also Kessels and Korthagen, 1996). They suggest that phronesis is knowledge that is more *perceptual* than conceptual because it is situation-specific and tied to the context where a problem is met or a need or concern arises. Thus the responsibility of the teacher educator is to heighten student teachers' perceptions to focus "the attention of the actor in the situation on certain characteristics of the situation, characteristics important to the question of how to act in the situation" (ibid., p. 7).

I had had no personal teaching experience of a "field-based" course and I naïvely thought that its *modus operandi* should parallel more traditional teaching. How to begin to tease out how candidates understood their practicum experiences and how those understandings should propel on-campus classes was a conundrum at best and a black hole at worst. I had not yet reached the point where I could trust my "knowing-in-action," what Schön (1983, p. 50) sees as one of the hallmarks of competent professionals, where the knowing is tacit, implicit in the action, and interactive with both action and outcome. Consequently, I was tentative when it came to actively negotiating content with candidates and aggressively soliciting topics that were most relevant and responsive to their needs and concerns.

In a series of focus groups conducted with elementary and secondary candidates at the conclusion of that 1997–1998 academic year, the first year of full implementation of the restructured program, the on-campus weeks met with vigorous protest. Candidates questioned their purpose and saw them as "a waste of time." The hoped-for opportunities to connect theory and practice did not appear to happen for any of the participants. They found that in "every single class, we talked about our experiences . . . for the first week." In the second week, they were frustrated by the absence of structure where "almost every class was . . . decide your own agenda for this class or decide a topic or choose from these topics." I appreciated that theory and practice should not be bifurcated, but I simply did not know how to orchestrate that delicate balance where theory and practice are carefully and thoughtfully interwoven such that each informs the other. A major pillar of the restructured program was, and continues to be, learning from experience, congruent with Dewey (1938), Schön (1983), and Lave and Wenger (1991). I can vividly recall some of my most able candidates saying that theory was all well and good and could be interesting, but asking how it really connected with their teaching in the schools. What they were asking for were applications, strategies, and particular ways to address the myriad challenges they were encountering in the schools. And what I struggled with was how to enable their learning from experience while contending with trying to learn from my own. Nothing in all my teaching experiences with children, adolescents, and adults had prepared me for the necessary kind and degree of reframing in thinking and in practice.

Recently I began reading the memoir of literary scholar Jane Tompkins (1996), entitled *A Life in School.* It is a rich exploration of her school history, from P.S. 98 in New York City through graduate school at Yale and on into the academic world. Her description of teaching as an "ego-battering enterprise" resonated for me:

Teaching, by its very nature, exposes the self to myriad forms of criticism and rejection, as well as to emulation and flattery and love. Day after day, teachers are up there, on display; no matter how good they are, it's impossible not to get shot down.

(ibid., p. 90)

For Tompkins, good teaching consisted of "brilliant ideas about the subject matter [because] this was the model I have been given, and it was what I tried to live up to" (ibid., p. 90). Similarly, Russell describes "frames" for the process of learning to teach as well established, "not just in the minds of those learning to teach but also in the minds of experienced teachers and faculty who teach those who are learning to teach" (2000, p. 239). As I reconsider and re-evaluate, it was my desire to produce "brilliant ideas about the subject" that was preeminent. After all, brilliance could protect against the slings and arrows of a student question that challenged, or even exposed, any cracks in one's knowledge base. Because I presumed that I knew more Theory, I could dazzle with that and shore up candidates' lesser store of "pure" knowledge. Korthagen and Kessels (1999) rather neatly skewer teacher educators for their *a priori* choices about what theory should be told. They contend that inherent to choosing and telling theory is the prevalent, traditional conception that there is a gap that needs to be bridged between theory and practice. But "it was the a priori choice that created this gap in the first place" (ibid., p. 6). Culpability is always hard to shoulder.

Learning to listen

I had the good fortune to be involved in the initial evaluation process of our restructured program as a facilitator for focus groups conducted with elementary and secondary teacher candidates. This experience provided an opportunity to begin to understand the reform experience through the voices of teacher candidates. Ironically, those who are centre stage in the process of becoming a teacher and who have so much to offer about its attendant challenges, complexities, and the quality of their pre-service preparation often receive the least attention. Cook-Sather (2002) argues that students' perspectives must be authorized. She contends that if students are indeed actively engaged in their own knowledge construction, then their voices must be heard to provoke a "conceptualization of teaching, learning, and the ways we study them as more collaborative processes" (ibid., p. 3). These focus groups taught me a great deal about candidates' commitment, passion, beliefs, and frustrations, as they also provided insights into where we were falling considerably short. They also underscored that dramatic program reform was far more difficult than anticipated. Had I not had the experience of facilitating these groups, I seriously question whether feedback from course evaluations would ever have been sufficient to propel the kinds of changes that I had to make if I were to begin to address Sarason's (1996, 1998, 2002) concern about creating contexts for productive learning. "The differences between contexts of productive and unproductive learning is the basic starting point which will allow us to see what we call our educational system in a more realistic way" (Sarason, 2002, p. 236). More pointedly, Sarason (2004) contends:

> *Unless, and until, on the basis of careful studies and credible evidence we gain clarity and consensus of the distinguishing features of classroom contexts of productive and unproductive learning, the improvement of schooling and its outcomes is doomed.* The history of reform efforts is testimony to the recognition that the bulk of American classrooms are contexts of unproductive learning, and the diverse efforts of reform had to have the goal of making them productive. They failed because they were not clear about what they meant by *productive, unproductive,* and *learning.*
>
> (ibid., pp. 1–2, emphasis in original)

Sarason's (2002) notion of contexts of productive and unproductive learning provides a vantage point to see more clearly how embedded learning is and must be in context and how closely every teacher must attend to it:

> One of the most important criteria of a context of productive learning: *wanting* to learn but not because learning is externally demanded. In the restaurant business they say success depends on three things: location, location, location. In schools the three things are context, context, and context. If you do not know the context, your explanation or judgment of what you see or what has been reported can be misleading or wrong.
>
> (ibid., p. 184)

A refrain that echoed throughout the 1997–1998 pre-service focus groups was, "Give us stuff, not fluff!" "Stuff" was not limited to resources *per se* but included expectations to be engaged in a rigorous exploration of the learning-to-teach process. Candidates spoke tellingly of their realization that teaching carries with it both power and responsibility, "We need to be asking, 'How dare you teach?' . . . that needs to be asked more often because it IS such a powerful position" (1998, Secondary). They spoke of their deep respect for the profession and, consequently, "for what it is we want to get out of [their program]" (1998, Secondary). Hence their concern for rigour: "You don't slap the assignments so that you can say the program is rigorous. You slap the assignments so that there is value to the program" (1998, Secondary). And they asked for respect and the chance to speak with a critical voice. Not surprisingly, they praised their practicum experiences as the most valuable component of their program "for the practicum is the only setting in which they can experience firsthand the delights, challenges and frustrations of life at the front of a classroom (Russell, 2004, p. 1).

And so I began my descent into the "swampy lowland" and those methods of inquiry that are not exempt from experience, trial and error, intuition, and muddling (Schön, 1983, p. 43). Schön's oft-quoted description of the landscape of practice resonated:

In the varied topography of professional practice, there is a high, hard ground where practitioners can make effective use of research-based theory and technique, and there is a swampy lowland where situations are confusing "messes" incapable of technical solution. The difficulty is that the problems of the high ground, however great their technical interest, are often relatively unimportant to clients or to the larger society, while in the swamp are the problems of greatest human concern.

(ibid., p. 42)

Cochran-Smith describes the "reciprocal, recursive, and symbiotic relationships of scholarship in teaching education as 'working the dialectic' " (2005, p. 219) (see also Cochran-Smith and Lytle, 2004). To do so requires an emphasis on the "blurring rather than dividing of analysis and action, inquiry and experience, theorizing and doing in teacher education" (Cochran-Smith, 2005, p. 219), all are reminders of the swampy lowlands. The line of inquiry that focused on giving voice to teacher candidates and learning to listen to their perceptions and representations has continued to develop and to be provocative and fruitful (see Martin and Russell, 2005). Of note, the initial broad organizational inquiry into the restructured pre-service program and the series of program evaluation studies that it yielded virtually ended after the 1997–1998 academic year, once full implementation was underway.

Perspectives

Goodlad raises what might be a "chicken and egg" dilemma when he asks, "What comes first, good schools or good teacher education programs?" (1991, p. 1). Lest we flounder, he quickly answers, "Both must come together. The long-term solution—unfortunately, there is no quick one—is to renew the two together . . . as equal partners in the simultaneous renewal of schooling and the education of educators" (ibid., pp. 1–2). In an effort to spur partnership, schools that accepted our candidates for placements would be called Associate Schools and would be accepting a cohort or school group, rather than 1 or 2 individuals. This meant that Associate Teachers within a school could confer about their roles and responsibilities, rather than working in isolation to mentor candidates. And candidates would similarly have the support of their peers. As public acknowledgment of their participation, these schools would be given a Queen's banner to display in their entrance hallway. The linchpin between the Faculty of Education and the Associate School was the Faculty Liaison, who usually was assigned to a cluster of schools. The liaison was responsible for supervising candidates, communicating with Associate Teachers and the school administration, and teaching one of the field-based courses, Theory and Professional Practice. Because of the length of the extended practicum, far more was demanded of the participating teachers. Cultivating and maintaining relationships were both more difficult and more important than it had been in the old program (Upitis, 2000a).

Numerous stakeholders were consulted prior to and during the pilot year and the first year of full implementation. These included school administrators, teachers, community members, federation representatives, and teacher educator colleagues outside of our Faculty. Following Hatch (1998) who suggests that the reform process is more complex when various stakeholders are consulted, our dean was clear that "it was a necessary process, for we sensed that if the reform was to be successful, resultant changes would have to be tailored to the unique features of the institution and supported by the larger community" (Upitis, 2000a, p. 52). Because the willing involvement of teachers in schools was crucial to the success of the reformed program, focus groups with elementary and secondary teachers and administrators were conducted during the planning stages with the intent of discovering concerns and working to address or redress them. These consultative groups provided such rich data that the same approach was used as part of the loosely coupled evaluations of the pilot year and the first year of full implementation (see Martin *et al.*, 1999; Martin *et al.*, 2000). In 1997–1998, in addition to facilitating focus groups with candidates, I conducted focus group interviews with administrators and field practitioners and subsequently analyzed those data sets. Recounting the full range of findings is beyond the scope of this chapter; but a brief synopsis points towards the critical importance of understanding varying perspectives and incorporating that understanding into one's teaching and learning.

A predominant message throughout this set of focus group data was a desire for partnership between the schools and the Faculty. Teachers and administrators valued the infusion of energetic candidates into their schools, and there was considerable support for the extended practicum since "teaching is a marathon" and being a "sprint runner for a couple of weeks" is not adequate preparation for the marathon. Participants spelled out the price of partnership pragmatically. They wanted faculty who would supervise candidates to be visible and to communicate regularly with them. They were concerned about criteria for assessing candidates over the course of the extended practicum placements, about how and when candidates' teaching responsibilities should be structured, about their own increased workload and additional responsibilities, and about in-school coordination given the size of the in-school groups. They predicted that without decided attention to implementation issues, many problems would arise. And so they did. Partnership was possible but far more daunting to achieve than we had thought. A secondary administrator's succinct assessment was representative: "The whole thing was a great plus to candidates, a plus to the school as a whole. It wasn't a plus to the individual associate teachers" (Martin *et al.*, 2000, p. 285). Overall, the field-based courses were poorly understood as "an infringement," as was the purpose of school group meetings that took candidates away from the classroom: "I don't have a good idea as to what they were doing, and when they're at the school we *should*."

Participants had many recommendations for tackling the pragmatics that they identified including open and continuous communication between the Associate Schools and the Faculty and changes to the structure of the extended practicum so candidates could experience the start-up of school, return to the Faculty to learn "the groundwork" and then go back to the schools. The field asked for recognition of their contribution to the profession as they struggled to meet the demands of the restructured program, "I felt like I *gave* a lot more than I got back." Teachers were torn by their professional responsibilities to their students and to their teacher candidates, but "my job, first and foremost, is for my students."

I found these data sets compelling and the process of data analysis reinforced my commitment to let the data speak if the voices of the participants were to be heard. I learned that one must be vigilant and remember that there are multiple perspectives and ways of seeing. I was reminded how deeply one becomes immersed in one's own community of practice and how great the divide between communities can be. A secondary principal spoke of the two cultures, the "ivory tower and the practical tower":

> We've got a long way to go to make the most of both of those in a much more connective kind of way, where the practitioners in the school have a bit more time and a bit more respect for the theoretical, and those who are engaged in the theoretical have a little more respect of knowledge from the actual, practical world.
>
> (Martin *et al.*, 2000, p. 295)

I realized that there are points of divergence that cannot be well negotiated nor should they be. Our principal responsibility is teacher education and our primary commitment is to our prospective teachers. For our colleagues in the schools, their principal commitment is to the learning of the students in their classrooms, followed by their commitment to the profession and to those who are becoming teachers. Notwithstanding, concerted attention must be directed towards each community of practice having "a bit more time and a bit more respect" for the other.

Giving credence to the authority of experience (Munby and Russell, 1994), I began to introduce specifically the notion of perspective into my courses and to work to have candidates consider the classroom dynamic from multiple points of view. As I thought harder about my own students' perspectives, I became more aware of the need to problematize what I was trying to do and introduced up-front statements of purpose. How could I expect my students to buy into what I was doing if they were unaware of why I was doing it? Consequently some of us who taught the Professional Issues course developed a list of discussion topics to guide the school-group meetings that took place at the Associate Schools. Candidates could then share the topics with their associate teachers. I started explaining why they needed to tell their associate teachers what they were doing in their school groups as well as what their assignments were for the Critical Issues course. By extension, if associate teachers were unaware of the purpose and content of school-group meetings, how could they ever sanction, let alone support, candidates' time away from the classroom. When I subsequently became a Faculty Liaison and began teaching the other field-based course, Theory and Professional

Development, I took to heart the recommendations from the field, in particular regarding more on-going and open lines of communication, and have worked to incorporate them.

Beliefs and values

The underlying rationale for the two field-based courses, Theory and Professional Development and Professional Issues: Equity and Exceptionality, built on the need to have contextualized experiences before abstractions from or about those experiences could occur (Upitis, 2000a). During the extended practicum, candidates were allotted three hours per week to work collaboratively in their school groups on course-related tasks. Candidates used their in-school experiences to begin to develop a critical stance, to address equity issues such as gender, social class, cultural diversity and to learn to understand the population of students with exceptionalities and necessary curricular adaptations, accommodations, and interventions. Additional topics for their school-group discussions included classroom management, board policies and procedures, and the overall school community.

Teaching the Professional Issues course made me realize that if candidates were going to develop a critical stance, then they needed to move beyond their assumptions about students' abilities, attitudes, or performance, assumptions that could be delimiting and ultimately not supportive of individual students' needs and abilities. But to do so meant challenging their beliefs and values and presenting opportunities for them to re-present their own school experiences in light of their often-contrasting practicum experiences. Secondary candidates (2000) spoke tellingly about learning how "eye-opening" it was to learn "different priorities" from their students who were not university or college bound. In contrast to their own experiences, candidates came to the realization that a "university degree [may not be] the best education"; therefore they needed to respect and address "other options" to prepare their students as "lifelong learners." As elementary candidates confronted challenges in their classrooms, they, too, found it to be eye-opening, "We're dealing with kids that are carrying weapons, and kids that will laugh in your face and swear at you, and call you names ... I was totally unprepared for it" (2000, Elementary).

If candidates were going to be able to confront their "taken-for-granted" assumptions, they needed to first identify what those were. And for that to happen, they had to feel safe enough to risk feeling vulnerable and exposed. The Professional Issues: Equity and Exceptionality course was required for all pre-service candidates and there was a prescribed set of topics. Many of these topics were emotionally laden, sometimes leaving candidates unsettled and distressed. I slowly began to understand that it had to be their issues, their challenges, their questions, and their dilemmas of practice that drove the course. I could set the topics; however, how they played out had to be contingent upon and in concert with candidates' own experiences. By giving credence to those, a context could be created that validated the authority of their experience (see Munby and Russell,

1994, for an explication of the concept of "authority of experience" and its pre-eminent role in an epistemology of practice). Acknowledging and validating candidates' practicum experiences with their attendant challenges and dilemmas meant that sufficient dissonance could be generated to spur conceptual change.

The focus group data revealed how much candidates' beliefs about learning-to-teach changed, "I learned the most by doing . . . I don't think anyone can really teach you how to *teach*. That's what I was expecting when I came here. Someone's going to teach me how to teach. But that's not how it works" (1998, Secondary). Participants in these focus groups acknowledged the complexity of learning-to-teach as they recognized that "There is no process or equation that you can plug factors into and get the right answer . . . You learn by *doing*. Often, you learn by doing wrong, and you need that forum, that opportunity to do wrong" (1998, Secondary, in Martin and Russell, 2005, p. 16). So, too, did I learn from experience, learn by doing, and learn by doing wrong. Perhaps most importantly, I came to realize that I had to step back. Although I knew that I could and should provide direction, I had to relinquish control. Tompkins makes the case that teachers need to "let go" and relinquish authority if a class is going to get to know itself.

> People's personalities won't be visible, their feelings and opinions won't surface, unless the teacher gets out of the way on a regular basis . . . To get out of the students' way, the teacher has to learn how to get out of her own way. To not let her ego call the shots all the time. This is incredibly difficult.
>
> (1996, p. 147)

Well described in the literature (e.g. Britzman, 1991; Bullough, *et al.*, 1992; Feiman-Nemser, 2001; Grossman, 1990; Huberman, 1993) is the trajectory of teaching, beginning with the necessarily egotistic survival phase where the focus is on oneself and delivering the curriculum, moving to a burgeoning awareness to look beyond oneself to *see* the students and their varying needs and abilities, and progressing to a full-fledged understanding of the critical importance of not only understanding one's students but wholeheartedly working to engage them and enable their ownership of their learning. But until I got out of the way and truly made room for their critical questions, concerns, and issues, it was sheer hubris to assume that engagement and ownership were remotely possible in any meaningful way and that any transformative learning could take place.

Contexts of productive and unproductive learning

Sarason contends that if teachers are to create contexts of productive learning, then of "bedrock importance" is the need to stimulate and support "a student's wanting to learn, to learn more, willingly to experience how such wanting takes him or her to domains of knowledge and actions that had been understandably so, not in the ken of the student" (2002, p. 186). He describes wanting to learn as "a door opener to heretofore unknown worlds" and charges the teacher to light "that kind of fire with the hope that it will rage and spread" (ibid., p. 186). Not leaving the reader in the lurch, Sarason goes on to frame some of the additional requirements for "that kind of fire" to flare. Foremost are knowing, appreciating, and respecting one's students since "school learning—whether adequate, inadequate, or worse—is never independent of the personal and cognitive history of students" (ibid., p. 217). For Sarason, a context of productive learning must be motivating; and if what is being learned is productive, then it will become self-sustaining over the short and long term. But "teachers teach under pressure, and kids learn under that pressure. We know it and they know it" (ibid., p. 209). Where he lays blame is, however, not with teachers but with those who prepare teachers, arguing that becoming teachers are socialized into a school culture that supports conformity and belies confrontation. Within Faculties of Education, little is done to dispel the hyperbole in the usual rhetoric that is espoused:

> Each child is a distinctive individual, each child can learn, the mission of the school is to help the individual fully realize his or her potential. It does not take long at all for that would-be teacher to understand that rhetoric is one thing, acting consistently with it is quite another thing, much like the difference between *your* fantasy and *your* reality.
>
> (ibid., p. 189)

The central issue here is not the impossibility of the teacher's task but avoiding or indirectly addressing how to approximate the goal: "It is not sinful to fall short of the mark, it is sinful not to have a mark. There is a difference between compromising your beliefs and caving in to the easy way out" (ibid., p. 190).

The following excerpts from the focus group data (Martin and Russell, 2005) reveal how absent were opportunities for candidates to deconstruct the rhetoric and to have a forum for their questions, "teachers need to know *how* to communicate with their students, and never has anyone brought up communication" (1998, Secondary). More pointedly, an elementary candidate (2000) lamented there were no opportunities to address whether, "in an inner city setting, . . . do you spend your time teaching the provinces of Canada or how to say please and thank you?" Without opportunities to consider broad-based education issues and principles of practice, they saw the program as "disjointed" with "no continuity." They were left feeling "herded through" because there was no "common ground, something that's bringing it together and having a focus" (1998, Secondary). "Knowing how to teach curriculum" was presented with "no handle on the history," no consideration of "political stance" or challenge of the status quo (2000, Elementary). Candidates asked where was the discourse that addressed substantive questions like, "What do we mean by education?" and "Who is education really for?" (2000, Elementary). Without "framed discussion [of] things that transcend curriculum—like pedagogy, learning styles, assessment, evaluation" (1998, Elementary), they felt ill prepared. They wanted help to integrate and consolidate their practicum experiences with their coursework, "The closer I get to the end, the less I feel I've learned about the fundamentals that I'm going to build my program on, and that's . . . scary" (2000, Elementary). These data were sobering as they too clearly exposed the three counts where we and I fell short: (1) in creating contexts of productive learning; (2) in disentangling the conceptual and instrumental differences between contexts of unproductive and productive learning; and (3) in reconsidering and re-presenting practicum experiences, using contexts of productive or unproductive learning as frames.

Teaching as a moral act

As I revisit the focus group data sets, I am struck by the intensity of feeling that resonates throughout, whether it is data from the field or from teacher candidates. There is praise, but there is certainly protest as well. The discrepancy between our views, as teacher educators, of the restructured program and those of candidates, associate teachers, and administrators reveal how complex teacher education is and how challenging systemic change is (Martin *et al.*, 2000; Martin and Russell, 2005). Context again is preeminent as no reform movement occurs in a vacuum. Reform movements are both reactive and visionary: reactive in their perception of an unsatisfactory state that requires change and visionary in their perception of a more desirable state (Sarason, 2002, p. 245). Not surprisingly, they can generate intense support and equally intense dissent, and this intensity requires at least some consideration of teaching as a moral act. Moral responsibility shapes teachers' beliefs and values, drives their pedagogy, and ultimately goes some way towards a determination of their actions as worthy and their teaching as valued.

Although the notion of the "moral dimensions of teaching" is inherently complex and defies any clear or simple answer, the moral is simply "everywhere" (Sanger, 2001, p. 683). Fenstermacher (1986) is helpful in teasing apart "good" teaching into a moral force and an epistemological force. Morally, "good teaching" asks what principles justify teaching actions that, in turn, could evoke principled action by students. Epistemologically, "good teaching" asks if there is a rational defense to what is being taught and whether there will be attendant value for students by contributing to their knowledge, beliefs, or understanding. Thus teaching as a moral act has several requirements. These include: (1) identification of moral precepts or "moral goods" (Fenstermacher, 2001, p. 640) such as respect, honesty, fairness, truthfulness, courage, compassion, and generosity); (2) consideration of the warrants for teaching actions; and (3) some sense of whether teaching actions could or would engender moral actions on the part of students. The epistemology of "good teaching" queries both declarative and procedural knowledge, asking whether there is intrinsic value in that knowledge such that students will benefit.

Unpacking the moral and epistemic aspects of "good teaching" is insufficient without considering teaching actions. Again, Fenstermacher (1984) is helpful. Using the notion of manner, he argues that teaching extends well beyond subject matter knowledge and requires a manner that is liberating. Such a manner can serve as a model for students. Such a manner can also represent a liberal education that can free the mind to see dogma, convention, and stereotype, thereby providing the capacity for students to make sense of and contribute to their world. Although Fenstermacher initially introduced "manner" to develop a more robust conception of teaching where manner would contrast with method, he later significantly altered his position. Drawing "attention away from method, directing it instead to manner, led to a far too rigid division between the two. It now appears that method is an extremely important means for fostering manner in students" (2001, p. 640).

This interplay between manner and method, what could be considered a moral dynamic, contextualizes candidates' assessment of their professors and the relevance of their coursework. The professors who were passionate, engaging, and modeled good practice were valued. "These professors were not about '*the* answer' but instead developed the questions with us . . . and sometimes you don't leave the classroom with an answer, but maybe more questions, and that's leading you towards finding the answer" (2000, Secondary) (Martin and Russell, 2005, p. 19). Those who did not "genuinely care about what they're doing and really [don't] want to prepare you for next year . . . wiped out . . . everything that we learn [about] what a good teacher is and how [to] create a positive learning environment" (2000, Secondary) (Martin and Russell, 2005, p. 19).

Many of the tensions inherent in teaching are driven by moral considerations and moral judgments. These considerations and judgments become an on-going part of teachers' lives and go some way towards shaping their professional identity. Unless they can be played out in a context where becoming teachers can confront and wrestle with them, teacher educators will sell candidates short and will certainly compromise their own moral responsibility.

Conclusion

In what I consider to be one of the best images of the ill-structured domain of teaching, McDonald (1992, p. 1) describes "real teaching" as happening "inside a wild triangle of relations—among teacher, students, subject—and the points of this triangle shift continuously."

> Yet, out of the uncertainty, craft emerges. The wildness of the triangle provokes it. . . . I craft a workable relationship for the moment [with my students] . . . I tune my stance continually to the values that seize me. Similarly, though I remain chronically unsure of what to teach and how to teach it, I develop an eye for productive linkage . . . [But] I can never be sure of the moves I must continually dare to make; the relations of teaching remain always skittish.
>
> (ibid., pp. 1–2)

I had to learn how to live with the skittishness in a very different way. I had to learn how to appreciate "back talk" on multiple levels and learn how to learn from experience and credit the authority of the experience. I had to learn how to learn from working the dialectic of research and teaching. I had to learn how to "let go" and trust the process itself. And, of course, what I now think of as my epiphany continues as a work always in-progress.

These realizations are hard won, the changes in my thinking and in my practice always accompanied by a sense of uncertainty and not inconsiderable angst. But if I am going to walk my talk and create contexts for productive learning, then my beliefs about the need for a community of learners with a shared sense of purpose, who will embrace challenge and accept risk, must be translated into practice. I need to be vigilant, so I continue to listen hard and, I hope, well and honourably to candidates' voices. I need to continue to ensure that multiple perspectives are also understood and credited. In so doing, I need to expose fully and unabashedly my passion for wanting to learn, for wanting my candidates to learn, and for wanting those whom they will teach to learn—well beyond their ken. Finally, as I enact new pedagogical strategies for teacher education, I need to continually question my assumptions, beliefs, and values, always acknowledging the essential tensions of teaching and respecting that teaching is indeed a moral act.

References

Britzman, D. (1991) *Practice makes practice: A critical study of learning to teach.* Albany, NY: State University of New York Press.

Bullough, R. V., Jr., Knowles, J. G., and Crow, N. A. (1992) *Emerging as a teacher.* New York: Routledge.

Bullough, R. V., Jr. and Pinnegar, S. (2001) Guidelines for quality in autobiographical forms of self-study research. *Educational Researcher, 30*(3), 13–21.

Cochran-Smith, M. (2005) Teacher educators as researchers: multiple perspectives. *Teaching and Teacher Education, 21,* 219–225.

Cochran-Smith, M. and Lytle, S. L. (2004) Practitioner inquiry, knowledge, and university culture. In J. Loughran, M. L. Hamilton, V. LaBoskey, and T. Russell (eds.), *International handbook of research of self-study of teaching and teacher education practices.* Dordrecht: Kluwer, pp. 602–649.

Cole, A. L., Elijah, R., and Knowles, J. G. (eds.) (1998) *The heart of the matter: Teacher educators and teacher education reform.* San Francisco: Caddo Gap Press.

Cook-Sather, A. (2002) Authorizing students' perspectives: Toward trust, dialogue, and change in education. *Educational Researcher, 31*(4), 3–14.

Darling-Hammond, L. (1997) *The right to learn: A blueprint for creating schools that work.* San Francisco: Jossey-Bass.

Darling-Hammond, L. (2000) Teacher quality and student achievement: A review of state policy evidence. *Education Policy Analysis Archives, 8*(1). Retrieved April 23, 2001, from http://epaa.asu.edu/epaa/v8n1/

Dewey, J. (1938) *Experience and education.* New York: Macmillan.

Feiman-Nemser, S. (2001) From preparation to practice: Designing a continuum to strengthen and sustain teaching. *Teachers College Record, 103,* 1013–1055.

Fenstermacher, G. D. (1986) Philosophy of research on teaching: Three aspects. In M. Wittrock (ed.), *Handbook of research on teaching,* 3rd edn. New York: Macmillan, pp. 37–49.

Fenstermacher, G. D. (2001) On the concept of manner and its visibility in teaching practice. *Journal of Curriculum Studies, 33*(6), 639–653.

Frye, N. (1957) *Anatomy of criticism: Four essays.* Princeton, NJ: Princeton University Press.

Giroux, H. and McLaren, P. (1986) Teacher education and the politics of engagement: The case for democratic schooling. *Harvard Educational Review, 56*(3), 213–238.

Goodlad, J. I. (1991) *Educational renewal.* San Francisco: Jossey-Bass.

Grossman, P. L. (1990) *The making of a teacher: Teacher knowledge and teacher education.* New York: Teachers College Press.

Hatch, T. (1998) The differences in theory that matter in the practice of school improvement. *American Educational Research Journal, 35*(1), 3–31.

Holmes Group (1995) *Tomorrow's schools of education.* East Lansing, MI: The Holmes Group.

Huberman, A. M. (1993) *The lives of teachers.* trans. J. R. Neufeld. New York: Teachers College Press.

Kessels, J. P. A. M. and Korthagen, F. A. J. (1996) The relationship between theory and practice: Back to the classics. *Educational Researcher, 25*(3), 17–22.

Knowles, J. G. and Cole, A. L. (1998) Setting and defining the context of reform. In A. L. Cole, R. Elijah, and J. G. Knowles (eds.), *The heart of the matter.* San Francisco: Caddo Gap Press, pp. 15–36.

Korthagen. F. A. J. and Kessels, J. P. A. (1999) Linking theory and practice: Changing the pedagogy of teacher education. *Educational Researcher, 28*(4), 4–17.

Lave, J. and Wenger, E. (1991) *Situated learning: Legitimate peripheral participation.* Cambridge: Cambridge University Press.

Loughran, J. (2006) *Developing a pedagogy of teacher education: Understanding teaching and learning about teaching.* London: Routledge.

McDonald, J. P. (1992) *Teaching: Making sense of an uncertain craft.* New York: Teachers College Press.

Martin, A. K., Hutchinson, N. L., and Whitehead, L. (1999) Gauging field support for a proposed innovative field-based program of teacher education. *Teacher Education Quarterly, 26*(2), 21–34.

Martin, A. K., Munby, H., and Hutchinson, N. L. (2000) Protests and praise from the field: Focus groups and predictive validity. In R. Upitis (ed.), *Who will teach? A case study of teacher education reform.* San Francisco: Caddo Gap Press, pp. 279–297.

Martin, A. K. and Russell, T. (2005) Listening to pre-service teachers' perceptions and representations of teacher education programs. In J. Brophy and S. Pinnegar (eds.), *Learning from research on teaching: Perspective, methodology, and representation:* Vol. 11. Advances in Research on Teaching Series. Oxford: Elsevier, pp. 3–41.

Munby, H. and Russell, T. (1994) The authority of experience in learning to teach: Messages from a physics methods class. *Journal of Teacher Education, 45*, 86–95.

Russell, T. (2000) Teaching to build on school experiences. In R. Upitis (ed.), *Who will teach? A case study of teacher education reform.* San Francisco: Caddo Gap Press, pp. 227–240.

Russell, T. (2004) Modeling what matters to future teachers: Self-directed learning, learning from experience, and community-building. Paper presented at the meeting of the American Educational Research Association, San Diego, CA, April.

Sanger, M. G. (2001) Talking to teachers and looking at practice in understanding the moral dimensions of teaching. *Journal of Curriculum Studies, 33*(6), 683–704.

Sarason, S. B. (1996) *Revisiting "The culture of the school and the problem of change."* New York: Teachers College Press.

Sarason, S. B. (1998) *Political leadership and educational failure.* San Francisco: Jossey-Bass.

Sarason, S. B. (2002) *Educational reform: A self-scrutinizing memoir.* New York: Teachers College Press.

Sarason, S. B. (2004) *And what do you mean by learning?* Portsmouth, NH: Heinemann.

Schön, D. A. (1983) *The reflective practitioner: How professionals think in action.* New York: Basic Books.

Schön, D. A. (1987) *Educating the reflective practitioner: Toward a new design for teaching and learning in the professions.* San Francisco, CA: Jossey-Bass.

Tompkins, J. (1996) *A life in school: What the teacher learned.* Cambridge, MA: Perseus Books.

Upitis, R. (2000a) How will we teach those who will teach? In R. Upitis (ed.), *Who will teach? A case study of teacher education reform.* San Francisco: Caddo Gap Press, pp. 45–60.

Upitis, R. (ed.) (2000b) *Who will teach? A case study of teacher education reform.* San Francisco: Caddo Gap Press.

Wilmore, E. (1996) Brave new world: Field-based teacher preparation. *Educational Leadership, 53*(6), 59–63.

Zeichner, K. M. and Liston, D. P. (1991) Traditions of reform in U.S. teacher education. *Journal of Teacher Education, 41*(2), 3–20.

12 Value-based teacher education

The role of knowledge, language and golden moments

Mieke Lunenberg, Fred Korthagen, and Martijn Willemse

> If tomorrow's teachers are to be responsible and effective conduits of moral education, teacher education programs must take up the challenge of moral education instruction.
>
> (Wakefield, 1997, p. 5)

The meaning of Wakefield's statement is crystal clear: if we want teachers to be responsible for moral education, then teacher education institutes must prepare them for this task. When seen in this light, it is remarkable how little has been written on this topic. At the international level, teacher educators and researchers appear to focus more on instructional methods in schools and in teacher education institutes than on the moral aspects of education, although this latter focus is more common in Europe. There is little empirical evidence on whether or not teacher education institutes are capable of preparing student teachers for the moral aspects of the teaching profession (Cochran-Smith and Zeichner, 2005; Fullan *et al.*, 1998). Moreover, there is considerable confusion about what constitutes moral education. Does it resemble issues such as facilitating identity formation and personal growth (emphasised by Loughran, 2006, p. 2) and, if so, how? The same question can be asked of the fostering of democratic values and skills (Cochran-Smith, 2004), or any of the related issues mentioned in the literature.

In order to develop a clear focus in this confusing area, we decided to concentrate on a single aspect of moral education in schools and teacher education, namely, the role of values. In this chapter we describe a four-year research project, during which we collaborated with 54 teacher educators in a teacher education institute for primary education. This institute's four-year programme combines subject matter with professional preparation. The aim of the research project was to investigate how teacher educators can prepare student teachers to provide an education that develops certain values in children. In this chapter we use the term *value-based education* for such education provided by teachers and the term *value-based teacher education* for the preparation of teachers for value-based education.

In the first part of the study we focused on the curriculum in one particular teacher education institute. During this phase we found that many curricular choices were made implicitly and that the curriculum as such contained few relevant ingredients. Accordingly, value-based teacher education proved to be largely dependent on teacher educators, whose professional background appeared to be of great importance. It became clear that preparing student teachers for value-based education requires specific knowledge, yet this seems to be a neglected aspect of teacher education throughout the world.

In the second part of the study we focused on the values that teacher educators say they consider to be an important part of value-based teacher education and on how they incorporate these values into their teaching practice. We also asked them whether their teaching practice emphasised support for the student teachers' personal development or for their professional development. The third part of the project involved an in-depth analysis of the daily practices of 9 teacher educators with specific expertise. An ability to exploit golden moments—unforeseen situations in which something is said or done that refers to value development or personal growth—was found to be of pivotal importance.

All participants agreed that our research project shows that preparing student teachers for value-based education is not easy. As many authors emphasise the importance of this pedagogical area in today's world (Grossman, 2005), specific staff development in teacher education seems necessary. We describe the details of such a staff development programme, carried out in the context of the second and third phases of the study, as we believe that this may be of interest to other teacher educators.

Theoretical background

> In educational encounters, a teacher's norms and values, and the extent to which they are enacted in practice, influence the manner in which students might develop their own. Thus personal relationship between teachers and students is crucial as identity formation and personal growth combine to shape the nature of pedagogy itself.
>
> (Loughran, 2006, p. 2)

We fully endorse this view, and we observe that there is little research on how this plays out in practice, either in schools or in teacher education programmes. In contrast, there is a considerable body of literature in which experts debate the role of values in both primary and secondary education (Willemse *et al.*, 2005a). However, no broad international consensus has been reached concerning the goals and contents of an educational programme which targets the development of certain values. There is a similar lack of consensus concerning appropriate pedagogical approaches. For example, in the literature we find at least 9 different terms describing such educational approaches as "value education," "moral education," "character education" and "personal and social education" (Vedder and Veugelers, 1999; Berkowitz, 1995). Moreover, this has excited the interest of several different disciplines (including education, theology, political science, philosophy, psychology and sociology) and of related intra-disciplinary and inter-disciplinary schools of thought.

For the purposes of our research project, we have summarised the diversity of interpretations, disciplines and schools of thought involved in the complex international debate into the following three themes (see also Willemse, 2005a):

1   *The legitimacy of value-based education*. At issue here is whether or not value-based education is actually a task for schools and teachers at all. The vast majority of studies on this theme answer this question in the affirmative (see, for example, Klaassen, 1996; Wardekker *et al.*, 1998).
2   *The content of value-based education*. While there is a variety of views about the role of values in education, at least in the Netherlands there does seem to exist a broad consensus that it encompasses both the personal domain (developing identity) and the social one (forging citizenship) (Biesta and Miedema, 2002; Ten Dam and Volman, 1999; Valstar and Veugelers, 1998; Veugelers *et al.*, 2002; Veugelers and Vedder, 2003). At the international level, there is also broad agreement that the development of values in children should not be considered as a separate subject or discipline, but rather that it should be seen as an integral part of the curriculum (Solomon *et al.*, 2001; Stephenson *et al.*, 1998).
3   *The design of value-based education*. Finally, there is the issue of how value development can be incorporated into everyday teaching. The results of research into the best way of doing this, however, have been ambiguous (Solomon *et al.*, 2001).

The literature review led us to conclude that there is no clear, generally accepted, practically proven and universally applicable theoretical framework for value-based education at either primary or secondary level, let alone for value-based teacher education.

We draw a distinction between two specific contexts to clarify the various terms used in the literature. Context A is that of value-based teacher education; context B is that of value-based education in schools (see Figure 12.1). The research project presented in this chapter deals with context A. More specifically, it concerns a teacher education institute for primary education.

The value-based teacher education provided by teacher educators must be based on a vision of the moral aspects of their own profession and that of the teacher. Such a vision is shaped in part by the teacher educators' ideological, cultural and personal backgrounds, and partly by their own values. These values embrace ideas, convictions and ideals in respect of good teacher education and good teaching. Consciously or subconsciously, they guide the educators' behaviour (Clark, 1995; cf. Hansen, 2001; De Ruyter *et al.*, 2003). In our view, it is important to draw a conceptual distinction between two sets of values. On the one hand, there are the teacher educators' own values. On the other, there are those that they wish to develop in their student teachers and those eventually imparted to pupils, once the students become teachers. We must

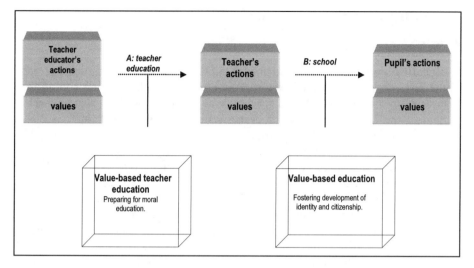

Figure 12.1 Value-based teacher education in relation to value-based education in schools.

acknowledge, however, that teacher educators' own values will inevitably influence the values they want to develop in their students and, ultimately, in their students' pupils.

The central question in our study was: How are student teachers prepared for value-based education through teacher education practices? Taking our literature survey as a basis, we formulated three assumptions for our study:

1 If a teacher education programme is intended to prepare student teachers for value-based education, then our first assumption is that this should be reflected in the curriculum and in the way in which the students' mastery of this material is assessed. In line with Kieviet (1993), Wardekker *et al.* (1998) and Vedder and Veugelers (1999), we also assumed that value-based teacher education is an integral part of the curriculum.

2 Our second assumption was that the development of the students' personal and professional identity is one of the focal areas of value-based teacher education (see Stephenson *et al.*, 1998; Ten Dam *et al.*, 2004). In respect of this latter point, the emphasis of the course should gradually shift from the personal to the professional identity. Student teachers should be encouraged to develop their own pedagogical view of education and of the role of values in their teaching (Kieviet, 1993; Ten Dam *et al.*, 2004; Vedder and Veugelers, 1999; Verkuyl, 2002).

3 Finally, we assumed that the person of the teacher educator himself or herself is an important factor in value-based teacher education (cf. Hansen, 2001; Buzzelli and Johnston, 2002). The next three sections describe the methods used to study these assumptions and the results obtained.

A teacher education curriculum

Design and methods

The first study focused upon the curriculum of Module 4. This is the final part of the first year of a teacher education programme at CHN, a teacher education institute in the Netherlands that specializes in primary education. This 12-week module was linked to a series of overall learning goals, five of which can be regarded as specifically value-based:

1   The student will be able to justify his or her contacts with the pupils in elementary schools.
2   The student will be able to clarify his or her teaching values and norms, and will be able to relate these to his or her teaching practice.
3   The student will be able to reflect continuously on his or her own attitudes, opinions and teaching and on new innovations, and will be prepared to change his or her own teaching through self-evaluation.
4   The student will be able to choose teaching objectives related to his or her own identity and to the identity of the school.
5   The student will have a knowledge and understanding of children's identity, and of their emotional, cognitive, creative, social, ethical, religious, cultural, and physical development. The student will also be able to stimulate such development.

The aim of this study was to identify the value-based education elements in part of the course curriculum and to examine the learning effects on the student teachers.

During this study we identified the value-based learning objectives formulated by the teacher educators responsible for developing the part of the curriculum under study (the designers). These objectives were derived from the value-based overall goals. We looked at how these teacher educators shaped the learning goals in those programme components of the curriculum that they designed. A record was also made of the teaching and learning methods that they selected for these components. We also looked at whether the teacher educators who actually taught the curriculum, and the students taking the module, recognised those goals, components, and teaching and learning methods as such.

The data were collected in a group interview with the designers and through questionnaires completed by the teacher educators and students at the end of the course. The student teachers and their mentors at the schools where the students' teaching practice took place were given questionnaires about the skills the student teachers were expected to use during their work placements. In all, 9 course designers, 20 teacher educators and 80 mentors (primary school teachers who supervised the student teachers during their teaching practice) took part in the process, together with 217 student teachers in the initial assessment and 164 in the final assessment.

Results and reflection

Starting with five value-based overall goals, the curriculum designers formulated 59 learning objectives for Module 4 of the curriculum. Based upon the distribution of those objectives over the various modules and programme components, our conclusion is that value-based teacher education seems to be mainly associated with problem-based learning tasks and religious education. It is rarely, if ever, associated with subjects such as music, mathematics and expression. This refutes one of the assumptions formulated for this study, that value-based teacher education forms an integral part of the curriculum as a whole. In broad terms, both the teacher educators and the student teachers recognised the 59 learning objectives. However, the two groups differed in their opinions as to which of those objectives were most recognisably part of value-based teacher education.

The course designers selected 13 programme components and 25 associated pedagogical methods as most characteristic of value-based teacher education. Their choice was largely recognised by both the teacher educators and the students. Problem-based learning tasks and portfolio assignments were regarded by all concerned as the most characteristic programme components. The teacher educators listed discussion and structures encouraging reflection as the most characteristic pedagogical methods. Both they and the students awarded the highest score to discussion. The choice of this method seems to correspond with what we find in the literature regarding suitable approaches to moral education in primary and secondary education (see Ling *et al.*, 1998; Solomon *et al.*, 2001).

Within the context of their five value-based overall goals, the course designers had also listed 19 skills that students ought to be able to apply during their period of teaching practice. Both the students and their mentors were of the opinion that those skills, as formulated by the course designers, were indeed displayed to a large extent during that practice. In particular, they believed those relating to reflecting upon classroom teaching were widely applied.

An important aspect revealed by our research is that, in this particular module, the choices in respect of the positioning of value-based teacher education within the curriculum appear to be partly implicit in nature. The group interview proved to be essential. As it generated an overview and forced the course designers to look for ways of making the concept of value-based teacher education more explicit, it compelled them to point out exactly where it could be found in Module 4. The course designers admitted that they found it difficult to be specific about exactly which parts of the curriculum included recognisable value-based teacher education. They also seemed to have made the implicit assumption that value-based teacher education (within the part of the curriculum studied) is confined primarily to the religious education module and to problem-based learning components, and that it has no real part to play in such subjects such as music and mathematics. Moreover, some teacher educators in these areas seemed to find it difficult to get a grip on the concept of value-based teacher education.

Looking at the results of this first study, we reached two preliminary conclusions. First, it seemed that not all teacher educators have the requisite knowledge to provide adequate value-based teacher education. Second, it appears to be necessary for teacher educators to communicate with one another in order to clarify their ideas about value-based teacher education. This in turn enables them to develop a shared language with which to discuss this theme.

Values and identity development

Design and methods

The second and third studies concerned the actual practices adopted by teacher educators. The aim of these studies was to develop an understanding of the ways in which they provide value-based teacher education. This might take place within or outside the context of the formal curriculum and it might be implicit or explicit, planned or unplanned. For the purposes of these studies we influenced the object of our research in various ways, in order to obtain greater insights. We postulated that a staff development programme based on a systematic reflection and discussion about actual practices could benefit teacher educators in two ways. First, it might enable them to convert their sometimes vague ideas about value-based teacher education into something more tangible. Second, it might provide the support that they need to further develop value-based teacher education. This approach makes use of the ALACT model. ALACT is an acronym derived from the initial letters of the five phases of a spiral model of systematic reflection (Figure 12.2). This model is an important component of the realistic approach to teacher education described by Korthagen *et al.* (2001).

Our starting points for the second study were the values that teacher educators consider to be important in the provision of value-based teacher education and how they incorporate these values into their teaching practice. All 54 teacher

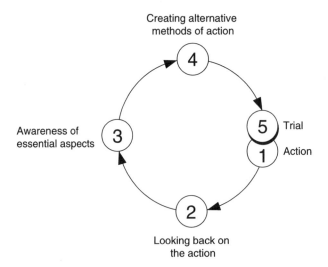

Figure 12.2 The ALACT model for reflection.

educators employed at the teacher education institute under study were asked to formulate values by building a "wall." They built a personal paper wall using handwritten cards, each identifying a value seen as important to value-based teacher education.

The instrument known as "The Wall" (see Figure 12.3) is based on a technique described by Korthagen *et al.* (2001, pp. 162, 167). The aim is to facilitate reflection on various educational goals or values that often remain implicit, and on the relations between them. Each teacher educator was given a number of blank paper "bricks." The teacher educators were invited to fill in these bricks with values they considered important for their own practice. In order to promote comparability of the various values, we encouraged the teacher educators to express each value as a complete phrase, using a subject and a verb. The following are examples of such phrases: "I will show respect to my student teachers," or "stimulating the development of student teachers' identity."

Next, we asked the participants to identify the most important values (up to a maximum of four) and place them at the base of their walls. These values represented the "foundation" of the wall. We then asked the teacher educators to copy these foundation values onto the back of the sheet (see Figure 12.4). They were then asked to indicate whether these values focused on supporting student teachers' personal development or their professional development, or possibly a combination of both.

Finally, the participants were also asked to decide which of their value foundations was the most important of all. They were then asked to give examples of how they put this value into practice.

Results and reflection

The 54 teacher educators' views of what constituted important values in value-based teacher education varied widely. They included such things as "respect," "collective responsibility for the world," "meeting," "openness" and "humour." The values are very diverse and not distinct (for example, "meeting" and "openness"). Moreover, most of these values are not specific to the area of education. The selection of generalized values such as "respect" and "humour" raises the question of how these values are translated into practice (see Willemse *et al.*, 2005b).

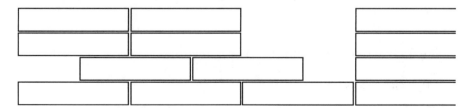

Figure 12.3 The Wall technique for concretising educational goals or values and their relations.

PLEASE MAKE A COPY OF THE BRICKS IN YOUR FOUNDATION (MAXIMUM OF FOUR BRICKS)			
Brick:	Brick:	Brick:	Brick:
Focus on: • personal identity • professional identity • both	Focus on: • personal identity • professional identity • both	Focus on: • personal identity • professional identity • both	Focus on: • personal identity • professional identity • both
From the bricks above, choose one brick (value) that you consider most important, and write this value below. Please also describe an example of the way in which you express this value in your practice.			
Most important brick:	Example:		

Figure 12.4 Foundation of the wall.

The practices followed in this teacher education institute appear to indicate a lack of shared values or a shared vision about what constitutes value-based teacher education. The process of building and discussing the walls seemed to be the first step in developing a common language that could be used to talk about those values in concrete terms. The teacher educators started to "think aloud" (Loughran, 2006, p. 47), albeit only for their colleagues and not yet for their student teachers.

At a more abstract level, however, there are some indications of shared values. We found two common themes running through the values put forward by the teacher educators. One was social development, and the other was personality development. The second assumption formulated for this study (that teacher educators focus upon both the personal and professional aspects of identity development) seemed to be correct. For most values, the teacher educators indicated that the focus was on supporting both personal and professional development. However, our second study provided no specific insights into ways of implementing these two aspects.

The daily practices of nine teacher educators

Design and methods

Nine teacher educators, for the most part pedagogues and theologians, volunteered to participate in a follow-up project. This phase, which consisted of three meetings, involved the use of the Moral Analysis Chart (MAC, Figure 12.5). The

0 Value	1 What do I mean by this value?	2 How do I put this value into practice?	3 What is my behaviour as a teacher educator?	4 What do I want student teachers to achieve?
		When/at which moments How/using which teaching and learning methods What topics		
5 Reflection:				

Figure 12.5 The Moral Analysis Chart.

MAC is based on the column technique described by Korthagen *et al.* (2001, pp. 168–169) and on an instrument for systematic reflection developed by Biesta and Verkuyl (2002). The MAC is used to encourage teacher educators to reflect on how they put their values into practice.

The teacher educators who participated in the follow-up phase completed the MAC on four separate occasions. This took place at the meeting with the entire staff of teacher educators and at the end of each of the three meetings in the follow-up project. In the intervals between these meetings, the teacher educators were challenged to reflect on how they put their values into practice. In doing so, they were asked to focus on any aspects that remained unclear.

In this third study, we asked the teacher educators to describe the following in their Moral Analysis Charts:

1   the specific meaning that they attached to the values they had identified as being the most important (Column 1);
2   those moments in which they felt that they had put their values into practice (Column 2);
3   the teaching and learning methods that they used when putting their values into practice (Column 2);
4   the specific topics that they taught when putting their values into practice (Column 2).

In addition, we asked them to describe their own behaviour (Column 3) and what they wanted their student teachers to achieve (Column 4).

The MAC was accompanied by a description of each column that guided the teacher educators in completing the charts. The facilitator who conducted the three meetings also explained how to fill in the MAC. In addition, video recordings were made of each of the teacher educators at work during a teaching session of their own choice. To ascertain the extent to which the values described in the MACs were actually put into practice, we then interviewed the educator concerned and two of their students concerning the session in question.

Results and reflection

The nine teacher educators who took part in the follow-up exercise gave expression to their values during subject-based meetings and when supervising students individually. In so doing, they made use of discussion, of conversation, and of methods that encourage dialogue and reflection. Our research makes it clear that, at the outset, those who participated in the follow-up exercise were not providing value-based teacher education in a consciously planned manner. Moreover, they found it difficult to say how often they adopted a value-based approach when working with students.

The finding that teacher educators struggled to formulate answers in their MACs, together with the diversity of these answers, seems to confirm the lack of a language that is adequate to the needs of value-based teacher education. This finding is consistent with the observation that the entire staff of teacher educators struggled to formulate their values in the Wall instrument. The teacher educators seemed not to possess what Van Manen and Li referred to as a "pathic language," a language that is "sensitive to the experiential, moral, emotional and personal dimensions of teaching and school life" (2002, p. 221). Our research further reveals that teacher educators have trouble making it explicit what they do or want to do when practising value-based teacher education. It was only in the context of this staff development programme that they started to think aloud (Loughran, 2006) and to develop a moral language related to actual educational practice. Educators can use this language to discuss the role of values in education with one another, and with their students. Both teacher educators and students can use it when talking about the relation of this issue with their own practices.

The fact that teacher educators initially did not provide value-based teacher education as a consciously planned subject does not mean that teacher educators did not provide such teacher education at all: they appear to make use of golden moments. In other words, if a student raises a value-laden problem or topic during subject-based classes, the educators attempt to turn it into a learning opportunity for the whole group. Interestingly, this is in line with paradoxes formulated by Palmer for the purpose of articulating his views of practice. One such paradox is "Invite the voice of the individual and the voice of the group" (1998, p. 74, cited in Loughran, 2006, p. 70), another is "Honor the 'little' stories of the students and the 'big' stories of the disciplines and tradition" (Palmer, 1998, p. 74). The second part of this paradox seems to represent the problem experienced by the teacher educators in our study. To a large extent, they lack both a knowledge and language of "the disciplines and tradition" that are relevant to value-based teacher education. Few teacher educators have a background in pedagogy or theology, so they lack the ability to connect theory with practice. As a result, student teachers miss an important opportunity to derive a broader, more general meaning from these golden moments.

Our research reveals that the educator's personal approach and attitude are important elements in value-based teacher education. This concurs with Loughran's (2006, p. 86) view that "teaching is a relationship." When questioned on this point, both the teacher educators and the students cite qualities (values) such as "showing an interest," "being available," "empathising," "having an open attitude" and "being on the student's wavelength." In the third study, both the teacher educators and students identified the specific moments in which these qualities were demonstrated. Furthermore, both groups indicated exactly the same moments. Interestingly, this seems to suggest that teacher educators and student teachers see teacher education practice in the same way. When teaching, however, teacher educators seldom present the underlying qualities or values in an explicit way. This raises the question of whether students really ever learn very much at all from the examples given them by their teacher educators. In a related study among teacher educators from another Dutch institution, Lunenberg *et al.* (in press) found the same phenomenon. Teacher educators are not accustomed to being explicit about their pedagogical choices, and whenever they are asked for such details, they seldom make connections with theory. Teacher educators therefore seem to overlook the importance of what Loughran described in the following words:

> Fundamental to all is the importance of communicating the *why* of [teacher educators'] practice so that students of teaching can make informed decisions about what they need to learn about *their* teaching in order to enhance the learning of their pupils . . . The implicit messages and intentions of teaching must be challenged, students of teaching need to know what we think are the intended outcomes from our practice and, as teacher educators, we need to be able to articulate not only what we are doing, but why we are doing it and how we are communicating that through our practice.
>
> (2006, p. 61)

We conclude that, in this respect, the teacher educators participating in this study still have a long way to go.

Knowledge, language and golden moments

In this chapter we have attempted to answer the question, *How are student teachers prepared for value-based education through teacher education practices?* On the basis of our literature survey we were able to formulate three assumptions for our study:

1   We assumed that if a teacher-education programme has the objective of

providing value-based education, then that aim should be reflected throughout the entire curriculum, and in the way in which students' learning of that
curriculum is assessed.

2   We assumed that the focus of value-based teacher education includes developing both the students' personal identity and their professional identity.
Furthermore, the emphasis of the course should gradually shift from the
former to the latter.

3   We assumed that the professional skills and personal qualities of teacher educators themselves are an important factor in value-based teacher education.

We draw three conclusions. First, with regard to that part of the curriculum that
we examined, we conclude that the teacher educators who paid most attention to
values-based teacher education were those involved in designing religious education components and some problem-based learning tasks. In the second study,
pedagogues and theologians volunteered to participate in the staff development
project. It seems that pedagogues and theologians as well as their colleagues
presuppose that value-based teacher education is mainly the field of pedagogues
and theologians because, based on their educational background and interest,
they have the necessary professional knowledge. However, Korthagen *et al.*
(2000) state that support should be given to all teacher educators to enable them
to develop expertise in this field. These authors also contend that reflection on the
moral aspects of teaching should be incorporated into the training given to all
teacher educators, as well as teachers.

Second, a moral language is missing in teacher education. The teacher educators in our study found it enormously difficult to name their practice (see
Loughran, 2006, p. 65). In our view, a practical and shared moral language is
needed to help both teacher educators and teachers reflect on their work. It
would also make them aware of their progress in developing values in their students or pupils (Campbell, 2003). Such a language would offer them the
opportunity to better communicate with each other, and to charge their teaching
with greater meaning. Moreover, a language of this kind could help them to
differentiate between different values, which would make their reflections and
discussion on the role of values in (teacher) education more specific. Student
teachers could also be encouraged to adopt this language, since that would
benefit their later professional practice (Sockett and LePage, 2002).

The instrument known as "The Wall" seemed to provide a first step in the
development of a common language for discussing educational values in concrete terms, at any level. Accordingly, this could be an important instrument in
the professional development of teacher educators (and that of teachers). The
same is true of the Moral Analysis Chart (MAC). This is a tool that can be used
by both teachers and teacher educators. It offers clear reference points that can
assist them in developing a moral language which can promote reflection and
terminological precision. For example, a discussion of Columns 2 and 3 of the
MAC can be combined with learning to use paradoxes and tensions, axioms,
summary statements, and assertions. As Loughran (2006, chapter 5) has shown,

this can support the development of a shared language. Hence, the explicit use of the MAC by teacher educators may offer their student teachers the meta-awareness that Loughran (2006) considers to be fundamental to teacher education.

Third, our research concerns the prominent role that individual teacher educators seem to play in value-based teacher education. This role was highlighted in our third study by the emphasis placed by educators and students alike upon such factors as "making time," "being available," "empathising" and "being on the student's wavelength." We assume that this involves a mixture of professional skills and personal qualities which teacher educators can develop still further. In order to improve the professional development of teacher educators, it may be important to encourage them to develop specific attitudes, or at least to stimulate their awareness of their own attitudes. This coincides with the views of Koster *et al.* (2005). In a study on the development of a professional profile for teacher educators, these authors state that

> Hence, in the future, it should be examined if and how the competence profile for teacher educators can be extended to include attitudes, motives and personal characteristics of the teacher educator, which would then cater for all the competence aspects that determine how effectively a situation is dealt with.

> (ibid., p. 173)

The prominent role of individual teacher educators is also reflected in the use that they make of so-called golden moments. When and how that is done depends upon the extent to which educators are able to create such moments in the course of their work, and/or to recognise and exploit them. We take the view that if teacher educators can improve their expertise in recognising, creating and using golden moments, then they will be better able to unpack them (Loughran, 2006). They will only be able to do so, however, if they can also obtain the theoretical knowledge needed to give meaning to such moments. The importance of unpacking and giving meaning is that they enable student teachers to learn how to make use of golden moments in their own practices. Korthagen *et al.* emphasise this in the following way:

> During teacher education, teachers should not only learn techniques associated with pedagogical professionality, such as leading a discussion about moral dilemmas, but they should also be able to bring value problems into education in a pedagogically sound way. In other words, they should be able to "make hay while the sun shines," namely, when in class, at school or in a broader community a moral dilemma occurs in a concrete (not artificial) setting. Then they should be able to discover, generate and discuss such a dilemma in the real social context.

> (2000, pp. 250–251)

References

Berkowitz, M. W. (1995) *The education of the complete moral person.* Aberdeen: Gordon Cook Foundation.

Biesta, G. J. J. and Miedema, S. (2002) Instruction or pedagogy? The need for a transformative conception of education. *Teaching and Teacher Education, 18,* 173–181.

Biesta, G. J. J. and Verkuyl, H. S. (2002) Woorden en daden: Het pedagogische analyse-schema [Words and actions: The moral analysis chart]. In G. J. J. Biesta, H. S. Verkuyl, and F. A. J. Korthagen (eds.), *Pedagogische bekeken: De rol van pedagogische idealen in het onderwijs.* Soest: Uitgeverij Nelissen, pp. 93–108.

Buzzelli, C. A. and Johnston, B. (2002) *The moral dimensions of teaching: Language, power and culture in classroom interaction.* London: RoutledgeFalmer.

Campbell, E. (2003) *The ethical teacher.* Milton Keynes: Open University Press.

Clark, C. M. (1995) *Thoughtful teaching.* London: Cassell.

Clark, C. M. and Peterson, P. L. (1986) Teachers' thought processes. In M. C. Wittrock (ed.), *Handbook of research on teaching,* 3rd edn. New York: Macmillan, pp. 255–296.

Cochran-Smith, M. (2004) The problem of teacher education. *Journal of Teacher Education, 55*(4), 295–299.

Cochran-Smith, M. and Zeichner, K. M. (eds.) (2005) *Studying teacher education: The report of the AERA panel on research and teacher education.* Mahwah, NJ: Lawrence Erlbaum Associates.

Dam, G. ten, Veugelers, W., Wardekker, W., and Miedema, S. (2004) *Pedagogisch opleiden: De pedagogische taak van de lerarenopleidingen* [Pedagogical teacher education: The pedagogical task of teacher education institutes]. Amsterdam: SWP.

Dam, G. ten and Volman, M. (1999) *Scholen voor sociale competentie: Een pedagogisch-didactische benadering* [Schooling for social competence: A pedagogical approach]. Lisse: Swets and Zeitlinger B.V.

Fullan, M. G., Gazuluzzo, G., Morris, P., and Watson, N. (1998) *The rise and stall of teacher education reform.* Washington, DC: American Association of Colleges for Teacher Education.

Grossman, P. (2005) Research on pedagogical approaches in teacher education. In M. Cochran-Smith and K. M. Zeichner (eds.), *Studying teacher education: The report of the AERA panel on research and teacher education.* Mahwah, NJ: Lawrence Erlbaum Associates, pp. 425–476.

Hansen, D. T. (2001) Teaching as a moral activity. In V. Richardson (ed.), *Handbook of research on teaching,* 4th edn. Washington, DC: American Educational Research Association, pp. 826–857.

Kieviet, F. K. (1993) *Onderwijs en opvoeding, enige kanttekeningen bij de zogenaamde pedagogische opdracht van het onderwijs* [Schooling and education: A few remarks on the so-called pedagogical task of education]. Leiden: Rijksuniversiteit Leiden.

Klaassen, C. (1996) *Socialisatie en moraal: Onderwijs en waarden in een laat-moderne tijd* [Socialization and moral: Education and values in a late modern era]. Leuven: Garant.

Korthagen, F. A. J., Kessels, J., Koster, B., Lagerwerf, B., and Wubbels, T. (2001) *Linking practice and theory: The pedagogy of realistic teacher education.* Mahwah, NJ: Lawrence Erlbaum Associates.

Korthagen, F. A. J., Klaassen, C., and Russell, T. (2000) New learning in teacher education. In R. J. Simons, J. van der Linden, and T. Duffy (eds.), *New learning.* Dordrecht: Kluwer, pp. 243–259.

Koster, B., Brekelmans, M., Korthagen, F., and Wubbels, T. (2005) Quality requirements for teacher educators. *Teaching and Teacher Education, 21*, 157–176.

Ling, L., Burman, E., and Cooper, M. (1998) The Australian Study. In J. Stephenson, L. Ling., E. Burman, and M. Cooper (eds.), *Values in education*. London: Routledge, pp. 35–60.

Loughran, J. (2006) *Developing a pedagogy of teacher education*. London: Routledge.

Lunenberg, M., Korthagen, F., and Swennen, A. (in press). The teacher educator as a role model. *Teaching and Teacher Education*.

Manen, van, M. and Li, S. (2002) The pathic principle of pedagogical language. *Teaching and Teacher Education, 18*, 215–224.

Palmer, P. J. (1998) *The courage to teach: Exploring the inner landscape of a teacher's life*. San Francisco: Jossey-Bass.

Ruyter, J. de, Conroy, J. C., Lappin, M., and McKinney, S. 2003) Ideals of ITE students at the University of Glasgow. *Teaching and Teacher Education, 19*, 771–785.

Sockett, H. and LePage, P. (2002) The missing language of the classroom. *Teaching and Teacher Education, 18*, 159–171.

Solomon, D., Watson, M. S., and Battistich, V. A. (2001) Teaching and schooling effects on moral/prosocial development. In V. Richardson (ed.), *Handbook of research on teaching*, 4th edn. Washington, DC: American Educational Research Association, pp. 566–603.

Stephenson, L., Ling. E., Burman, E., and Cooper, M. (eds.) (1998) *Values in education*. London: Routledge.

Valstar, J. and Veugelers, W. (1998) Waarden leren leren: De pedagogische opdracht van de lerarenopleiding [Learning to learn values. The pedagogical task of teacher education]. *VELON Tijdschrift voor Lerarenopleiders 19*(2), 4–7.

Vedder, P. and Veugelers, W. (1999) *De pedagogische functie van het onderwijs. Waarden-vormend onderwijs in een multiculturele en pluriforme samenleving* [The pedagogical task of education. Value education in a multicultural and pluriform society]. Den Haag: NWO/PROO.

Verkuyl, H. S. (2002) *Lesgeven in pedagogisch perspectief: Een werkboek voor leraren-in-opleiding* [Teaching from a pedagogical perspective. A workbook for student teachers]. Soest: Nelissen.

Veugelers, W., Miedema, S., Zwaans, A., Dam, G. ten, Klaassen, C., Leeman, Y., *et al.* (2002) *Onderzoek naar de pedagogische functie van het onderwijs op klas- en schoolniveau* [Research on the socio-pedagogical task in education at class level and at school level]. Den Haag: NWO/PROO.

Veugelers, W., and Vedder, P. (2003) Values in teaching. *Teachers and Teaching: Theory and Practice, 9*, 377–389.

Wakefield, D. (1997) *Who's teaching teachers about character education instruction?* LaGrange, GA: LaGrange College. ERIC Document Reproduction No. ED 429 068.

Wardekker, W., Biesta, G., and Miedema, S. (1998) Heeft de school een pedagogische opdracht? [Does the school have a socio-pedagogical task?]. In N. de Bekker-Ketelaars, S. Miedema, and W. Wardekker (eds.), *Vormende lerarenopleidingen*. Utrecht: SWP, pp. 11–21.

Willemse, T. M., Lunenberg, M. L., and Korthagen, F. A. J. (2005a). Values in education: A challenge for teacher educators. *Teaching and Teacher Education, 21*, 205–217.

Willemse, M., Lunenberg, M., Korthagen, F., and Beishuizen, J. (2005b). The moral aspects of teacher educators' practices. Paper presented at the meeting of the American Educational Research Association, Montréal.

13 How experience changed my values as a teacher educator

Tom Russell

After almost 30 years as a teacher educator, I believe that I understand in complex rather than superficial ways the essential changes in perspective required of a new teacher and how pre-service practicum experiences interact with education courses. While teaching often looks easy, acquiring habits of good teaching and making explicit the principles of one's pedagogy take time. Acquiring the habits of good teacher education and making explicit the principles of a pedagogy of teacher education add further layers and additional time. I now understand more fully the evolution of my own practices and my own values in response to the complexity and challenges of pre-service teacher education. Personal experiences in the teacher education classroom and in school classrooms as practicum supervisor have stimulated major changes in my values. In addition, my research on learning to teach has enabled me to listen to those who are learning to teach in ways that would not have occurred in the education classroom alone.

As I help teacher candidates learn to study their own development as teachers, studying my own practice has become an increasingly important part of giving genuine meaning to reflective practice and constructivist teaching approaches. Creating and sustaining a teaching-learning relationship with each student is now the fundamental goal from which all else follows. That relationship evolves as we come to understand, through shared experiences and the sharing of experiences, the significant messages conveyed to students by how a teacher or teacher educator teaches. Constructivism, metacognition, and reflective practice are simply idle terms and phrases until they come to life through appropriate pedagogy, in the teacher education classroom as well as in the school classroom.

In this chapter I describe how my values have developed in response to my students' reactions to my changes to my teacher education practices in the physics methods classroom and in practicum supervision in schools. There seems to be a common assumption that research findings inspire new practices that are easily added to one's teaching when the evidence is clear and when the new practices match one's values as a teacher. My own experience has been otherwise. Only by significant effort over several years am I able to fully understand the potential benefits and personal consequences of a change recommended by research, and only through self-study research am I able to achieve that understanding. Most new practices do eventually become regular features of my teaching, but only when I gain personal evidence that they make my students' learning more productive. Thus I speak of practice changing my values, rather than values changing my practices. Personal values inspire me to introduce potentially productive changes, but only after I have successfully changed my practices do my values evolve further as I gain personal understanding of the reasons why new practices are more productive. As in most significant and enduring learning, experience precedes understanding.

In the first section of this chapter, I describe a number of ways that I have changed my teacher education practices. I include comments about my reasons for trying to change and about the consequences of each change for my students. In the second section of the chapter I speak more broadly about experienced-based changes in my values and about my evolving perceptions of the many challenges associated with enacting a pedagogy of teacher education.

Changing my practices

Probing students' views of teaching and learning

Trying to talk less and listen more inspired me to probe students' views of teaching and learning, in schools and in teacher education. In response to in-service work with experienced teachers prior to becoming a pre-service teacher educator, I began with a determination to talk less than most teachers seem to talk when they are teaching. We have a century of classroom research showing that teachers talk a great deal. For example, Flanders' "rule of two-thirds" suggested that two-thirds of the time, someone in a classroom is speaking, and two-thirds of the time the person speaking is the teacher. The teachers I helped to study their own teaching came to two conclusions: (1) they had no idea they spoke as much as they did; and (2) they had no idea that it would be so difficult to reduce the extent to which they speak. My earliest classes of would-be teachers were genuinely puzzled by my teaching, for it also seemed clear that I could not tell them that I was trying to talk less than they expected. Less talking inevitably led to more in-class activities and to more listening on my part, and I invented an open-ended "mid-course evaluation" that generated comments to which I could then respond, having created a context for opening up my approach. Inevitably, one particularly frustrated student blurted out the question, "Why didn't you tell us you weren't going to tell us?" I was well on my way to having practice shape my values.

Learning from practicum supervision

Personal experiences observing new teachers in practicum settings soon confirmed that words do not change behaviour. My teaching assignment has always included supervision of pre-service teaching. Even though I was not doing a great deal of "telling" people how to teach, I was trying to help them develop their expectations for their own teaching. Practicum observations quickly showed me that what we do in education courses has little impact on early teaching behaviour; we may influence the veneer, but rarely does our influence extend far beneath the surface. This insight drove me to pursue reflective practice and reflection-in-action as described by Schön (1983), whose ideas appeared in print just as I was becoming increasingly frustrated by the extensive differences I was observing between what we did in education classes and what teacher candidates subsequently did in school classrooms. Although my personal values have moved beyond the default assumption that education courses will make a profound difference, I sense that most pre-service programs have retained that assumption in practice.

Reflecting-in-action and the meaning of reflective practice

Pursuing the personal meaning of Schön's (1983) concept of reflection-in-action taught me that I had to study my own teaching to understand whether I really was changing my teaching and whether my students perceived me as modelling new practices and reflective practice itself. As I worked to understand what reflective practice is in the context of daily teaching and to discover how reflective practice can be fostered, it became increasingly obvious that I needed to study my own teaching in relation to my values. It is far too easy to assume that one's values are being expressed in one's teaching; it is equally easy to be blind to evidence to the contrary. We may actually change what we do, but we should never assume that the change is having its intended effects. It may be the most enduring impact of Schön's (1983) book is that those learning to teach are urged to be reflective practitioners; becoming a critically reflective practitioner appears to be even more desirable. In the program in which I teach, I usually sense that there is far more urging than there is teaching of reflective practice and how reflection-in-action is different (profoundly different) from everyday reflection, which all prospective teachers seem to sense is vague and effortless, and certainly not intellectually demanding or rigorous (Russell, 2005).

Listening to my students

Listening to students was a value that became an active part of my teaching through making "Tickets Out of Class" a practice in almost every class. In the last three or four minutes of each class, I give each person an index card or small piece of paper and ask for responses to questions such as "What is the main idea you are taking from today's class?" and "What further questions do you have about something we did or discussed?" As the year proceeds, there are times when comments are entered anonymously on an electronic bulletin board, where all members of a class may read them. I have always thought that my teaching required listening to my students and asking them to play back to me the effects of my teaching on their learning. As I worked to make this way of listening a routine in my personal practice, I began to sense that many teachers in schools and many faculty members in universities do not share my opinion. I have urged ways of listening to students on those I am teaching, and a few have returned saying that they were actively discouraged by associate teachers from requesting students' comments. Having recently made "Tickets Out of Class" a regular practice at the end of every class, I am impressed by the value of this practice as a way of fostering clear communication between teacher and students and also among students.

Finding meaningful ways to relate to earliest teaching experiences

The uncertainty and complexity of showing students what they might need to know after five years of experience, when they were wisely and rightly focused entirely on the first days and weeks of teaching taught me to seek not a commitment to radical change but a commitment to a few innovative teaching moves in the earliest days of the school year. Teacher educators can easily fall into a trap of expecting far too much far too soon, particularly when they look on new teachers as "the best hope for the future" of school improvement and reform. While I continue to develop the big picture for the long term in as many ways as I can, listening to recent graduates in their first or second year of teaching has convinced me that the challenges of that first year of teaching are beyond anything any of us quite remember.

My return to the high school classroom in 1991 and 1992 was an intense and invaluable exercise in self-study (Russell, 1995) that helped me to see that every teacher has a unique window of opportunity during the first week of school, when students are adjusting to their new teachers and are inclined to accept virtually any teaching procedure that contributes to their learning. I now ask my students to prepare a "First Four Days' Action Plan" that they can take out as the opening of school approaches and they brace for that exciting first day as a "real teacher." Experience has shifted my focus from long-term to short-term perspectives, recognizing that those learning to teach already have most of the values of an innovative teacher. Sustaining and enacting those values calls for specific ideas for challenging and engaging teaching moves that can become comfortable for both students and teacher early in school year (Loughran, 2006).

Experience first as an approach to fostering reflective practice

Years of trying to foster reflective practice with mixed and modest results taught me to show people how to reflect before I told them that was what they were doing (Russell, 2005). Most of the changes to my practice as a teacher educator have involved reaching a better understanding of my own values as a result of listening to my students, and then moving on to create new practices in response to what I heard. Several years ago one person who sent me weekly notes from his practicum took note of the large number of people stressing the importance of "being a reflective practitioner" and then commented that we might be far more successful if we modelled reflective practice ourselves and if we helped people learn how to reflect rather than assuming that reflection was clearly understood at the outset. This comment transformed my practice as I changed assignments to ones that provided a clear set of questions appropriate to various stages of the pre-service program together with a straightforward way for me to comment clearly about what further thinking they might want to do. I avoid mentioning "reflective practice" until the end of the program, when they have the experience of reflection before them as a way to understand my comments and suggestions about how reflective practice can contribute to their development as a teacher.

Finding ways to foster self-directed learning

Russell's Rule of Structure gradually evolved into explicitly fostering Self-Directed Learning. As I worked to shape my teacher education classrooms into places where both my students and I could accept my teaching practices, I began to attend to the degree of "structure" I was providing and how I was providing that structure. A graduate student, later a colleague, put a name to the rule I seemed to be using, and Russell's Rule of Structure was stated as "If no one is complaining about lack of structure, then I'm providing too much." It takes many people a moment to see what those words are trying to say, but they serve as a reminder that it is difficult for a teacher to know when she or he might be providing far more structure than students require to continue their work. In 2002, listening to one student helped me to realize that my attention to learning from experience also called for a significant element of self-directed learning—not abandonment to working entirely alone but space in which to take personal responsibility for what needed to be learned and for how and how quickly it should be learned.

Seeing teaching as creating contexts of productive learning

First and foremost, teaching calls for creating "contexts of productive learning" (Sarason, 2002). Kohn (1999) has highlighted the importance of intrinsic motivation in children's learning, in contrast to the heavily emphasized external motivation of grades and rewards for good grades. Both Sarason and Kohn develop the fundamental theme that learning is productive when students are engaged by their work and when their work leaves them wanting to learn more. They develop this theme in reaction to the observation that after three or four years of schooling, children's intrinsic motivation for classroom activities seems to decline steadily to the end of high school. Teachers bemoan students' lack of interest, and professional development talks about motivating students to learn, but few seem able to make the link to the pressure to cover the curriculum and increase scores on achievement tests. In the context of my work as a teacher educator, I must regularly ask myself, "Is my teacher education classroom a context of productive learning for the pre-service teachers I am working with?"

Changing my values

Like every teacher and like every teacher educator, I was "lost in school" when I began my work in these fields (Martin and Russell, 2006). Virtually all of my teaching moves were default responses, made normal and comfortable by the many teachers I watched for many years with little or no access to their thinking. (A high school English teacher did use an unforgettable phrase, "pedagogical prerogative," to justify a particular teaching decision, but this was little help.) As teachers and as teacher educators, we do tend to teach as we were taught. As teacher educators, we commonly aspire to change those many familiar patterns that Sarason (1971) describes as the culture of the school. Teacher educators generally believe that the quality of classroom interaction and learning can be improved; rarely do we seem to appreciate the extent to which changes must begin in the teacher education classroom, not in the classroom of the first-year beginning teachers we have recently taught (Munby and Russell, 1994). Transmission of new ideas can never have the impact and authority of direct experience. Whether we are encouraging new teachers to explore alternatives to the Socratic method or considering cases such as Sarason's account of teachers' responses to the introduction of "new math" as a curriculum, enacting a new practice is always far more challenging and engaging than listening to a description of a new practice.

Recognizing patterns of teaching and learning as cultural

As Sarason (1971, 1996) has argued for more than three decades, life in schools is usefully thought of as a culture. We can be told about the practices of a culture different from our own, but we cannot begin to understand that culture until we experience it personally. We learn a culture by living in it, but when it is the only culture we know, identifying and understanding the influence of that culture is very challenging. While new teachers are experts at the student experience of the school culture, the teacher experience of school culture is profoundly different. Would-be teachers enter a teacher education program thinking that they know little or nothing about how to teach, yet they have watched their own teachers for more than 15 years and are acutely aware of good and bad teaching behaviours. As each year of pre-service teaching passes, I become more aware of how much prospective teachers already know, in the form of preconceived ideas about teaching. I also notice that they erroneously believe, initially, that they know very little. One way to account for this belief that they know little involves recognizing that, when teachers teach, they typically reveal very little about how they think about teaching. This usually leaves their students—including those who will choose to become teachers—viewing teaching as both easy and mysterious. When practicum assignments finally provide pre-service teachers with first-hand experiences of teaching, they may quickly leap to thinking they know a great deal, only to discover later that a little knowledge can be a dangerous thing. Andrea Martin's account in Chapter 11 of insights gained from dramatic program changes reminds me of the power of early practicum experiences to shift teacher candidates from passive consumers of teaching ideas to active critics whose personal experiences of teaching inspire entirely new sets of important practical questions.

While he identified features of the culture of the school in hopes of showing others how to improve the quality of students' learning, Sarason (1998) now appears to have accepted the realistic conclusion that our "system" of schools, universities, and teacher education is not likely to change:

> What finally convinced me was the recognition that no one—not teachers, not administrators, not researchers, not politicians or policymakers, and certainly not students—willed the present state of affairs. *They were all caught up in a system that had no self-correcting features*, a system utterly unable to create and sustain contexts of productive learning. . . . There are no villains. There is a system. You can see and touch villains, you cannot see a system . . . The reform movement has been about parts, not about the system, not about how the purposes of parts are at cross-purposes to each other, not about how the concept of purpose loses both meaning and force in a system that is amazingly uncoordinated and that has more adversarial than cooperative features.
>
> (Sarason, 1998, p. 141, emphasis added)

The importance of acknowledging that we are "lost in school"

My use of the phrase "lost in school" is inspired by Nuthall's (2005) account of cultural myths identified in a review of his career researching events in classrooms:

> Through nearly 45 years of research on teaching and learning in school classrooms, I have slowly become aware of how much of what we do in schools and what we believe about teaching and learning is a matter of cultural routines and myths. What is more, much of the research on teaching and learning in classrooms is itself caught up in the same rituals and myths and sustains rather than challenges these prevailing beliefs.
>
> The underlying theme, which the reader should keep constantly in mind, is that so long as we remain unaware of the extent to which our hidden culture determines how we practice, think about, and do research on teaching, attempts at reform are likely to be ineffective.
>
> (ibid., p. 896)

The phrase "lost in school" could easily be misinterpreted as suggesting that teachers and teacher educators in some sense do not know what they are doing. Please recall that I began this section by indicating that I was lost in school when I began to teach and again when I began to teach prospective teachers. The phrase is meant to highlight the extent to which we are unaware that many of the teaching and learning behaviours in schools and in teacher education programs are habitual and were not chosen deliberately or purposefully. Lortie (1975, p. 62) captured the situation with these words:

> Students are undoubtedly impressed by some teacher actions and not by others, but one would not expect them to view the differences in a pedagogical, explanatory way. What students learn about teaching, then, is

intuitive and imitative rather than explicit and analytical; it is based on individual personalities rather than pedagogical principles.

Nuthall continues his analysis with this recommendation:

> It is important to search out independent evidence that the widely accepted routines of teaching are in fact serving the purposes for which they are enacted. We need to find a critical vantage point from outside the routines and their supporting myths . . . The approach I have learned to take is to look at teaching through the eyes of students and to gather detailed data about the experiences of individual students.
>
> (2005, p. 925)

Much of my research since 1990 has been grounded in self-study methods, inspired by returning to the physics classroom to remind myself of the work for which I was preparing my students. Much of the evidence I collected drew on the experiences of those I teach, as Nuthall recommends. The more I work to listen to former students, even as they move into their fifth and sixth years of teaching, the more I have come to believe that *virtually all teacher educators dramatically underestimate and erroneously conceptualize the nature of a teacher's professional learning in the earliest years of teaching.* By default, just like teachers in schools, we tend to tell and then assume that theory will be enacted in practice. Kane, in her chapter, has creatively termed this the "immaculate assumption."

Enacting a pedagogy of teacher education

My own perspectives on enacting a pedagogy of teacher education focus on the following: (1) modelling my educational values, implicitly and explicitly ("walking my talk"); (2) naming features of school and university culture early and often; (3) listening to my students and playing what they tell me back to them as a way of challenging them to clarify issues and assumptions; and (4) building on their practicum experiences, rather than attempting to talk over the experience gap that inevitably separates my perspective from theirs.

This chapter seeks to account for the evolution of my own values and practices as a teacher educator as I gradually learned how and why I needed to listen closely to the impact of experience on those learning to teach. As I become more sensitive to the importance of learning as an intrinsically rewarding and motivating activity, I realize that my own professional learning has become more rewarding and motivating for me personally. Thus it becomes increasingly important for me to create intrinsically rewarding and motivating learning contexts for new teachers and to help them launch personal careers that will be intrinsically rewarding. Teachers rely heavily for encouragement and support on those moments when children "get it." Teachers need similar "aha" moments in their own professional learning. Most formal education focuses on learning new content, which requires coming to see events (literary, historical, scientific, etc.) from new perspectives. Teacher education needs to focus on learning to see one's students' learning experiences from new perspectives, and my personal view of enacting a pedagogy of teacher education certainly includes developing new teachers' ability to recognize and interpret moments when they achieve a new way of thinking about learning (Korthagen *et al.*, 2006).

Preparation for the profession of teaching tends to be the shortest professional preparation course in our universities. Teaching looks easy, and good teaching looks very easy. It follows that learning to teach and teaching new teachers must also be very easy. Why, then, do I and the other contributors to this collection seek to make the simple complex and why do we argue that enacting a pedagogy of teacher education is complex rather than simple? Enacting a pedagogy of teacher education might sound as simple and straightforward as teacher education itself is assumed to be. Prospective teachers enter a pre-service program with clear expectations that first they will be told how to teach well and then they will go to their practicum schools to teach as they were told. Why should they expect anything else? Virtually all of their previous schooling has involved transmission-based teaching approaches in which teachers tell students what they need to know, assign exercises for practicing what they have told them, and then test them to see how much they remember. The penultimate test for the new teacher is the pre-service practicum, which is quickly followed by the ultimate test, the first year of teaching. How we enact our pedagogy of teacher education is crucial to what follows the first year of teaching experience, for that is when we need to ask whether anything remains of what we try to teach in our pre-service programs (Zeichner and Tabachnick, 1981).

Enacting a pedagogy of teacher education is a big-picture enterprise calling for continuous and creative attention to the importance of challenging prospective teachers to consider both what they will teach and how they will teach it. Enacting a deliberate pedagogy of teacher education does not come naturally to anyone. Our experiences of many years as students in school and university, our own pre-service teacher education experiences, and our experiences as teachers and teacher educators have inadvertently but successfully taught us to focus on what we teach. Those experiences also seem to teach us that, when we teach subjects or teach new teachers, we are endowed with special magical powers that enable us to talk over, around, and through the experience gap—the gap between our own successful experiences and the experiences that students and prospective teachers have not yet had. Experience has authority that is often ignored in formal learning. When we overlook the contributions of experience to learning, we also ignore our professional responsibility to help new teachers understand the cultural patterns of our schools and resist becoming lost in school. We need to move beyond the myth that teachers provide students with right answers, so that productive classroom learning can be encouraged. Similarly, we need to resist the myth that teacher educators provide right answers about teaching, such as teaching tips and resource packages, so that productive professional learning can begin. New teachers can take charge of identifying and making explicit their own development as they gain teaching experience. Enacting a pedagogy of teacher education challenges us to create classroom environments in which it is safe, appropriate and necessary to consider how we learn as well as what we learn.

Acknowledgement

This chapter draws on data collected under a grant from the Social Sciences and Humanities Research Council of Canada.

References

Kohn, A. (1999) *The schools our children deserve: Moving beyond traditional classrooms and "tougher standards."* Boston: Houghton Mifflin.

Korthagen, F., Loughran, J., and Russell, T. (2006). Developing fundamental principles for teacher education programs and practices. *Teaching and Teacher Education, 22*(8), 1020–1041.

Lortie, D. C. (1975) *Schoolteacher: A sociological study.* Chicago: University of Chicago Press.

Loughran, J. (2006) *Developing a pedagogy of teacher education: Understanding teaching and learning about teaching.* London: Routledge.

Martin, A. K. and Russell, T. (2006) "Lost in teachers' college"—Deconstructing the teacher education façade: A case study of collegial self-study. In L. M. Fitzgerald, M. L. Heston, and D. L. Tidwell (eds.), *Collaboration and community: Pushing boundaries through self-study.* Proceedings of the Sixth International Conference on Self-Study of Teacher Education Practices. Cedar Falls, IA: University of Northern Iowa, pp. 186–189.

Munby, H. and Russell, T. (1994) The authority of experience in learning to teach: Messages from a physics method class. *Journal of Teacher Education, 4,* 86–95.

Nuthall, G. (2005) The cultural myths and realities of classroom teaching and learning: A personal journey. *Teachers College Record, 107,* 895–934.

Russell, T. (1995) A teacher educator and his students reflect on teaching high school physics. *Teacher Education Quarterly, 22*(3), 85–98.

Russell, T. (2005) Can reflective practice be taught? *Reflective Practice, 6,* 199–204.

Sarason, S. B. (1971) *The culture of the school and the problem of change.* Boston, MA: Allyn and Bacon.

Sarason, S. B. (1996) *Revisiting "The culture of the school and the problem of change."* New York: Teachers College Press.

Sarason, S. B. (1998) *Political leadership and educational failure.* San Francisco: Jossey-Bass.

Sarason, S. B. (2002) *Educational reform: A self-scrutinizing memoir.* New York: Teachers College Press.

Schön, D. A. (1983) *The reflective practitioner: How professionals think in action.* New York: Basic Books.

Zeichner, K. M. and Tabachnick, B. R. (1981) Are the effects of university teacher education "washed out" by school experience? *Journal of Teacher Education, 32*(3), 7–11.

Index

16–17, 107–108, 110–112, 121, 162,
169, 178; learning 146, 148, 189, 190;
self-understanding of teachers 111;
struggles 107; trust 86
Professional Development Schools 28
professional knowledge 43–44, 46, 51,
139, 178; of student teachers 138; tacit
nature of 83; of teachers 4, 6, 11
program: structure 150
prospective teachers 31–34, 36–43
psycholinguistic 98
pupil learning 26, 28

Quality Assurance Bodies 62

rationalization 46–49
reading and writing: how children
understand 96
reconceptualized: practice 149
reconstructionist 149
reflect 170, 175, 178; on problems 47
reflection 45–56, 58, 106–108, 111–116,
118, 121–122, 171–178; in action 51,
78, 79, 81, 84, 184
reflective practice 182, 184, 185, 191
reflective stance 54; critical 52
reform 149–150, 153–154, 156, 161,
163–165
reform movements 161
reframe 24, 32, 38, 40, 145, 148
relationship 77–81, 83, 89–91, 138–139,
145–148, 155, 167, 177; between
subject matter and pedagogy 45;
between teaching and learning 7, 68
religious education 171, 178
research 16, 18–20, 23–29
researcher 20, 25–26, 71; of teacher
education 61, 70, 73
researching practice 32
resilience 73
resource packages 190
risky business 121
Rogoff, B. 99, 100–101, 105
rookie professor 131
Russell, T. 13, 48, 58–59, 78, 83, 151,
153–164, 178–185, 186, 191
Russell's Rule of Structure 186

Samaras, A. 6
Sarason, S. 83, 94, 142, 148, 153–154,
159, 161, 164–165, 186–188, 191
scaffolding 33, 37, 39, 40, 42
scholars 71
scholarship 14, 15, 63, 69

Schön, D. 6, 32, 44, 49, 59, 80, 82, 87, 94,
151–154, 165, 184, 191
school: community 90; literacy test 82; lost
in 188; urban 100
Schuck, S. 6, 87
Science Curriculum Improvement Study
96, 104
seating plan 142, 143
secondary: education 108, 112; school
students 117
seeing through students' eyes 9
self-actualization 109, 110, 122
self-directed learning 186
self-evaluation 170
self-study 13–15, 23, 25, 27, 29, 32–33,
43–44, 77, 87–88, 92–94, 107, 182,
185, 189, 191; autobiographical forms
of 151
Senese, J. 5, 45, 51–52, 57–59
shared: experiences 13; readings 55
Shulman, L. 14–15, 67, 71, 75
small-group discussion 19
Smart, M. 96
social studies teachers 37
social: development 174; efficiency 149;
justice 64, 66, 72, 75
social-pedagogical task 107
sociocultural theory 98, 99, 100
Sockett, H. 178
Socratic lessons 78
Socratic method 187
staff development programme 167, 172,
176, 178
static electricity 143–144
status quo, challenge to 160
student: behavior 51; concerns about 83;
learning styles 132; learning 48, 50, 103,
146–147, 183, 187, 190
student teachers' preconceived notions of
teachers and teaching 71
students of teaching 1–8, 11–14
studying my own practice 182
subject matter knowledge 53, 89
survival: patterns 111, 116; phase 159
swampy lowland 154–155
Swennen, A. 177, 181
syllabi 125

Tabachnick, B. 138
tacit 152; making explicit 4
teacher 17, 124–130, 132–136; of teachers
32
Teacher Education Programs 11
teacher education; alternative view of 31; as